THE CENTER FOR SOUTH AND SOUTHEAST ASIA STUDIES of the University of California is the coordinating center for research, teaching programs, and special projects relating to the South and Southeast Asia areas on the nine campuses of the University. The Center is the largest such research and teaching organization in the United States, with more than 150 related faculty representing all disciplines within the social sciences, languages, and humanities.

The Center publishes a Monograph Series, an Occasional Papers Series, and sponsors a series published by the University of California Press. Manuscripts for these publications have been selected with the highest standards of academic excellence, with emphasis on those studies and literary works that are pioneers in their fields, and that provide fresh insight into the life and culture of the great civilizations of South and Southeast Asia.

RECENT PUBLICATIONS
OF THE CENTER FOR SOUTH AND SOUTHEAST ASIA STUDIES

Edward Conze
The Large Sutra on Perfect Wisdom

William G. Davis
Social Relations in a Philippine Market

Stanley A. Kochanek
Business and Politics in India

Daniel S. Lev
Islamic Courts in Indonesia

Sylvia Vatuk
Kinship and Urbanization: White-Collar Migrants in North India

VILYATPUR 1848–1968

This volume is sponsored by the
CENTER FOR SOUTH AND SOUTHEAST ASIA STUDIES,
UNIVERSITY OF CALIFORNIA, BERKELEY

TOM G. KESSINGER

VILYATPUR 1848-1968

SOCIAL AND ECONOMIC CHANGE
IN A NORTH INDIAN VILLAGE

UNIVERSITY OF CALIFORNIA PRESS
BERKELEY, LOS ANGELES, LONDON

University of Califorina Press
Berkeley and Los Angeles, California
University of California Press, Ltd.
London, England
Copyright © 1974, by
The Regents of the University of California
ISBN: 0-520-02340-4
Library of Congress Catalog Card Number: 72-89788
Printed in the United States of America

To

V.C.K., W.C.K., C.C.K.

and the people of Vilyatpur

CONTENTS

	Preface	xi
	Introduction	1
I	Rural Administration and Society Under the Mughals and the Sikhs	11
II	Vilyatpur in 1848: A Reconstruction	46
III	Demographic Change, 1848–1968	84
IV	Economic Change, 1848–1968: Agriculture	102
V	Economic Change, 1848–1968: New Opportunities and the Use of New Incomes	154
VI	Social Change, 1848–1968: Family and Kinship	178
	Conclusion: Social and Economic Change, 1848–1968	202
	Glossary	221
	Index	225

TABLES

1	Caste of Zamindars Responsible for Revenue *ca.* 1596	28
2	Villages in Possession of Various Castes, 1851	30
3	Residential Groups, 1848	50
4	Occupational Structure, 1848	55
5	Size of Agricultural Holdings, Owned and Used, 1848	63
6	Caste and Property Groups, 1848	64
7	Occupation and Property Groups, 1848	65
8	Traditional Shares, 1848	69
9	Population Growth, 1855–1961	86
10	Effects of Insecurity of Life, 1848–1968	88
11	Location of Migrants from Vilyatpur, 1848–1968	91
12	Vilyatpur Caste Composition, 1848–1968	95

13   Development of Public Works, 1868–1892   106

14   Size of Agricultural Holdings (Ownership), 1848–
       1968   114

15   Cultivated Land, Per-Capita, in Vilyatpur, 1855–1968 115

16   Size of Farms (Operating Units), 1848–1968   116

17   Increases in Agricultural Production, 1848–1968   119

18   Capital in Agriculture, 1848–1968   122

19   Land Sales and Mortgages, 1885–1966   133

20   Relative Size of Farms to Holdings, 1848–1968   141

21   Property Group Size and Composition, and Land Use,
       1848–1968   142

22   Property Group Size and Composition, and Land Use,
       1848–1968   143

23   Property Group Size and Composition, and the
       Amount of Land Put Out on Rent, 1848–1968   145

24   Migration and Land Ownership, 1848–1968   146

25   Occupational Structure, 1848–1968   156

26   Resident Males Working Outside Vilyatpur, 1848–
       1968   161

27   Occupations of Emigrants, 1848–1968   164

28   Caste and Place of Migration, 1848–1968   166

29   Migration Patterns of Baseline Families, 1848–1968   168

30   Acquisition of Land by Baseline Families With Dif-
       ferent Histories of Migration, 1848–1968   172

31   Average Size of Household, 1848–1961   185

32   Family Composition, 1848–1968   189

33   Family Composition and Eligibility, 1848–1968   191

34   Family Composition and Eligibility Including Kins-
       men Living Outside the Village, 1848–1968   193

35   Family Composition Adjusted for Eligibility, 1848–
       1968   194

36   Origins of New Families, 1848–1968   197

37   Occupation of Family Head and Family Composition
       Adjusted for Eligibility, 1848–1968   200

MAPS AND FIGURES

Map 1: Punjab (1930): railways, canals, rivers   12

Map 2: Punjab (1901–47): Administrative and Natural
Divisions   13

Figure 1: Local Administration of the Mughals in the
Punjab   17

Figure 2: Organizational Chart of Administrative and Political Structure of the Punjab in Jullundur   23

Figure 3: Caste Structure of the Jats of Vilyatpur   37

ABBREVIATIONS USED IN THE NOTES

S.R., 1851. Richard Temple, "Settlement Report of the Jullundur District" in, India; *Selections From the Records of the
Government of India, General Report on the Administration
of the Punjab, for the Year 1849–50 and 1850–51* (London:
Court of Directors of the East India Company, 1854).

S.R., 1892. W. E. Purser, *Final Settlement Report of the
Jullundur District* (Lahore: Civil and Military Gazette Press,
1892).

D.G., 1904. *Punjab District Gazetteers. Jullundur District.*
(Lahore: Civil and Military Gazette Press, 1908).

P.A.R. *Report on the Administration of the Punjab* (Lahore:
Superintendent of Government Printing, Punjab, 1860–1937).

Punjab Census. Punjab Volumes in the *Census of India* (Superintendent of the Census, 1872–1961).

PREFACE

To those familiar with the Punjab, the Punjabis, and the literature about them, I feel that I must explain the form and style of this account of life in rural Punjab during the past one hundred and twenty years. The Punjabis are a vigorous and colorful people with a fascinating past—excellent subject matter for almost any kind of book. A number of authors have captured these qualities and produced works that are at once informative and a pleasure to read, appreciated by scholars and laymen alike. I find myself unable to continue this tradition because of my own background and the nature of the subject I have selected for detailed consideration. Since I have neither the literary skills of Kushwant Singh and G. D. Khosla, nor the insider's perspective of Prakash Tandon, nor long personal experience in the administrative service (like Malcolm Lyall Darling, Pendryl Moon, and M. S. Randhawa), I have relied on my training as a social scientist and historian, and produced an account full of "issues" and "numbers" which may appeal to only a few specialists.

The nature of my subject also prevents me from following the tradition of the literature on the Punjab; this, perhaps, may be the study's redeeming feature. My focus is the people who have comprised an ordinary village in Jullundur district since the middle of the past century. In general, they have been small-scale farmers, laborers, artisans, and petty traders—people of modest means who worked with their hands to support their families, not reflective men who kept diaries, records, and personal papers, the historian's conventional source materials. Others have described villagers as they saw them at particular moments in time, and retold folk tales and stories which can still be heard in rural communities today. But the absence of historical sources has meant that to date there are no historical studies of ordinary village people, the bulk of the country's population, except at a general level of exposition. I have attempted to fill this void by examining the decisions and behavior of the people of Vilyatpur from 1848 to 1968, as recorded in numerous official documents. Although the study falls short of the standards of narrative accounts of rural Punjab, I have been able to examine the quality of life in the village over time by building directly on the tradition of empirical research into rural conditions established by the Board of Economic Inquiry, Punjab, in the 1920's, and maintained in India by the Economic and Statistical Organization, Punjab, and in Pakistan by the Board of Economic Inquiry.

In the course of the training and research that went into this study, I acquired debts to individuals and institutions. Two men who influenced my career in different ways at its beginning are Wallace T. MacCaffrey, now of Harvard University, my undergraduate advisor, who inspired me to a career as a historian, and Tejwant Singh Bolaria, former principal of the Gram Sewak Training Center, Nabha, Punjab, who guided me during my first trip to India as a Peace Corps volunteer in 1961–1963 and taught me most of what I know about Punjab agriculture. I must also acknowledge the contribution of A. L. Fletcher, I.C.S., then financial commissioner for development, for the many opportunities to learn about rural Punjab as a development worker. I am indebted to the people of Vilyatpur who tolerated endless interviews and my insistence on detail, and made my family and me feel at home during our ten-month stay in the village. I particularly want to thank Shiv Singh Sahota, *surpanch* of the village, for taking the trouble to see that our visit was both productive and pleasant. S. Daljeet Singh, I.A.S., secretary to the Punjab government for education during the period of my research (1968–1969) and a friend of many years, was a constant help. Professors B. N. Goswamy and Victor DeSouza of Punjab University were both generous with their time and the resources of their institution, and H. S. Kwatra, superintendent of census, Punjab, went out of his way to be of assistance. To Tek Chand and Shanker Singh I am thankful for yeoman work copying village records, and I thank the *sadr kanungo,* Jullundur, and his staff, for making the locating and duplicating of a large number of records as uncomplicated as it was. S. Gurbachen Singh Chawla's affectionate care and logistic support exceeded beyond measure the already stringent requirements of a Punjabi brother-in-law.

I have benefited from the assistance and advice of many people as this study took its final form. C. M. Naim, my language teacher, and Louise Rehling of the Computation Center, University of Chicago, both made special contributions. I profited from discussions with

Josef J. Barton, Wilfred Malenbaum, Walter C. Neale, and Raymond
T. Smith during the course of writing; from the detailed comments
of Michael Pearson, Alan W. Heston, and Shanti Tangri on particular chapters; and from the comments of Philip Kuhn, Morris D.
Morris, and Bernard S. Cohn on the entire manuscript.

In a first book, particularly one that is essentially a thesis, one's
teachers deserve acknowledgment. I have been fortunate in my association with the faculty and students of the South Asia program at
the University of Chicago, who together created a truly remarkable
educational experience. This book is a product of the interdisciplinary tradition that characterizes Chicago and is reflected in the South
Asia program. Raymond T. Smith introduced me to general anthropology and guided my first research effort in Guyana in the summer
of 1967, thereby influencing the direction of my research. To Bernard
S. Cohn, my teacher, adviser, and friend I must give credit, above
all, for inspiration and guidance, both by direct instruction and
through the example of his own scholarship. Without his direction,
interest, and care, this book would never have been conceived, re-
searched, or written.

The Foreign Area Fellowship Program, the Danforth Foundation,
the National Science Foundation (GS 3141), and the Committee on
Faculty Research, University of Virginia, have all contributed funds
for this project. They are in no way responsible for any of its findings
and conclusions.

                                                          T.G.K.

INTRODUCTION

The Problem

Historians interested in the social and economic history of rural India or, to adopt the terminology of the social scientists, interested in social and economic change, have been confronted with a shortage of source materials. This does not mean that available published and unpublished materials are limited in volume. Numerous official commissions and committees produced gigantic reports dealing with rural conditions in India. The Famine Commission reports are probably the best known nineteenth-century examples and the Royal Commission on Agriculture one of the most important since the turn of the century. There are the massive statistical series of all-India coverage, most of which date from the 1880's, including the census and the annual compilations of statistics on agriculture, irrigation, education, and the like. These materials have formed the basis for important studies, a partial list of which includes: Bhatia and Srivastava on famines; Narain and Blyn on agriculture; Zachariah on internal migration; Krishnamurty and Thorner on the labor force; Bose on urbanization; Desai on the size and sex composition of the population; and Paustian on irrigation.[1] All these contribute to our knowledge of the social and economic history of South Asia by consolidating masses of material and recognizing trends for extended

[1] B. M. Bhatia, *Famines in India, 1860–1965* (2nd. ed.; New York: Asia Publishing House, 1967); M. N. Srivastava, *The History of Indian Famines* (Agra: Sri Ram Mehra, 1968); Dharm Narain, *The Impact of Prices on Areas Under Selected Crops* (Cambridge: University Press, 1966); George Blyn, *Agricultural Trends in India, 1891–1947: Output, Availability and Productivity* (Philadelphia: University of Pennsylvania Press, 1966); K. C. Zachariah, *A Historical Study of Internal Migration in the Indian Sub-Continent* (New York: Asia Publishing House, 1964); J. Krishnamurty, "Changes in the Composition of the Working Force in Manufacturing 1901–51: A Theoretical and Empirical Analysis," *Indian Economic and Social History Review,* VI (1969), 1–16; Daniel and Alice Thorner, *Land and Labour in India* (London: Asia Publishing House, 1962); Ashish Bose, "Six Dacades of Urbanization," *Indian Economic and Social History Review,* II (1965), 23–41; P. B. Desai, *Size and Sex Composition of Population in India, 1901–1961* (New York: Asia Publishing House, 1969); P. Paustian, *Canal Irrigation in the Punjab* (New York: Columbia University Press, 1930).

periods of time. Those like Krishnamurty's and Narain's that restrict themselves to a limited number of well-defined questions are particularly successful. Yet these authors concentrate on single aspects of social or economic change (those covered in the series of records they are using) at an aggregate provincial or all-India level, making it difficult to study cause and effect by relating their findings to either a specific historical or geographic context, or to other historical developments.

Two recent studies at the regional level demonstrate the importance of a specific social and cultural context for the study of the history of social and economic organization. Dharma Kumar, in *Land and Caste in South India*,[2] and Ravinder Kumar, in *Western India in the Nineteenth Century*,[3] both rely heavily on an understanding of local institutions for their treatment of developments during the nineteenth century. The authors sources are different from those in the works cited with all-India coverage for an extended period of time. The strength of regional and local records—the gazetteers, settlement reports, memoirs of civil servants, proceedings of various departments of the provincial administration, and district records—is their rich and detailed coverage of specific institutions at an important moment in time. Dharma Kumar's extensive use of the papers on "agrestic servitude" for her analysis of landless labor in early nineteenth-century South India, and the importance of detailed studies of several villages in western India just after British annexation in 1818 for Ravinder Kumar's account of changes in rural political and social structure, illustrate the strength of regional and local materials. Both books contribute to our knowledge of conditions in rural India in the early nineteenth century. Dharma Kumar's discovery of a sizable class of landless agricultural laborers in South India at the turn of the century challenges a basic element in the classical view of Indian economic history, and compels a rethinking of accepted ideas about the effect of British rule on rural society and economy. Yet as analyses of the process of change, the works are less satisfactory, both suffering from the limitations of their sources. Because they are

[2] Dharma Kumar, *Land and Caste in South India* (Cambridge University Press, 1965).

[3] Ravinder Kumar, *Western India in the Nineteenth Century* (London: Routledge and Kegan Paul, 1968).

based on particular official files, they cannot examine the extent and ramifications of changes other than those stemming from specific British policies.

Conception and Argument

This study combines the perspective and methods of the historian and the anthropologist in an attempt to break into the anonymity of rural Indian social and economic history, and transcend the limitations of conventional published and archival sources. The selection of a single village for a case study, a common anthropological technique, provides a laboratory for examining the working of such representative processes as migration, commercialization, differentiation of occupations, and population growth in rural Punjab for the past one hundred and twenty years.[4] Working with a single community and its constituent families makes it possible for the first time to use official landownership, tax, and census records that exist in abundance in a historical study. It also facilitates a structural-functional analysis of the interrelationship between different developments, villagers' changing behavior, and their underlying value structure. The history of migration from the village, for instance, examined in Chapters III and V is of intrinsic interest, amplifying Zachariah's all-India findings. Yet the real contribution is in the documentation of the interdependence of the patterns and goals of migration with family size, the extent of the family's land holding, and the importance of the community as a referent for measuring success. All-India studies are appropriate for the study of trends in urbanization, the spread of new technology, and the like. The case study shows how these changes occurred in the context of the village, and the consequences of one type of transformation for other aspects of social and economic organization.

Although the study draws heavily on anthropology, its perspective is emphatically historical. The purpose is not to show that village life in the Punjab is changing today, which it certainly is, but to follow the course of developments for an extended period and con-

[4] For a fuller discussion of the theoretical and methodological framework of this study, see Tom G. Kessinger, "History and Anthropology: The Study of Social and Economic Change in Rural India," *The Journal of Interdisciplinary History*, III (1972), 313–322.

sider what factors—government policies and programs, population growth, villagers' innovations, and the like—caused the pattern of events at particular times. A specific starting point is the first requisite. To measure change of any kind—land ownership, cropping, migration, family organization, to list a few of the topics considered in the following chapters—a baseline is needed comparable in specificity and rigor to the data used in the rest of the study. The model of the "traditional Indian village" found commonly in anthropological studies and some works in economic and administrative history is of little value because of its generality and timelessness. Ideas and institutions in India that are commonly labeled traditional are actually the product of long-term historical change, and do not transcend time. Even when something like "the village," or caste appears unchanged in form, its meaning in a new social, economic, political or cultural context may be different.[5]

The baseline for the study—the village in 1848—is established in Chapter II. This consists of a detailed description of village social and economic organization as it existed then. The choice of the year 1848 is dictated by the availability of data, and implies nothing about the history of the preceding period. In 1848 British revenue officials conducted their first survey of Jullundur district and produced a detailed set of village records which I have used to construct my account. Available information on the Mughal and Sikh periods indicates a range of important developments. Enough is known to trace in Chapter I the origin of Vilyatpur, the social and political organization of its settlers, and the political and administrative context of the village. But there is insufficient detail to form a baseline for the rest of the study, and I am therefore compelled to begin with 1848, two years after British annexation.[6]

Chapters III through VI examine topically the history of demographic trends, agriculture, occupational structure, and family organization. A series of thirty-seven tables derived from material in village records and interviews provide the data base for the findings about the consequences of the insecurity of life in the nineteenth

[5] Toru Matsui, "On the Nineteenth Century Indian Economic History—A Review of a 'Reinterpretation,'" *The Indian Economic and Social History Review*, VI (1969), 30.

[6] Jullundur was part of the territory annexed following the first Sikh War in 1846. The bulk of the Punjab did not come under British administration until the final defeat of the Sikhs in 1849.

century and population growth in the current one, technological change in agriculture and the growth of village production, patterns of migrational and occupational change, and the relationship between the family and economic activity. Several themes, developed throughout the topical chapters, integrate the study, providing its over-all direction. The basic framework and referent is the history and changing meaning of the Indian village as a community. The family and the family farm in rural Punjab, and the relationship between developments outside the village and changes in Vilyatpur are the other recurrent concerns. The themes of the community, the family and family farm, and the interaction of change in different arenas, show social change and economic development in rural Punjab, 1848–1968, to have been an incremental process, involving substantial modifications in villagers' behavior. This conclusion, together with specific findings on such issues in rural history as tenancy, indebtedness, land sales, innovation, investment, constitute the study's principal contribution to the understanding of social and economic change since the middle of the past century.

The conceptual and methodological approach employed in the study has at least one limitation. The focus is on the village of Vilyatpur and its inhabitants. The community is related to the outside world through a series of ties—kinship, family members who have migrated, government agencies, transportation facilities, and the market. The relationship between the village and the outside world, two arenas in which villagers participate on very different terms, changes throughout the period under study. Having selected a single community for detailed examination, however, I can only show the changing interaction from the village perspective. I must also add that the material presented here is a preliminary report on the principal themes in the social and economic history of rural Punjab, and is not intended as a comprehensive statement on all aspects of the village, 1848–1968. I have chosen to publish the material in this form as a background to more specific, problem-oriented studies, and because there are few historical accounts of rural India.

The Sources

The sources which provided most of the historical data on the village—census, tax, ownership and agricultural records—are part of the permanent record maintained in every district in North India

for official reference and use in the courts. Since I have described
the materials available in rural Punjab in detail elsewhere, I will
only list the principal ones and their contents to clarify references in
the text, footnotes, and tables.[7]

Jamabandi: Official record of the title to all land in the village,
which also serves as the tax list, and a record of all leases and mortgages of land, rents, and agreements for the division of the produce
of the land among co-owners where applicable. A new *jamabandi* is
drawn up every four years by a paid government employee (*patwari*).
This record is available in the Revenue Record Room, District Commissioner's Office, Jullundur for 1848–1849, 1884–1885, 1898–1899,
and every four years thereafter. The 1848–1849 record is particularly
detailed, including among other things an account of the origin of the
village.

Shajra Nasib: Official genealogical tree of all families who own
land or are permanent tenants in the village. Since 1884–1885, the
shajra nasib has been drawn up with each new *jamabandi* by the
patwari.

Lal Kitab: Official village notebook with annual statistics on the
cultivated area, area irrigated, area used for each crop, value of land
sold and mortgaged, and the number of wells in the village. The results of the quinquennial livestock census, and the decennial population census are also in the *Lal Kitab* which is stored in the Tehsil
Record Office in Phillaur.

Khanna Shumari: A household census conducted in 1848 as part
of the first revenue survey. The census is appended to the *jamabandi*
for that year, and is available in the Revenue Record Room, District
Commissioner's Office, Jullundur.

Pilgrimage records: Registers of the names and genealogies of all
pilgrims from Vilyatpur kept by Brahmin record keepers at several
important places of Hindu pilgrimage. The records also contain a
general history of each caste group in the village.

Interviews with the head of each family in the village in 1968–1969
formed the other source of information on the history of the Vilyat-

---

[7] Tom G. Kessinger, "Historical Materials on Rural India," *The Indian Eco-
nomic and Social History Review,* VII (1970), 489–510; and Tom G. Kessinger,
"Sources for the Social and Economic History of Rural Punjab," in Kenneth
Jones (ed.) *Sources for Punjab History: A Bibliographic Anthology* (East Lansing:
Asian Studies Center, Michigan State University, 1973).

pur's residents. During our ten-month stay in the village I spent from four to eight hours with each family, collecting biographical information on each person in the genealogy as far back in time as possible.[8]

The Method

The genealogies of all male members of the community provided the basic framework for the collection, organization, and analysis of the data in the village records and interviews. With the information in the *shajra nasibs,* pilgrimage records, and interviews, I reconstructed the genealogy for the males of almost every family that has lived in the village for more than one generation since approximately 1750, including members who have emigrated but retain some connection through family ties or continued ownership of property. The *khanna shumari* (household census) for 1848 supplies the names of the individuals in each genealogy resident in the village at that time and to whom a date was therefore assigned. The record provided a specific dated framework of names of men and their relationships to one another for the period 1848–1968 which I then filled in with biographical information drawn from the village records and interviews. The information included: birth date, age, age at death, education, occupations, travel and migrations, marital history, and land ownership and use.[9]

The data were collated by computer by assigning a number to each family in the village in the baseline year, 1848, and a second number to each of the descendant families for the next one hundred and twenty years. Each piece of information relating to a specific family was coded with its number for collating. The data were processed in three different forms to examine different aspects of the village's social and economic history, and each table in the study indicates the file from which it is derived. "Family biographies," the largest file, is a series of cross tabulations on the different variables listed above.

[8] For a description of the interview's format, see Kessinger, "Historical Materials," 504–507.

[9] For the code used in the study and a discussion of data processing in general, see Tom G. Kessinger, "Vilyatpur 1848–1968: An Historical Study of Social and Economic Change in a North Indian Village," Unpublished Ph.D. dissertation, University of Chicago, June, 1972, Appendix III, "Data Processing Techniques," 365–382.

The "land file" is relatively straightforward computations of agricultural statistics: size of holdings and farms, tenancy, rents, and the like. The "family profiles" is a simple listing of all information for each individual family in the village, 1848–1968, organized according to the baseline family from which it is descendant, giving the total for that group of families.

I selected nine dates in the period as points of observation, or "reference years," for the analysis and presentation of the data. The availability of revenue records was the principal consideration in the selection of the years 1848, 1884, 1898, 1910, 1922, 1934, 1946, 1958, and 1968. The first three are the only nineteenth-century dates for which I could locate *jamabandis* in Jullundur District. Thereafter I used every third jamabandi to get intervals of roughly twelve years or their multiple for the whole period. Because the four-year intervals at which material exists since 1898 are unnecessarily short for examining the trend of developments for such an extended period of time, twelve-year periods, which work out to be roughly half a generation, are used to catch the individual in rural Punjab at distinct stages in his life career.

Throughout, the analysis is concerned only with the males who comprised the village of Vilyatpur, a practice which requires some explanation. My concern is with the family, its ownership of property, and the transmission of property through time. Family membership is traced through men only, and until recently, only men customarily inherited property. A fundamental Punjabi value, the continuity of the family, its name, and place in village society, depends entirely on male heirs. Yet neither these aspects of Punjabi society nor the omission of women from the sample of individuals studied should be construed to suggest that women do not participate very directly and effectively in the decisions and behavior studied. They were also instrumental in the research that went into it, contributing their knowledge of past events in their own and their husbands' families. In general women were better at associating events in the family's history to well-known events, a technique that I employed for facilitating the dating of occurrences and computing individuals' ages.[10]

[10] For the dating technique employed, see Kessinger, "Historical Materials," 507–510.

Conventions Employed in the Text

The following are the principal conventions I have used to simplify exposition:

1. The repeated changes in the Punjab's boundaries in the past one hundred years make it difficult to select a definition that is both relatively precise and stylistically acceptable. For the period before 1947 I have employed two usages. In all specific references (using statistics, drawing contrasts between different provinces and the like), "the Punjab" refers to the province as constituted between 1911 and 1947; that is, excluding Delhi (separated in 1911) and the North-West Frontier Provinces (separated in 1901). In more general statements, "the Punjab" simply means those districts administered from Lahore at that particular moment. For the post-independence (and partition) period "the Punjab" refers to that part of the old province incorporated in the Republic of India. Pakistani Punjab will be designated as such and I will not distinguish between Punjab and Haryana because this last division occurred after the 1961 census.

2. I will use tribe and caste interchangeably for the Punjabi term *zat* (Hindi *jati*) because this usage is common in the literature on the Punjab, particularly with reference to the landed groups. Similarly I will translate the Punjabi *got* (Hindi *gotra*) as both clan and sub-caste. Many authorities consider the *got* among the landed *zat* in Punjab to be fundamentally different from the *gotra* of the Brahmins. See Denzil Ibbetson, *Punjab Castes* (Lahore: Superintendent Government Printing, Punjab, 1916), pp. 20–22. While the two may differ in origin, they are identical in their place in the marriage system.

3. For the translation of caste names I have followed H. A. Rose, *A Glossary of the Tribes and Castes of the Punjab and North-West Frontier Province* (Patiala: Languages Department, Punjab, 1970). (This is a reprint of the 1911–1919 edition.) The translations for caste names given in parentheses denote the group's "traditional occupation," and not the actual occupation of its members at any particular time. Whenever the English equivalent of the caste name is used it will be capitalized to distinguish it from occupation, which will be in lower-case letters.

4. I used the common English renderings of Hindi, Punjabi, and Urdu words rather than attempting a systematic transliteration. Each term is defined after its first occurrence in the text, and in the glossary.

5. In the tables I used three dashes (– – –) to differentiate instances where the percentage worked out to be less than 1 percent from those where the value was actually zero.

Chapter I

RURAL ADMINISTRATION
AND SOCIETY UNDER THE MUGHALS
AND THE SIKHS

The Punjab¹ and Jullundur District

The Punjab lies in the angle between two mountain ranges that
divide the India subcontinent from the rest of Asia, the Himalayas
on the north and the Sulaimans on the northwest. The most important part of the province consists of the northwestern end of the
Indo-Gangetic plain, a vast, level, extremely fertile and heavily populated tract stretching from the Punjab to Bengal following the
course of the Ganges river and its tributaries. These two geographic
features had profound consequences for the region's history until
British annexation in the nineteenth century. Situated near the
passes which provide the only access through the mountain barrier
from Asia, and at the head of North India's richest area, the Punjab
experienced almost continuous incursions of central Asian peoples
and provided the site for numerous important battles which decided
the fate of much of North India.

Before the last decade of the nineteenth century, when numerous
projects to develop the Punjab's soil and water resources were con-
summated, the region consisted of four geographically distinct zones:
the Himalayan, the sub-Himalayan zone, the Indo-Gangetic plain,
and the northwest dry area.² The hills received the greatest annual
rainfall, but owing to the difficulty of the terrain, supported a small
population. Westward from the Himalayan foothills, each of the
other three zones was progressively drier. Population density rose
sharply in the sub-Himalayan and Indo-Gangetic plains—the latter
supporting almost half of the Punjab's population—and then declined rapidly in the dry zone. Until the turn of the century the
Indo-Gangetic plains contained the richest and most heavily cultivated agricultural lands, with the sub-Himalayan a close second. The
first application of modern technology to manipulate the Punjab's

¹ See convention number 1 in the introduction.
² *Punjab Census,* 1921, I, 95.

11

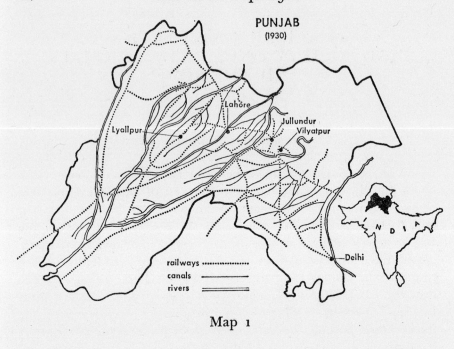

PUNJAB
(1930)

Map 1

environment and alter the distribution of the population came in 1892 when the Punjab government opened the first of its major irrigation works in the northwest dry area. Canals had existed in the region in the Mughal period, and the British had constructed several new works after annexation in 1849, but all these facilities served tracts where settled agriculture had been carried on for centuries. The new departure, dating from the end of the last century but with the greatest expansion in the 1920's, was the construction of hundreds of miles of canals through previously barren districts that had supported nomadic pastoralists with a density of less than ten persons per square mile. Together, British engineers and Punjabi colonists transformed the northwest dry area into the richest agricultural tract in the subcontinent producing a steady increase in the population and productivity of northwestern Punjab.[3] By 1947 the four zones were no longer distinct in population density and agricultural productivity; the only real contrast was between the hills and the other

[3] *Punjab Census*, 1931, I, 5.

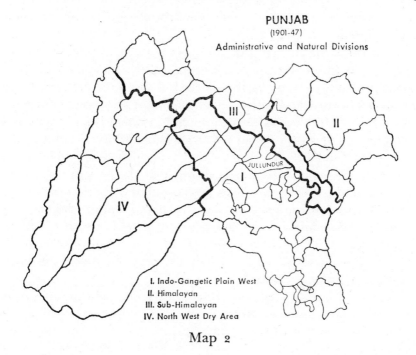

PUNJAB
(1901-47)
Administrative and Natural Divisions

I. Indo-Gangetic Plain West
II. Himalayan
III. Sub-Himalayan
IV. North West Dry Area

Map 2

three.[4] The government's construction of roads and development of the hilly areas for orchards and other tree products have reduced even this disparity since Independence.

The Punjab's many rivers divide the region into tracts, each possessing a measure of ecological and historical unity. Mughal, Sikh, and British officials used these natural divisions for administrative boundaries. Vilyatpur is situated in the southern end of the *doab* (area between two rivers) between the Sutlej and Beas rivers, in what was regarded as the central area of the old British Punjab and is now part of the Punjab state in the Republic of India. Jullundur *doab* was administered as a unit under both the Mughal and Sikh regimes, forming a separate *sarkar* (district) under the two governments. After annexation of the *doab* in 1846 following the first Sikh War, the British divided the tract into three districts, Jullundur in the plains, Hoshiarpur in the submontane area, and Kangra in the hilly portion.

[4] For a complete discussion of the development of irrigation in the Punjab, see Paul Paustian, *Canal Irrigation in the Punjab* (New York: Columbia University Press, 1930).

With minor modifications, these administrative divisions continue
to the present.

Except for some low-lying areas subject to flooding along the rivers,
most of Jullundur district is a flat, unbroken, alluvial plain. Soils
vary considerably, but more than three-fourths of the cultivated area
consists of heavy loams which, if irrigated, are very productive.[5] Because of the district's proximity to the hills, rainfall is fairly constant,
averaging about 25–30 inches a year, a figure which is close to the
average for Punjab.[6] The district also has a high water table (10 to
27 feet in 1885 and rising slowly throughout the period) due to the
location of the Sutlej and Beas rivers and the narrowness of the
doab.[7] Even when lift technology was relatively simple, the nearness
of subsoil water allowed the construction of wells which enhanced
the productivity of the district. The use of the Persian wheel, a series
of buckets on a continuous rope-chain driven by bullocks, was noted
as early as 1526 in the area.[8]

The combination of regular rainfall, rich soils, and extensive areas
irrigated from wells made Jullundur one of the richest areas in North
India throughout the Mughal and Sikh periods.[9] In the words of one
British official writing on the resources of the Punjab in 1847,

It is acknowledged by everyone that the Jullundur Doab was the most
favoured Province of the Sikh dominions. Parts of the [central districts],
equal it in fertility, but no continuous tract of the same extent can be
said to exceed it.[10]

A further indication of Jullundur's productivity is the high tax assessments on its agricultural lands. Throughout the nineteenth century, until the extensive canal-irrigated tracts of western Punjab were
developed, Jullundur paid the highest rate per acre in the province.[11]
This resource base supported the densest population in the province,
a position the district maintains to the present day. In 1850 there

[5] D. G., 1904, 149–152.

[6] *Punjab Census*, 1921, I, 95.

[7] S.R., 1892, 106.

[8] Zahirud-din Muhammad. *The Memoirs of Babur*, trans. Annette S. Beveridge
(London: Luzac and Co., 1921), II, 486.

[9] Abul Fazl-I-Allami. *Ain-I-Akbari*, trans. H. S. Jarrett, corrected and further
annotated by Jadu-Nath Sarkar. (Calcutta: Royal Asiatic Society of Bengal,
1949), II, 316.

[10] *Selections from the Records of the Government of the Punjab and Its De-
pendencies*. New Series, No. XVI. "Notes on the Revenue and Resources of the
Punjab." (Lahore: Punjab Government Civil Secretariat Press, 1880), 49.

[11] See P.A.R., 1892, xxii–xxiii.

were 420 persons per square mile; in 1861 the figure reached 914.[12] By nineteenth-century standards, Jullundur was heavily populated and fully developed. From their first experience with Jullundur, British officials regarded it as densely settled and farmed to capacity, designating it as a recruitment area in the 1890's when settlers were selected from "congested" districts to colonize the newly irrigated tracts in western Punjab.[13] This mid-nineteenth century characterization of Jullundur must be kept in mind through the following chapters as we trace the developments of the period 1848–1968. Despite the pressure of population on the district's resources and the fact that agriculture was already intensive at the time of annexation, considerable economic growth has taken place—a point of importance for an understanding of Punjab's social and economic history, and of consequence for the future of independent India.

Jullundur district has always been well served with roads and transportation facilities. The Grand Trunk road, of ancient origins but substantially improved during Akbar's reign (1556–1605), passed through the district connecting it with Lahore and Delhi and thereby with all principal trade routes to Persia, Tibet, and South India. Although neither the city of Jullundur nor the surrounding country side produced any special manufactures, there was some trade in hand-woven cloth. In addition a limited trade in agricultural produce existed from Jullundur to nearby markets.[14] The Grand Trunk road was paved in the decade from 1850 to 1860 and in 1870 a railway line running through Jullundur from Lahore to Delhi was completed with the construction of suspension bridges over the Beas and Sutlej rivers.[15] Since the turn-of-the-century and up to the time of Independence, sixty miles of feeder roads were built, beginning the process of tying rural communities into the mainstream of the economic and political life of the district.[16] But from the point of view of most villagers in Jullundur, the major developments in transportation did not come until after Independence. In 1967 there were

[12] P.A.R., 1849–50, 121; Punjab Government. *Punjab, District Census Handbook, No. 10, Jullundur District* (Chandigarh: Government of Punjab, 1966), 25.

[13] Punjab Government. *Punjab District Gazetteers, Gazetteer of the Chenab Colony, 1904* (Lahore: Punjab Government, 1905), 29, 36.

[14] Sujan Rai, "Khulasatu-T-Tawarikh," trans. Jadunath Sarkar, in Jadunath Sarkar, *India of Aurangzib* (Calcutta: Bose Brothers, 1901), 83, and S.R., 1851, 225.

[15] S.R., 1892, 45.

[16] Punjab Government. *P.W.D. Administration Report* (B. & R., 1942–43 (Lahore: Superintendent Government Printing, Punjab, 1943), Table III.

485 miles of paved roads in the district and plans had been made to link every village by an all-weather road in the next few years.[17] It is common to see buses and trucks within a few miles of most villages, three-wheeled Tempos (Punjabi *tempu*) filling in on routes without sufficient traffic to warrant regular service by larger vehicles. In 1968 two new four-lane bridges over the Sutlej and Beas replaced their nineteenth-century predecessors, facilitating the flow of truck and bus traffic that has increased so much in recent years.

Rural Jullundur under the Mughals and the Sikhs

Although Mughal and Sikh documents have recently been found,[18] little detailed information exists about the social and economic history of rural Punjab before British annexation, particularly in contrast to the abundance of facts available for the period after 1849. The pre-British revenue records that exist relate primarily to the central revenue office of the earlier regimes, telling little about the organization of rural society and economy.[19] Even where local records have been located and examined, they yield little more than a glimpse into the organization of the revenue administration and the level of taxation because the records were only concerned with taxes, and did not, like their British counterparts, constitute an official title to the land.[20] Additional efforts along the lines of Goswamy's and Grewal's work will unearth more documents from private collections, and materials stored in official archives will eventually come to light.[21] But until this happens it is impossible to examine important aspects of Vilyatpur's history with the same detail as the British period, and a

[17] Goverment of Punjab (India). *Statistical Abstract of Punjab*, 1967. (Chandigarh: Economic and Statistical Adviser to Government, Punjab, 1968),

[18] B. N. Goswamy and J. S. Grewal, *The Mughals and the Jogis of Jakhbar* (Simla: Indian Institute of Advanced Study, 1967), and *The Mughal and Sikh Rulers and the Vaishnavas of Pindori* (Simla: Indian Institute of Advanced Study, 1969).

[19] Sita Ram Kohli, "Land Revenue Administration under Maharajah Ranjit Singh" in *Journal of the Punjab Historical Society*, I (1918), 74.

[20] S.R., 1851, 262. I have considered the types of records available in the context of the nature of rural Punjabi society and the administrative systems of the Mughals and the Sikhs in, Jones, *Sources for Punjab History*.

[21] For instance Jullundur's first settlement officer, Sir Richard Temple, mentions finding and using the *mauzinas* (village registers) dating from the Mughal period in his early assessment of many of Jullundur's villages, but never states where he stored them. I am sure that they still exist in some archive or office.

Figure 1

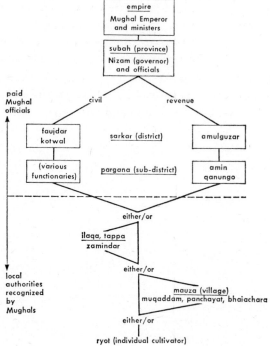

consideration of the administrative and political history of rural Jullundur from 1600 to 1846 based on general accounts of Mughal and Sikh rule and other published works, must suffice. The treatment of the Mughal period will be particularly sketchy, but, in conjunction with the somewhat more complete materials on the early nineteenth century, will provide an outline of social and economic organization in rural Punjab, and indicate something about the nature and extent of change in the pre-British period. This background is useful for evaluating developments over the one hundred and twenty years from 1848 to 1968.

Politically and administratively, the *doab* was an integral part of the Mughal empire from its founding (1526) until the Afghans, Marathas, and Sikhs turned the Punjab into a battleground in the mid-eighteenth century. As a subdivision of the Lahore *subah* (province), the administration of Jullundur *sarkar* (district) followed the pattern found in all of the more settled parts of the empire.[22] Figure 1 shows

[22] This account is adapted from P. Saran, *The Provincial Government of the Mughals* (Allahabad: Kitabistan, 1941), 207–211.

two variations in the administrative system. Throughout the empire a hierarchy of appointed officials with distinct functions were responsible for civil and revenue administration and the preservation of law and order. In *khalisa* (crown) lands these officials were the only authority; they administered the emperor's orders and collected revenue for the royal treasury. But a considerable amount of the territory of the empire was granted as *jagirs* to individuals who were empowered to collect the revenues for themselves in return for service to the emperor, and in these areas the official hierarchy was duplicated by the *jagirdars'* functionaries. The administrative system of the Mughal empire was quite refined. Even at the *pargana* level civil and revenue administration were separate; the revenue branch was particularly specialized with an *amin* responsible for the collection of taxes, and a *qanungo* for the maintenance of records. No general statement about how *jagirdars* managed their grants is possible since assigned land varied so much in area and conditions of grant. Petty states of semi-autonomous rulers and extensive tracts given to high officials fall into this category; a number of villages attached to a temple or school and a few acres given to a local priest, though technically different, were functionally the same. Rajas and some of the large *jagirdars* often had administrations patterned after the emperor's, but most had agents who were less formally organized and without specialized responsibilities. Both systems had a number of intermediaries who were either part of the government or appointed by it to carry out its functions.

Scholars of Mughal India agree that below the *pargana* there was no other official unit of administration. In most areas Mughal officials are thought to have relied on the assistance of village headmen (*muqaddams*), village elders (*panchayats*), and village record keepers (*patwaris*), in both revenue matters and problems of keeping the peace in the fairly numerous villages (*mauzas*) in each *pargana*.[23] The *muqaddam* was a local man, not a government official, although he could be punished for not assisting Mughal authorities.[24] Similarly, "the village panchayat . . . was popular in origin, but recognized by the government." [25] The *patwari* was a paid functionary,

[23] Saran, pp. 207, 212; Irfan Habib, *The Agrarian System of Mughal India* (New York: Asia Publishing House, 1963), 130–135.

[24] Habib, 130–132.

[25] Saran, 207.

but in contrast to his counterpart under the British, received his remuneration from the village rather than the government.

In this sense, Mughal government in rural areas was essentially military and fiscal,[26] designed to maintain its position and collect state taxes. Whether out of "conscious foresight or political expediency, [the Mughals] did not attempt to interfere with . . . the local government of the village communities."[27] As in other premodern states, there was little direct interaction between most individuals and the government. The administration dealt with each group in society through that group's own leaders, and refrained from interfering in the group's internal affairs unless there was a threat to overall Mughal dominance and the orderly collection of revenue.[28] But one point is not clear in this general outline of rural administration and the relationship of the village to the state apparatus. None of the authorities on the period indicate exactly what is meant by "village community." Is it a village as designated in the revenue records (*mauza*), a populated place (*abadi*), a discrete settlement (*pinda*), or a group of settlements bound together by ties of caste and kinship (*ilaqa, thapa,* etc.)? To what extent does the model of semi-autonomous groups within the state coincide with the familiar picture of the Indian "village republics"? The nature of the village and its significance in the social, political, and economic life of Punjab's rural population is a theme that will run throughout the account of Vilyatpur, 1848–1968. We will return to the subject after completing the outline of rural administrative and political structure in the pre-British period.

Although there was no formal level of administration linking Mughal officials in the *pargana* to cultivators living in the villages, zamindars[29] who performed this function existed over much of the empire. The origins of the *zamindars* and their relations to the state

[26] Kashi Singh, "The Territorial Basis of Medieval Town and Village Settlement in Eastern Uttar Pradesh, India," in Association of American Geographers, *Annals,* LVIII (1968), 218.

[27] Saran, 239.

[28] This point is a major theme in Michael N. Pearson's work "Commerce and Compulsion: Gujarati Merchants and the Portuguese System in Western India, 1500–1600," unpublished Ph.D. dissertation, University of Michigan, 1971.

[29] The term is used here as it occurs in the literature on Mughal India, and not in the sense common in the Punjab at present where it simply means "cultivator."

varied greatly from one region to another.[30] Caste and lineage groups
that either conquered or settled an area, officials who were able to
turn their land grants into hereditary holdings, Rajas who had been
deprived of their official position but still held land, and the descendants of holy men who had received a land grant, are a few examples.
The crucial factor was state recognition of the responsibility for the
collection and transmission of the revenue throughout a specified
area. From the local point of view the *zamindars* were important elements to be reckoned with; they possessed official sanction, forts, and
small contingents of men to enforce their rights. In much of the
Jullunder *doab* under the Mughals, lineages of Muslim Rajputs held
the position of *zamindar* over extensive tracts containing many villages inhabited by other caste and religious groups.[31] These Rajputs
gained their position when, sometime in the early fourteenth or
fifteenth century, they conquered the area as a lineage group. Ties
of kinship and caste provided a continuing source of cohesion against
the local population and outside intruders—a common pattern
throughout North India in this period.[32]

There is apparently little information in Mughal sources on the
relationship between the *zamindars* and the cultivators in the villages. In his general account, Irfan Habib, the leading authority on
the period, sees no connection between the *zamindar* and the village
community with its *muqaddam* and *panchayat*. There is no information on the internal organization of the village; *zamindars* are de-
picted as dealing with individual peasants.[33] This might be true in
smaller *zamindaris* where the *zamindar* was in close proximity to a
small number of cultivators and functioned as the *muqaddam* himself, but not in most areas.[34] In the villages around Vilyatpur, the
Muslim Rajputs came from their forts periodically to collect taxes
from the *muqaddams,* and did not directly supervise land use or
community affairs.[35] In their own and nearby villages, the *zamindars*
participated directly in the supervision of agriculture and village

[30] Habib, 159–169.
[31] Abul Fazl-I-Allami, II, 320–1; S.R., 1892, 75–78.
[32] Habib, 163, 167.
[33] Habib, 165.
[34] *Ibid.*, 134.
[35] B. R. Grover, "Nature of *Dehat-i-Taaluqa* (Zamindari Villages) and the Evolution of the *Taaluqdari* system during the Mughal Age" in *The Indian Economic and Social History Review*, II (1965), 261–263.

life in general. In other probably more distant villages, they functioned more specifically as revenue-collecting intermediaries between the state and other caste groups who controlled cultivation. From a local point of view, the political developments of the years 1750–1849 meant freedom from *zamindars* of rival caste status and alien religion.

Punjab's history in the last half of the eighteenth century is a chronicle of the rise of the Sikhs as a military and political power, and of continued struggle among these successors to Mughal authority in the region. For nearly fifty years the Sikh *misls* (armed bands) fought first the Afghan governors of Punjab and then each other for control of different parts of the province. Because of its subdivision between various *misls,* whose area of control remained in flux, it is difficult to treat Punjab's political and administrative history as a whole for the period from 1759 to 1799. The *misls* had no formal government or administrative apparatus. They were composed of a leader with his "relations, friends and volunteers," [36] to whom subordinate chiefs were affiliated, each with his own followers.[37] The composition of any particular *misl* always remained fluid:

The chief was to lead in war, and act as arbiter in peace; he was respected and treated with deference by inferior *sirdars* (leaders), but these owed no obligation to obey, beyond what they might consider to be their own reciprocal benefit, or for the well being of the *misul.*[38]

Subordinate chiefs frequently shifted allegiance between one *misl* and another to improve their circumstances, severing connections on occasion in an attempt to raise themselves to the level of independent chiefs without obligation to other leaders.[39] The villages under the control of a *misl* were parceled out to subordinate chiefs to support them and their followers, each subchief collecting taxes from several communities. The Punjab was ruled by a confederation without a head. The *misls* coalesced against outsiders like the Mughals and the Afghans, and fought with each other over territory in the interim.

For most of the last forty years of the eighteenth century the south-

[36] Thomas Thornton, *History of the Punjab* (London: Wm. H. Allen & Co., 1846), I, 224.

[37] D. G., 1904, 31.

[38] Thornton, I, 225.

[39] Joseph Davey Cunningham, *A History of the Sikhs* (Delhi: S. Chand & Co., 1966), 96.

ern end of the Jullundur *doab* was dominated by the Dalawala *misl.*[40]
Vilyatpur and several neighboring villages were controlled by a subchief named Gulab Singh, a local leader from the village immediately
to the north.[41] Gulab Singh was a member of the Sahota *got* (clan)
of the Jat *zat* (caste), the same as cultivators in Vilyatpur and several nearby villages.[42] He remained an affiliate of the Dalawalas until
about 1780 when he was able to establish his independence in the
fluid political conditions of the period.[43] For the next twenty years
Gulab Singh—and after his death his family—were able to maintain
their position by playing one *misl* off against another. Their control
of Vilyatpur and its environs was finally brought to an end in 1806
with their defeat by the Ahluwalia *misl* and the confiscation of all of
their holdings.[44] Vilyatpur finally came under the direct administration of Ranjit Singh, Maharajah of the Punjab, when he defeated
the Ahluwalias in 1811 and annexed their territories as he had annexed those of the other *misls* since 1799.[45]

The activities and organization of the *misls* eliminated the two
official levels of administration which had existed at the *sarkar* and
pargana under the Mughals.[46] In the area around Vilyatpur these
officials and the Muslim Rajput *zamindars* were replaced by a single,
low-level, military and political leader who was a local man with
caste and kinship ties in the area under his dominance. Once Ranjit
Singh extended his control over the *doab*, however, he reestablished
a formal administrative apparatus (Figure 2). As in the Mughal system, some areas were administered only by officials appointed in
Lahore and responsible directly to Ranjit Singh's government, others
were granted as *jagirs*. The duties of revenue collection and general
administration were combined at each level, the *nazim* and *kardar*
in the *sarkar* and *pargana* respectively.[47] The *diwan* was charged

[40] D. G., 1904, 35.

[41] *Ibid.*, 66.

[42] These terms, and local caste organization in general, will be considered in
detail below.

[43] D. G., 1904, 39.

[44] *Ibid.*, 66.

[45] *Ibid.*, 39.

[46] Percival Spear, *Twilight of the Mughals* (Cambridge University Press, 1951),
115.

[47] This account of the Sikh administrative and revenue hierarchy is adapted
from Kohli, 87–88; Hugh Kennedy Trevaskis, *The Land of the Five Rivers*
(Oxford University Press, 1928), 180; Gulshan Lall Chopra, *The Punjab as a
Sovereign State* (Hoshiarpur: Vishveshvarandand Vedic Research Institute,
1928), 82.

Figure 2

ORGANIZATIONAL CHART OF ADMINISTRATIVE AND POLITICAL
STRUCTURE OF THE PUNJAB IN JULLUNDUR *Ca.* 1580–1845

Territorial division	Mughal (1580–1730)	Sikh Misl (1750–1810)	Ranjit Singh (1810–1845)
subah (province)	Nizam (governor) and officers	none	Maharajah and court
sarkar (district)	appointed officials[a] (specialized functions)	Sirdar and subchiefs of Dalawala Misl	appointed officials[b] (specialized functions)
pargana (subdistrict)	appointed officials[a] (specialized functions)		appointed officials[b] (specialized functions)
ilaqa, etc.	Muslim Rajput zamindars	subchiefs/Gulab Singh	none
mauza (village)	muqaddam/panchayat	muqaddam/panchayat	muqaddam/panchayat

[a] Jagirdars are not shown since there is no record of Vilyatpur ever having been included in an assignment to a Jagirdar.

[b] In the years immediately after Maharajah Ranjit Singh gained control of the doab, the tax collection was farmed out. He soon established a regular administration.

with the maintenance of revenue records for the *sarkar,* the *qanungo* being his *pargana* subordinate. Where the revenues were assigned to a *jagirdar,* he employed his own assistants to make collections. In both instances, however, under Ranjit Singh's officials and his *jagirdars,* the *muqaddam* and *patwari* functioned on the local level as they had under the Mughals. Organizationally and functionally, the official part of the Sikh revenue system was a direct copy of its Mughal predecessor.[48] The formal structures of the two were identical. From the vantage point of the village cultivator they were similar as well since the position of the village was essentially the same in both. In the linkage between the state's administrative apparatus and the village, important changes occurred between the Mughal period and the Punjab under Maharajah Ranjit Singh. In Jullundur the Muslim Rajput *zamindars* were never able to regain their stature as revenue-collecting intermediaries.

Although Ranjit Singh at times employed a number of unrefined

[48] Kushwant Singh, *The History of the Sikhs* (Princeton University Press, 1963), I, 203.

means to collect taxes—including tax farming and cutting half the standing crop—his regular administration reached high levels of efficiency. Rup Lal, the *nazim* in Jullundur from 1832 to 1839, exemplified how competent some Sikh officials were. His revenue records attest to the thoroughness of his administration. They were so complete and well organized that British settlement officers used them for a temporary assessment of the revenue for Jullundur district in 1846–1847—the year of Jullundur's annexation—and as a guideline in the regular settlement for thirty years.[49]

Continuity and Change in Pre-British Punjab

The history of Jullundur from 1600 to 1846 shows trends which are of significance in considering the nature and extent of change from 1848 to 1968.

Under all three governments and systems of revenue administration—the Mughals, Sikh *misls,* and Maharajah Ranjit Singh—the structural position of the village remained unchanged (Figure 2). Even during the dencentralized rule of the *misls* which brought many changes in administration, the village level in the administrative and political structure retained its formal integrity as long as revenue was paid and other demands of local chiefs were satisfied.[50] Formal integrity, since saying that there was no structural change in *the* village does not mean that individual villages were not destroyed by adventurers or vindictive chiefs. Relatively few communities had really long histories of settlement, generation after generation, by the same group of families. Calculations made on the basis of genealogical evidence indicate that only about one fourth of Jullundur's villages in 1885 dated from Akbar's reign (1556–1605).[51] Yet despite the vicissitudes of individual communities, the village continued as a basic structural type in rural Punjab, both in relation to the state administrative apparatus and as a social setting.

This view of Punjabi society does not imply that the village was

---

[49] D. G., 1904, 254–6.

[50] Moreland finds this to be the case in the decentralized conditions of the United Provinces in the eighteenth century. W. H. Moreland, *The Agrarian System of Moslem India,* 2nd. ed. (Delhi: Munshiram Manoharlal, 1968), 175.

[51] S. R., 1892, 85.

a "self-sufficient" and "independent" entity. In 1830 Charles Metcalfe stated:

The village communities are little republics, having nearly everything they want within themselves, and almost independent of any foreign relations. They seem to last where nothing else lasts. Dynasty after dynasty tumbles down; revolution succeeds to revolution; Hindoo, Patan, Mogul, Mahratta, Sik, English are all masters in turn; but the village communities remain the same. In times of trouble they fortify and arm themselves: an hostile army passes through the country: the village communities collect their cattle within their walls, and let the enemy pass unprovoked. If plunder and devastation be directed against themselves, and the force employed be irresistible, they flee to friendly villages at a distance; but when the storm has passed over they return, and resume their occupations. If a country remain for a series of years the scene of continued pillage and massacre, so that villages cannot be inhabited, the scattered villagers nevertheless return whenever the power of peaceable possession revives. A generation may pass away, but the succeeding generation will return. The sons will take the places of their fathers; the same site for the village, the same positions for the houses, the same lands, will be occupied by the descendants of those who were driven out when the village was depopulated; and it is not a trifling matter that will drive them out, for they will often maintain their post through times of disturbance and convulsion, and acquire strength sufficient to resist pillage and oppression with success.[52]

Metcalfe's statement confuses the village as a structural type and the experience of particular communities. Although revenue officers collected an abundance of detailed ethnographic and historical information in the late nineteenth century, most of it appeared in unpublished reports and reference works on land tenure and customary law, and Metcalfe's conception has persisted.[53] A more accurate

[52] Great Britain, Parliament, *Parliamentary Papers* (House of Commons), 1830–1831, Vol. XI, Cmnd. 735 III, "Report from the Select Committee on the Affairs of the East India Company," Appendix 84, "Minute of Charles T. Metcalfe," 7 November 1830, 331–332 (Readex Microprint edition).

[53] Walter C. Neale, *Economic Change in Rural India* (New Haven: Yale University Press, 1962), 45. For a discussion of the various social ties uniting the village with wider society see M. N. Srinivas and A. M. Shah, "The Myth of the Self-Sufficiency of the Indian Village, *Economic Weekly*, XII (1960), 1375–1378; for the dynamic relationship between village culture and all Indian culture see McKim Marriott, "Little Communities in an Indigenous Civilization" in McKim Marriott (ed.) *Village India* (University of Chicago Press, 1955), 171–222; and for

characterization of the community which makes the distinction is by
Mark Wilks, written in 1810 on the basis of his experience with
Thomas Munro in South India. After a series of statements that may
have been Metcalfe's source, Wilks makes the kind of qualification
that would fit Vilyatpur's history under the Mughals and the Sikhs:

It is not intended to assert that the village in our contemplation may not
have produced the Caesar of his little world; the rights of the inhabitants
may have been invaded by [the headman, local officials or the king]: each
or either of these persons may have attempted, or have succeeded, or have
failed, in persuading or forcing an augmentation of the proportion of
money or of grain paid by the township [village] to the state, but con-
quests, usurpation, or revolutions, considered as such, have absolutely no
influence on its condition. The conqueror, or usurper, directly or through
his agents, addresses himself as sovereign or representative of the sovereign to the head of the township; its officers, its boundaries, and the
whole frame of its interior management remain unalterably the same;
and it is of importance to remember that every state in India is a con-
geries (sic) of these little republics.[54]

Rajput *zamindars* and Sikh *sirdars* disrupted the autonomy of the
village repeatedly in the pre-British period.

Yet we must refine more than the accepted ideas about the political
autonomy of the Indian village. The description below of Vilyatpur's
settlement will illustrate how difficult it is at times even to determine
where one village physically ends and another begins. We will see
that if economic self-sufficiency ever existed in rural Punjab, it involved clusters of villages around a *qasbah* (a larger village with a
permanent *bazaar*), an area considerably larger than a single settlement.[55] Revenue-collecting land-controllers dominated the village.
They were as frequently government appointees, who had made their
position hereditary, as products of indigenous settlement and conquest.[56] An extreme example of the state's power to shape rural so-

---

the history of the study of Indian villages see Bernard S. Cohn, "Notes on the
History of the Study of Indian Society and Culture," in Milton Singer and
Bernard S. Cohn, *Structure and Change in Indian Society* (Chicago: Aldine Pub-
lishing Co., 1968), 18–25.

[54] Lt. Mark Wilks, *Historical Sketches of South India* (Mysore: Government
Branch Press, 1930), I, 139. (This is a reprint of the 1810 edition.)

[55] Miriam W. Smith, "Social Structure in the Punjab," in M. N. Srinivas (ed.),
India's Villages, 2nd. ed. (New York: Asia Publishing House, 1960), 172.

[56] Louis Dumont, "The Village Community from Munro to Maine," *Contributions to Indian Sociology*, IX (1966), 88.

ciety at the local level comes from the Deccan in western India, where "government policies in pre-British times actually created lineage group estates in villages of whole regions where no such estates had previously existed." [57]

There was structural continuity at the village level through the Mughal and Sikh periods of Punjab's history, but there was also structural change. While the Sikh *misls* dominated the Jullundur *doab*, local chiefs collected taxes directly from villages, eliminating the official administrative structure at the *sarkar* and *pargana* and disappropriating, in effect, the Rajput *zamindars* whom the Mughal authorities had recognized.[58] Later, Maharajah Ranjit Singh restored the revenue system along the lines of its Mughal predecessor. Yet the two were similar only on the official levels. A basic change in the relationship between the village cultivators and government officials occurred at the level of the *zaminders*. The change is of importance for the study of the Sikh period (on which little detailed information is available) and for the development of land tenure in the Punjab after 1849 (Figure 2).

Table 1, computed from the data recorded in the *Ain-i-Akbari*, shows the subcaste of *zamindars* responsible for the payment of revenue at the close of Akbar's reign.[59] The Rajputs had a near monopoly in the area which became Phillaur *tehsil* and were clearly dominant in the *doab*. Although these figures refer to the late sixteenth century, they are indicative of the situation that lasted into

---

[57] Marriott, 187.

[58] The British attributed the by-passing of the *zamindars* to two different aspects of Ranjit Singh's revenue policy. On the one hand his heavy assessments were thought to have absorbed all of the cultivators' surplus, leaving nothing for the *zamindar*, S. R., 1851, 277; James M. Douie, *Punjab Settlement Manual*, 4th ed. (Lahore: Superintendent, Government Printing, Punjab, 1930), 57. On the other hand the *zamindars* were oppressed to weaken their position as potential competitors to the Maharajah. S. R., 1851, 264–265; Douie, 61; Trevaskis, 183.

[59] "The caste given as responsible for payment of revenue, probably meant numerical predominance or clear majority, but omits others who also paid revenue in the *parganas*." Bernard S. Cohn, "Structural Change in Indian Rural Society, 1596–1885" in Robert E. Frykenberg (ed.), *Land Control and Social Structure in Indian History* (Madison: University of Wisconsin Press, 1969), 56. The use of the *Ain-i-Akbari* data and the contrast drawn in Tables 1 and 2 are inspired by Cohn's essay. One difference in the two cases is that the Settlement reports have made the identification of the particular lineages possible for Jullundur.

TABLE 1

CASTE OF ZAMINDARS RESPONSIBLE FOR REVENUE, *ca.* 1596

(N. = percent of *mahals*, A. = percent of total area, R. = percent of total revenue)

	Jats			Jats & Rajputs			Rajputs			Afghans			Rajputs & Afghans			Khokars			Not given		
	N.	A.	R.	N.	A.	R.	N.	A.	R.	N.	A.	R.	N.	A.	R.	N.	A.	R.	N.	A.	R.
Phillaur tehsil[a]							67	96	95										33	4	5
Jullundur district[a]							43	55	46				14	35	38				43	10	16
Jullundur doab	3	4	5	2	2	1	52	43	54	2	3	5	2	14	11	2	5	4	37	29	20

SOURCE: Abul Fazl-I-Allami, II, 320–321.

[a] The two units consist of those *mahals* (revenue estates) situated for the most part in what became Phillaur *tehsil* and Jullundur district according to the findings of D. G. Barkley, *Punjab Notes and Queries*, III, 804, 878.

the eighteenth century as long as Mughal rule remained effective in the Punjab. The same Rajput lineages listed in the *Ain-i-Akbari* are mentioned in the reports of the British officers charged with Jullundur's first and second revenue settlements.[60]

Table 2 outlines the holdings of various subcaste groups on completion of the British revenue settlement of 1851. The dramatic reversal of the positions of the Jats and the Rajputs, particularly in Phillaur, but also, to a lesser extent, in the district, means that during one hundred years of Sikh rule, the Jats virtually replaced the Muslim Rajputs as the district's main revenue payers. But this is not the result of any significant movement in the area's population. Neither the unpublished village records nor the revenue reports and gazetteers suggest any migrations or changes in the caste-composition of Jullundur's villages either during the rule of the *misls* or under Maharajah Ranjit Singh. The Jats and the other caste groups with impressive gains—Gujars and Raens, in particular—merely formed the population of village cultivators in communities from which the Rajput lineages held the right to collect the land revenue but did not actually supervise agriculture and participate in local affairs. The Rajputs' possession of 7 percent of the villages in Phillaur in 1851 represents those communities where the *zamindars* actually resided, controlling agriculture and collecting the revenue.[61]

The effect of one hundred years of Sikh rule was to remove a layer of *zamindars* who were never replaced. The combination of a deliberate policy against former *zamindars,* who were seen as a political threat,[62] and Ranjit Singh's practice of frequently transferring officials,[63] militated against any redevelopment at this level of rural society. This change represents more than the substitution of *zamindars* from one particular family, lineage, caste, or religious group for those drawn from a different background—a process that was common in other parts of India in the pre-British period.[64] The elimination of the position of *zamindar* constituted a fundamental change in the structure of rural society in the Punjab. This change was a basic

[60] S. R., 1851, 288–289; S. R., 1892, 75–78.

[61] *Ibid.*

[62] Trevaskis, 183, Douie, 61; Census 1881, I, 52.

[63] D. G., 1904, 249–251.

[64] For a detailed case study of this process see Bernard S. Cohn, "Political Systems in Eighteenth Century India: The Banaras Region," *Journal of the American Oriental Society,* LXXXII (1959), 312–320.

TABLE 2

VILLAGES IN POSSESSION OF VARIOUS CASTES, 1851

(N. = percent of villages, A. = percent of total area, R. = percent of total revenue)

	Jats			Rajputs			Afghans			Gujars			Raens			Awans			Others		
	N.	A.	R.	N.	A.	R.	N.	A.	R.	N.	A.	R.	N.	A.	R.	N.	A.	R.	N.	A.	R.
Phillaur tehsil	64	59	73	7	10	7	3	2	1	7	6	3	13	16	11	1	1	1	6	7	4
Jullundur district	51	48	56	15	17	15	4	3	3	4	4	2	14	16	14	5	3	4	8	9	8

SOURCE: S. R., 1851, 334.

factor in the development of a system of land tenure under the British in which village cultivators who owned and farmed small holdings were predominant.[65] As a "land of peasant proprietors," the Punjab is strikingly different from much of northern and eastern India where *zamindars* and *taluqdars* obtained ownership rights under the British. This generalization must be cautiously interpreted since a considerable amount of land in the Punjab has always been cultivated by tenants, and some holdings were quite large. Yet the control of estates consisting of numerous villages by single families or small groups—common in Bengal, Bihar, and the United Provinces—is not found in the Punjab with the exception of the Native States of the Princes, a special case.[66]

During Ranjit Singh's reign, the extent of structural change in rural Punjab was limited by the substantial tracts granted as *jagirs* to officials and political favorites.[67] At any moment, a Sikh *jagirdar* was the functional equivalent of a Rajput *zamindar,* both acting as intermediaries between village cultivators and the state. The completion of the process of change had to await British annexation and the implementation of British revenue policies and procedures.

The evolution of British land-revenue policy in India contributed to the final elimination of *zamindars* in the Punjab. The British government, as had all of its predecessors, depended upon land revenue for most of its income. In each newly annexed territory, British officials had to determine how much revenue to assess and whom to make responsible for its payment.[68] These procedures were known as the land-revenue settlement. Their twofold nature remained constant from the 1790's to the 1860's as various parts of the subcontinent were brought under British administration. But the policy used to determine the principles for making assessments and deciding which groups or types of individuals to regard as revenue payers varied greatly over time, depending on British perceptions of

[65] The effect was equivalent to a land reform in the sense of the simplification of tenures through the elimination of intermediaries between the cultivator and the state, and the distribution of land in small holdings rather than large estates.

[66] Throughout the British period about one-fourth of Punjab's area, with one-eighth of its population, was administered by various Native Princes under treaty and often with direct British supervision.

[67] D. G., 1904, 262.

[68] Douie, 2.

local tenures and traditions in a particular region, and on the current British ideology.[69]

Two different policies developed independently in Bengal and South India, the first areas to come under direct British administration.[70] In Bengal the settlement was influenced less by a knowledge of local institutions than by the necessity for creating a system requiring little administrative machinery. The large area to be dealt with and Lord Cornwallis' commitment as a Whig to a dominant role for a landed gentry, contributed to the designation of the *zamindars,* a group of diverse origins in Bengal numbering about three thousand, as owners of estates comprised of hundreds of villages. At the same time in Madras, guided by a romantic paternalism and a simplified view of village organization, Thomas Munro developed the system of settlement with the cultivators (*ryots,* hence *ryotwari*).

Later policies were based on experience gained in Bengal and the south. The Banares region of the United Provinces received a *zamindari* settlement on the Bengal model while Bombay followed the *ryotwari* pattern because, in both cases, the British officers involved had received their training in Bengal and Madras respectively. In the 1820's revenue policy took a new direction in the North-West Provinces that proved important for the Punjab. The British in the northwest realized that villages organized around a corporate body of proprietors from a single subcaste, as described by Metcalfe, were the most common type. The decision to settle with the corporate body as a group (*mahal:* village, hence *mahalwari* settlement) rather than various intermediaries (*taluqdars, zamindars* and the like) was influ-

---

[69] There are a number of studies of the evolution of British land-revenue policy in India. For an examination of the impact of British ideology on land-revenue policy see Eric Stokes, *The English Utilitarians in India* (Oxford University Press, 1959). Studies of the development and implementation of policy in different parts of India are: for the south, Nilmani Mukherjee, *The Ryotwari System in Madras* (Calcutta: Firma K. L. Mukhopadhyay, 1962); for Bombay, Kenneth Ballhatchet, *Social Policy and Social Change* (London: 1957); for the United Provinces, Thomas R. Metcalf, *The Aftermath of the Revolt* (Princeton University Press, 1964). It must be noted, however, that none of these studies are concerned with the examination of rural social organization or the actual effects of British policy on rural society. There may be less difference between one region and another than these studies suggest. See Bernard S. Cohn, *India: The Social Anthropology of a Civilization* (Englewood Cliffs: Prentice-Hall, 1971), 82.

[70] The next paragraph draws heavily on Metcalf, 36–45.

enced partly by a paternalism reminiscent of Munro, but largely by the impact of utilitarian ideology and the Ricardian theory of rent which held all intermediaries to be "useless drones on the soil." [71] Many Punjab revenue officials, including Richard Temple (later knighted), Jullundur's first settlement officer, received their training in the North-West Provinces. To the Punjab, they brought a strong orientation toward "the village community" and a prejudice against all intermediaries. Thus the tendency of the early Punjab settlements:

> was to commute the superior rights where they were established into a moderate percentage on the revenue, and to take engagements from the inferior proprietors and allow them sole management of the estate. The latter were looked upon as the valuable element in the community, the former as an interesting survival of a state of society which had passed and should not be revived.[72]

During the initial revenue surveys throughout the Punjab, officers were directed to inquire into the basis of all grants of revenue-collecting authority.[73] In Jullundur two sorts of claims existed: the old Rajput *zamindars'* and the Sikh *jagirdars'*. In numerous instances Rajput lineages were able to prove that their *zamindari* rights had not been completely extinguished under the Sikhs, by showing that they had continued to receive *malikhana* (a token fee traditionally paid by cultivators to the *zamindar*) even though they did not actually collect revenue.[74] The British designated these claimants as *taluqdars* (overlords), allowed them to collect *malikhana* but stripped them of all other rights and privileges.[75]

The claims of the Sikh *jagirdars* received closer scrutiny. In Jullundur many *jagirs* were resumed, only the grants found to have been made for military or religious purposes were upheld and even these, only for the lifetime of the incumbents.[76] In numerous instances *jagirdars* went to court in an effort to prove proprietary claims to their estates similar to those of the Rajputs.[77] To substantiate such claims, *jagirdars* argued they had performed many of the same functions as the *zamindars:* rent collection, participation in management of the estate, construction of wells, and interference in community affairs.[78] But the British officials refused to recognize the *jagirdars* because it proved

---

[71] Metcalf, 41.   [72] Douie, 58.   [73] *Ibid.,* 53.   [74] S. R., 1851, 289.
[75] *Ibid.*   [76] *Ibid.,* 260.   [77] *Ibid.,* 278–279.   [78] *Ibid.,* 279.

impossible to divest the *jagirdars* of their official character; they were, in fact, the trustees of the government; and the government used to do nearly all the things above enumerated, but did not consider itself as owner of the land nevertheless. So might the *jagirdar* act, and yet not thereby become proprietor.[79]

Obviously Sikh rule did not last long enough to establish in the eyes of the British the kind of hereditary claims recognized in the United Provinces and among the Rajputs in Jullundur. The origin of many of the *zamindars* was no different, only further removed in time. Had a few more generations passed before British annexation, it is likely that a group of *jagirdars* would have been sufficiently established to warrant official support. Because the basis of their claims could easily be traced to service or favor of the Sikh state, the *jagirdars* were pensioned off, completing the process of structural change initiated under the Sikhs.

Vilyatpur's Social Structure and Settlement
Jat Social Structure

The settlement and organization of villages in the Punjab is so much the product of caste structure that an account of Vilyatpur's origins must start with a description of the caste which settled it.

Vilyatpur's founders were members of the Sahota *got* (clan or subcaste) of the Jat *zat* (tribe or caste).[80] The Jats have been an important element of Punjab's population in its recent history, and they have been the predominant caste since the decline of Mughal authority in the eighteenth century. Under both the *misls* and Maharajah Ranjit Singh, they dominated Punjab politics, forming the backbone of the Sikh army and administration. At least during the British period, when census figures became available, they were the largest single tribe in the province,[81] and were heavily concentrated in rural areas where they were famous as landowners and cultivators. "In fact, in [Jullundur district], as in other places a man of this tribe

---

[79] *Ibid.*

[80] See convention number 2 in the introduction.

[81] In 1868 the Jats comprised 18 percent of the population of British Punjab, excluding the Native States and including the North-West Frontier Provinces. The figure for the Punjab in 1931 was 24 percent. *Punjab Census*, 1868, General Statement III, *Punjab Census,* 1931, II, Table XVII.

does not call himself a *Jat,* but a *zamindar* or agriculturist, if he does not give the name of his clan." [82] Sir Denzil Ibbetson, Punjab's ethnographer and later Lt. Governor, summed up British opinion of this important caste: "From an economical and administrative point of view he is the husbandman, the peasant, the revenue payer *par excellence* of the province." [83] The Jats, known by the British for their fighting skills from two wars with Ranjit Singh, were intensively recruited for the British Indian Army.

Among the Jats, as with most of the castes in North India, the *zat* is a nonlocalized endogamous unit comprised of numerous exogamous *gots.* Membership in the *got* is determined according to patrilineal descent, and residence is generally patrilocal. Jat clans varied greatly in size, distribution, and importance. Some, like the Sindhus and the Gills, numbered more than 100,000 persons each in 1881 and formed the dominant cultivating population in villages in ten or twelve districts.[84] The Sahotas, in contrast, were a relatively small and geographically compact *got,* numbering less than 5000 in 1881.[85] All Sahota villages were concentrated in the Jullundur *doab* until 1894, when a new community was settled in the newly irrigated tract of western Punjab.[86]

Although some attention has been given to the origins of the Jats (they have been identified with the Indo-Scythians who entered the subcontinent shortly before the beginning of the Christian era),[87] there is little discussion of the origin and relationship between the various *gots*—the more functional, structural unit. Ibbetson's suggestion that the creation of new clans might be related to the acquisition and settlement of a new territory certainly fits the evidence on the Sahotas.[88] The clan does not have a mythological history, found among many higher castes like the Brahmins and the Rajputs, tracing the clan's origin from an event in India's epical past. But there are traditions, common to many villages in North India, that account for the Sahota's settlement and ownership of each community they inhabit.[89] At Hardwar, an important pilgrimage center on the

[82] D. G., 1904, 61.   [83] Ibbetson, *Punjab Castes,* 102.   [84] *Ibid.,* 120–121.
[85] S. R., 1892, 74.
[86] D. G., 1904, 66; Punjab Government. *Punjab District Gazetteers,* Hoshiarpur District, 1904 (Lahore: Civil and Military Gazette Press, 1904), 45.
[87] Ibbetson, *Punjab Castes,* 97.
[88] *Ibid.,* 16–18.
[89] See Bernard S. Cohn, "The Pasts of an Indian Village," *Comparative Studies*

Ganges in western Uttar Pradesh (which the Sahotas have visited
regularly for more than three hundred years), the *bahis* (registers)
compiled by recording the genealogy of each pilgrim, trace the history of the *got* from its origin.[90] According to the accounts kept by
the *panda* (Brahmin record keeper), all members of the clan are
descendants of the twenty-one sons of Sahota who migrated from
western Punjab to the Jullundur *doab* thirty-one generations ago.
Membership in the *got* is therefore defined by descent from Sahota,
even though individual members of the clan cannot trace the connection genealogically themselves. Nothing more is known of the
clan's progenitor or the Sahota's relationship to other Jat *gots*. The
clan dates from the migration to Jullundur, and is a closed group,
at least for the period for which any evidence is available.

The internal structure of the Sahota clan mirrors that of other
Jat *gots* perfectly (Figure 3). Each clan is divided into a number of
als (maximal lineages)—localized descent groups—whose members
can at least theoretically trace their relationship to a common ancestor.[91] Unlike the *got,* the maximal lineage is not a fixed group and
instances of the creation of new *als* occur repeatedly in village oral
tradition[92] and even in the period covered in village records. In part,
the formation of new lineages is associated with the establishment of
new settlements. By leaving the parent settlement, Vilyatpur's first
residents created a new *al* which for the first three generations included all the Sahotas in the settlement. Vilyatpur now has three
maximal lineages, each forming a separate *patti* (kinship and resi-

in *Society and History,* III (1961), 243–244; Adrian Mayer, *Caste and Kinship in
Central India* (Berkeley: University of California Press, 1960), 161–163; V. N.
Mandlik, "Account of the Founding of the village Muruda in South Konkan"
cited in Ravinder Kumar, "Rural Life in Western India on the Eve of British
Conquest," *Indian Economic and Social History Review,* II (1965), 202.

[90] For a detailed description of these and all village records used in this study,
see Kessinger, "Historical Materials."

[91] D. G., 62. On Jat social structure in general see: M. C. Pradhan, *The Political
System of the Jats of Northern India* (New York: Oxford University Press,
1966), 58–60; Murry J. Leaf, "Ideas, Rites and Action in Sidhupur Kalan: A
Sikh Village in Punjab," unpublished Ph.D. Dissertation, University of Chicago,
1966, 57–79; Charles Morrison, "Dispute in Dhara: A Study of Village Politics
in Eastern Punjab," unpublished Ph.D. Dissertation, University of Chicago,
1965, 83–89.

[92] Oscar Lewis, *Village Life in Northern India* (New York: Vintage Books,
1965), 24.

Figure 3

CASE STRUCTURE OF THE JATS OF VILYATPUR

I	II	III	IV	V	VI
zat (caste)	got (sub-caste)	al/patti (maximal-lineage)	khandan (minimal-lineage)	tabbar (family)	ghar (household in Vilyatpur)

Jat

Sahota

Mema

→many others →many others

→many others

→many others

→many others →many others

→many others

Lakhu

→many others →many others

→many others →many others

→many others

→many others →many others

→many others

Gudr

→many others →many others

→many others →many others

→many others →many others

→many others

→(other Sahota lineages in other villages)

└(many other sub-castes)

└(many other castes)

dential grouping) in the village. Four other Sahota villages in the neighborhood also have three *als*, and the rest have four or more.

Of the numerous other kinship groups recognized by the Jats, only the *khandan* (minimal lineage), *tabbar* (family), and *ghar* (literally: house, here: household) require mention. The *khandan* generally consists of patrilineally related kinsmen who can trace their descent from an ancestor one or two generations earlier. Each *khandan* is made up of a number of *tabbars,* a smaller group ranging from a couple with their unmarried children to a three-generation cluster of lineally related kinsmen. The *khandan* and the *tabbar* are kinship units, not localized residential groups. Individuals living outside the village, temporarily or permanently, are still considered part of the *khandan* and the *tabbar,* and even the *tabbar* may be represented by several *ghars* in the village. The *ghar* is a purely residential group made up in most cases of close relatives, though occasionally including a servant or some more distant, often maternal, kinsman.

These groups, from the *khandan* to the *ghar,* are both progressively less stable and progressively more important in daily life. Change in each occurs as the consequence of the normal cycle of birth, marriage, procreation, and death.[93] For example, a *khandan* might be composed of five senior members (the sons of two brothers) and their offspring, some of whom are married and have children. As the number of progeny increases and the senior generation dies out, the *khandan* becomes too large to maintain solidarity at the time the linkage provided by its elders is disappearing. When the *khandan* disintegrates it is replaced by two new ones, each consisting of all of the descendants of each of the two brothers—the fathers of the generation that has just died out. This same cycle exists in the *tabbar* on a smaller scale. With the death of the father, married sons generally divide the *tabbar's* property to create new families. The *ghar* experiences the most frequent changes; alterations in living and cooking arrangements often occur as the result of domestic disputes and temporary migrations. Although in most instances changes in all three units occur in a series of divisions, recombinations occasionally take place, usually in response to some calamity in the *ghar, tabbar,* and, on occasion, even in the *khandan*. A brother who has established a separate family may on the death of his wife rejoin his brother.

History of the Sahotas

Reckoning from the genealogy of the clan maintained by the panda at Hardwar, the Sahotas migrated to the Jullundur *doab* in the fifteenth century. In 1443, thirty generations ago, a number of Sahota's sons founded a village named Gardiwala about sixty-five miles to the northeast of Vilyatpur in what is now Hoshiarpur district.[94] Three generations, or about one hundred years later, a group of five brothers obtained permission from local Muslim officials to clear some land for settlement in the southern end of the *doab* in what under Akbar

[93] The seminal work on this cyclical development is Meyer Fortes, "Time and Social Structure: An Ashanti Case Study" in Meyer Fortes (ed.), *Social Structure: Studies Presented to A. R. Radcliffe-Brown* (Oxford: Clarendon Press, 1949). For a number of studies examining this process in different settings see Jack Goody (ed.), *The Development Cycle in Domestic Groups* (Cambridge University Press, 1958); and for an application to Indian society see Harold A. Gould, "Time-Dimension and Structural Change in an Indian Kinship System: A Problem of Conceptual Refinement," in Singer and Cohn, 413-422.

[94] *Hoshiarpur District Gazetteer,* 217.

became the *Dhakdar Mahal.*[95] The *mahal* was sparsely populated, covered for the most part by a forest of *dhak* trees for which it was named, and apparently remained largely uncultivated even in Akbar's reign.[96] The village the brothers founded, the oldest Sahota community in the area, became the parent village for the clan's later settlements in the neighborhood.[97] Although originally known as Kuleta, the Sahota's referred to the village as *Barapind* (literally: big village), the name which now appears in all official documents. According to the genealogies collected for all of the villages in Jullundur district as part of the land-revenue settlement in 1885, Barapind is one of the three oldest in all of Jullundur district.[98] Now twenty-seven generations old, Barapind was probably founded in the early sixteenth century.

During the next four hundred years, the Sahotas founded five other villages in the area and settled with Jats of other *gots* in three more. These communities were established as cultivation was extended from Barapind by clearing away more of the forest in the *Dhakdar Mahal.* Six of the settlements share common boundaries; the other three are only a few miles away. In each new community, the Sahotas were the principal settlers and became the land-controllers and cultivators. Laborers and artisans either accompanied the settlers from the parent village or migrated from outside to take advantage of new opportunities.

While the settlement of a large tract by villagers of one *got* was not common in the Jullundur *doab,* this type of clan-settlement was well-known elsewhere in the Punjab[99] and North India.[100] Baden-Powell, in his compendium on Indian land tenure, suggests two patterns for the establishment of a clan in a new territory and its eventual spread over the environs of the parent community. In some cases a clan would conquer an area already populated and cultivated by

---

[95] *Misl haqiat* (record of rights), village Kuleta (Barapind), 1849.

[96] S. R., 1892, 21.

[97] *Ibid.,* 85; and *shajra nasibs* (genealogical register), 1884, for villages Rurka Khurd, Dhulaita, Chak Sahibu, Chak Indhian, and Atta.

[98] *Ibid.*

[99] S. R., 1892, 74; B. H. Baden-Powell, *The Land Systems of British India* (Oxford: Clarendon Press, 1892), II, 611; Denzil Ibbetson, *Report of the Revision of Settlement of the Panipat Tahsil & Karnal Parganah of the Karnal District* (Allahabad: Pioneer Press, 1883), 74.

[100] Baden-Powell, *Land Systems,* II, 134–37; Kashi Singh, 203–205.

another group, and then parcel it out among the clan's lineages for
further settlement, tax collection, and control of cultivation.[101] The
formation of the "little kingdoms" of the Rajputs in eastern Uttar
Pradesh illustrate this process.[102] In the second pattern, a small group
of settlers move into a previously uncultivated tract, establish their
claim by clearing and cultivating the land, thus providing a base
from which the clan can spread into the uncultivated land on the
edge of the original settlement. After their founding, satellite villages maintain connections with the parent community; the cluster
of related communities (*thapa* or *ilaqa*) forms a cohesive group in
relation to the government or any external threat.[103] The preeminence of the parent village often was recognized in annual rites during which a turban or token gift of money was paid to the *muqaddam*
of the parent village.[104] The history of the Sahotas in Barapind follows this second pattern of development: the pattern occurs repeatedly in Jat areas on the plains of the Punjab.[105] When Gulab Singh,
a local leader from Barapind, consolidated his power enabling him
to attach himself to one *misl* after another and finally to exist independently for more than twenty years, he drew on these kinship and
historical ties between the parent village and the other villages in the
ilaqa.

Vilyatpur's Settlement

The founding of satellite villages around Barapind was a continuous
process rather than the result of a particular event. New settlements
were established between the twenty-second and eleventh generations
in the clan's genealogy. The founding of each village, as recorded in
the revenue documents, shows important similarities suggesting that
a common factor was operative in the settlement process. Barapind
was settled by a group of five brothers from the Sahota village of
Gardiwala. A segment of a maximal lineage in their own village, the
brothers split off to settle Barapind, thereby founding a new village

---

[101] Baden-Powell, *Land Systems,* II, 636.
[102] Kashi Singh, 204; Cohn, *Political Systems.*
[103] Ibbetson, *Karnal Settlement,* 74–75.
[104] *Ibid.,* 75.
[105] See for Karnal District, Ibbetson, *Karnal Settlement,* 74–76; for Ludhiana
District, T. Gordon Walker, *Final Report on the Revision of Settlement of the
Ludhiana District* (Calcutta: Calcutta Central Press, 1884), 46.

and their own lineage. The settlement of the satellite villages was a continuation of this pattern. Vilyatpur's early history illustrates the principle of repeated segmentation in the village's founding and internal differentiation, and also demonstrates the role of the government in the creation of new villages.

Seventeen generations ago, Phal, a Sahota Jat and a "cosharer" of lands in Barapind, quarrelled with his lineage mates and took up residence with his three sons in fields on the southern edge of the village. At first the new settlement consisted of a single lineage, including all of the descendants of Phal's three sons. After only three generations, another quarrel took place, splitting the new community into three new lineages, each comprised of the descendants of one of the sons. This division took place in the third generation: just at the point that the *khandan* would be expected to disintegrate. The lineages existed as three separate settlements until a Mughal revenue official regrouped them, presumably for administrative convenience, into a single village with three *pattis,* each inhabited by one of the lineages and named after a prominent man in the lineage at the time of the quarrel. The official also divided the village's land—agricultural, residential and waste lands—between the three groups, making each responsible for the management of its share and for the payment of the revenue through its own *maqaddam.*

Vilyatpur's early history illustrates the importance and ramifications of the segmentary kinship system of the Jats. In a segmentary system, division into separate political and social groups occurs in a regular pattern along cleavages in kinship lines.[106] The founding of Vilyatpur by a segment of a maximal lineage from the parent community following a dispute, and then the differentiation within Vilyatpur, conforms to this model. The same principle is operative in the gradual continuous division of the *khandan* into new, derivative *khandans.* Yet there is also an aggregative aspect to the pattern. Although at any level, similar units tend to oppose one another—for instance one *khandan* against another within the maximal lineage—they will unite in disputes with another lineage jut as all lineages will function together against another village, or all of the Sahota

---

[106] The classic account of acephalous segmentary political systems is E. E. Evans-Pritchard, *The Nuer* (Oxford: The Clarendon Press, 1940). For an application to Indian village politics see Ralph W. Nicholas, "Structures of Politics in the Villages of Southern Asia," in Singer and Cohn, 271.

settlements against an outside threat. Gulab Singh's career is an illustration of the aggregative aspect of the segmentary system in the
pre-British period; so is the analysis of land control in the village
before 1848 in the next chapter.

Unfortunately, the history of the settlement of other caste groups
in Vilyatpur cannot be analyzed with the same detail as the Sahotas'.
To an extent this results from the nature of available records. British revenue records are concerned with the ownership and use of land,
and therefore relate primarily to the Sahotas, whose background and
history was an important element in their proprietary claim. But the
paucity of information on the other castes is a function of the settlement process. Each satellite village attracted the laborers, artisans,
and village servants needed for cultivating its fields and serving its
population. With the exception of two of the three largest caste and
occupational groups among Vilyatpur's non-Jat population—Chamars (Leather-workers) and Julahas (Weavers)—families of artisans
and servants moved in and out of the village frequently in the pre-
British period.[107] The Hardwar *bahis* contain a series of fragmentary
genealogies for Nais (Barbers), Jhinswars (Water-carriers), Sonihars
(Goldsmiths), Tarkhans (Carpenters), and Lohars (Blacksmiths) which
seldom contain more than two generations before 1848. In most cases
a number of different *gots* appear for each caste, indicating that the
discontinuity in Vilyatpur was real, and not an artifact of the pilgrimage and records system. Apparently the nonlanded found it possible or necessary or both to migrate with considerable frequency in
the politically fluid conditions of eighteenth and nineteenth century
Punjab.

The Brahmins, the third largest group in the village in 1848, all
belonged to the Tugnait clan which claims to have come to the Punjab from the Deccan. Tugnait Brahmins were found in all Sahota
villages in the Jullundur *doab* where they served as *prohits* (family
priests) to the Jats. They migrated from Gardiwala to Barapind along
with the Sahotas, and from there to Vilyatpur and the other villages.
Even after most of the Sahotas became Sikhs in the late nineteenth
century, the Tugnait Brahmins retained their prominence throughout the *ilaqa*. Little is known of the Chamars, who were second only
to the Jats in numbers in the village. Most of those who visited

---

[107] See convention number 3 in the introduction.

Hardwar from Vilyatpur before 1848 were members of either the Summan or Sund *gots,* two widespread North Indian clans; most of the Chamars now living in Vilyatpur are their descendants.[108] Neither clan was associated with the Sahotas in Gardiwala, but both were represented in Barapind and later in all but three of the satellite villages. Local tradition has it that the Sund and Summan Chamars came to the village as a group, but does not specify if this occurred at the village's founding or afterwards. The only other large group in the village, the Weavers, were represented by four different *gots* in 1848. The two largest *gots* were also found in Barapind; there were no Julahas in any of the other Sahota villages.

What Is a Village?

To discuss the history of Vilyatpur's settlement, it is necessary to consider the social structure of the Sahotas. The segmentary character of Jat kinship accounts for the process by which the village was founded, the internal organization of the community, and the nature of its relations with neighboring villages. The Sahotas established their claim to the area by clearing the land and founding a number of settlements over a long period of time. Barapind was colonized by a segment of the Sahota *got* from a village in Hoshiarpur district, and Vilyatpur, like the other satellite villages, was created as a continuation of this process. Following a dispute between *khandans* in one of Barapind's lineages, Phal started living in the fields, beginning a new lineage and forming what ultimately developed into a separate village. Internally the Sahotas' role as the original settlers and controllers of the land defined their position vis-à-vis the other caste groups in the community. Relations among the Sahotas followed the pattern of the segmentary kinship system with various levels at the *ghar, tabbar, khandan,* and the village's three lineages. Vilyatpur was connected with surrounding villages in the *ilaqa* through kinship ties of the Sahotas, a network that proved its importance in the *got's* settlement of the area and the political flux of the eighteenth and early nineteenth centuries.

When did Vilyatpur become a village? Certainly, in the sense of Charles Metcalfe's conception of the "village republic," the answer is

[108] Pandit Faqir Chand, Chamarawala Pandit, Gao Ghat, Hardwar, private interview, May, 1969.

never. If an economically self-sufficient and politically viable unit ever existed, it was the group of Sahota villages in the *ilaqa,* not any single community. Nor did Phal's act of settling in his fields suffice to create a village. *Abadis* of this type have always been numerous; some developed into villages while others remained small hamlets populated by a single *khandan.* At present there are seven such *abadis* in Vilyatpur. Unfortunately, it is hard even to say when the settlement became a village in the eyes of the administration. In the Mughal, Sikh, and British revenue systems, the *mauza* referred to an officially designated area of land that might contain several settlements but might also be uninhabited. Even now the census lists numerous villages that are uninhabited, comprised of agricultural lands cultivated by surrounding communities.[109] There is no indication in existing records whether Vilyatpur was treated as a *mauza* by the Mughal and Sikh administrations, or if Vilyatpur's revenues were paid by its own elders or through Barapind's *muqaddam.* In some instances where an area was settled by a single *got,* revenues were remitted on behalf of the whole clan by its council of elders or headman.[110] In view of Gulab Singh's success in appropriating the revenues of the Sahota villages, this might have been the case around Barapind.

Although it is difficult to say when Vilyatpur became a village in a spatial or administrative sense, a structural and cultural definition can be devised. The Punjabi term most commonly used for village is *pind;* the word is related to a Sanskrit term meaning a ball of rice offered at the *sraddhs* (funeral ceremonies) by the nearest living relatives. *Pind* also refers to the *sapinda* (group of kinsmen) considered ritually eligible to perform this oblation.[111] The Sahotas in Vilyatpur can be considered a *pind* at the time when they no longer conceived of their clansmen in Barapind as sufficiently closely related to perform this important ritual. This stage probably occurred once the Sahotas in Vilyatpur divided into three separate lineages. As long as

[109] See for instance *Punjab District Census Handbooks, Jullundur District,* "Village Directory," liv–lxxix.

[110] Pradhan, 106–107.

[111] Sir Monier Monier-Williams, *A Sanskrit-English Dictionary,* new edition (Oxford University Press, 1899). I am grateful to Professor Donald Nelson, Department of South Asian Languages and Culture, University of Chicago, for his assistance in working out this derivation.

there was only one lineage in the settlement, Vilyatpur was structurally just an extension of the parent village.

The history of Vilyatpur's settlement indicates the difficulty of
finding any general definition of the Punjabi village. In its establishment and growth, the character of the *pind* continued to change.
At times the role of the administration was crucial to this process,
as when the Mughal revenue official regrouped the three lineages
into a single community with three *pattis*. British ideas, policies,
and revenue procedures led to further changes in the village. As
part of this development, shifts occurred in the role and importance of aspects of Jat social structure described in this chapter. A
detailed look at the community as it existed in 1848—the year the
British revenue officers came to Vilyatpur—will provide a further
opportunity to consider the nature of the village. This profile of the
village at a specific time will also constitute a baseline for the study
of change after 1848, including the consideration of some of the
immediate effects of the coming of British rule.

Chapter II

VILYATPUR IN 1848:
A RECONSTRUCTION

Introduction

The general history of the Jullundur *doab* in the Mughal and Sikh periods and the account of the settlement of the village highlight the continuities and changes before 1846 and the process by which Vilyatpur was established. The focus was on events occurring over a long time to stress their developmental nature, and to emphasize the historical and structural ties between the village, villages in a wider area, and the mainstream of events in the Punjab. But the lack of adequate source material meant that the discussion was at a general level, and was based on the work of others—hardly an adequate starting point for the systematic, historical study of a village and its constituent families.

This chapter will attempt a detailed reconstruction of Vilyatpur's internal economic, social, and political life as it existed in 1848. In contrast to the rest of the study, the picture presented here will be static—a snapshot, with no effort to discern what is changing and what is not. Although, if material existed, a dynamic account would be preferable, a synchronic description does make it easier to grasp the relationships between different aspects of village life and organization. The chapter's primary purpose is to augment the description of the village's background because a prerequisite for measuring change after 1848 is a baseline comparable in specificity to the later material. An account of the village at the time of annexation has intrinsic value as well. Most studies about rural India prior to British rule contain little data and many undocumented generalizations.

There are several historical accounts of villages and rural life in the pre-British or early British periods using detailed empirical evidence.[1]

---

[1] I am only considering those accounts that draw on detailed descriptive or statistical evidence for a well-defined geographical area. Those based primarily on literary materials or concerned with rural life at a general level are not included.

Most are reconstructions based on official records. Only one contemporary account of an individual village in this period is known —a socio-economic survey of a community in Poona District in 1819 by Thomas Coates, a British doctor employed by the British East-India Company.[2] Scholars have approached the writing of historical accounts of villages in two different ways, either by dealing with a specific village or, in a more generalized way, with villages in a particular region. To an extent the procedure used depends on the type of sources available. G. S. Ghurye, working primarily with Coates' material, chose to concentrate on the village of Lony,[3] while Percival Spear dealt with "Delhi Territory" on the basis of a more general report by one of the British officers in Delhi in the early nineteenth century.[4] Yet it is equally true that the nature of the sources is not the only determinant of a study's focus, since Ravinder Kumar also draws heavily on Coates in his discussion of rural life in western India,[5] and Ghurye elaborates on his earlier studies of local religious practices in supplementing and interpreting available information on religion in Lony in 1819.[6] The choice between a detailed account of a single village—based on available statistical materials, supplemented with insights and conclusions from studies of other villages in the region—and a more general account about a number of communities (also with detailed information), is usually determined according to the writer's preference and the context of his study. Because both approaches rely on a combination of different types of materials, neither is inherently more accurate.

Given the central concern of this study—the social and economic change of a single village during an extended period of time—I have opted for the first alternative, a profile of the village itself at a specific moment. Since there is no descriptive account comparable to Coates' report on Lony, this will be a reconstruction based primarily on the rich qualitative and quantitative materials in Vilyat-

[2] Thomas Coates, "Account of the Present State of the Township of Lony," *Transactions of the Literary Society of Bombay* (London, 1823, reprinted 1877).

[3] G. S. Ghurye, *After a Century and a Quarter* (Bombay: Popular Books, 1960).

[4] Percival Spear, "The Rural Life of the Delhi Territory," *Twilight of the Mughals*, Chapter VI, 115–136.

[5] Ravinder Kumar, *Western India*, Chapter I, "The Poona Districts in 1818," 1–42.

[6] Ghurye, 44–69.

pur's revenue records for the initial survey of the village in 1848.[7]
Although these records were collected by the British two years *after*
annexation, I will assume that with a few notable exceptions they
approximate the general situation in the community in the late
Sikh period. To supplement and interpret information in the revenue records, I will also draw on discussions of village organization
and land tenure in various nineteenth century works by British
administrators, and recent studies by social scientists of important
village institutions.

The Village

When the British settlement officer and his numerous Indian assistants approached Vilyatpur in 1848, they travelled along one of the
four wagon tracks that connected the village with neighboring communities over almost flat terrain. Aside from occasional clumps of
trees amid the fully cultivated fields, the only break in the horizon
was the *abadi* itself, a compact settlement located on a slight rise
in the center of the village's 500 acres. A wall surrounded the village,
pierced by three gates—two small portals facing the southwest and
southeast with the main gate opening to the north.[8] The wall and
the whole village was constructed of *adobe* bricks covered with
plaster made of cow dung, clay, and straw. On closer inspection it
was clear that there was no separate wall, only a connected series of
windowless walls of the houses on the village's perimeter. There were
no buildings outside the central settlement, except a few sheds dot-
ting the fields next to some wells used for irrigation (to give shelter
to man and beast during the noonday heat), a somewhat larger structure just outside the main gate (used by one of the carpenters as
a workshop during the day), and a small shrine in a cluster of trees
called "the old man's garden" about two hundred yards to the west
of the *abadi*. Just outside the village wall there were a series of
small fenced enclosures for threshing, for the sugarcane presses

[7] For historical reconstructions of single villages based on revenue records, see
H. H. Mann, "A Deccan Village Under the Peshwas," Harold H. Mann, *The
Social Framework of Agriculture,* Daniel Thorner (ed.), (Bombay: Vora & Co.,
1967), 123–138; and S. A. Qadir, *Village Dhanishwar,* Technical Publications,
No. 5 (Comilla: Pakistan Academy for Rural Development, 1960).

[8] For a general description of villages in Jullundur district in the 1880's, see
S. R., 1891, 58–60.

during the harvest months, for storing cow dung cakes (the most common form of fuel), and for compost throughout the year.

To enter the *abadi* the revenue party had to pass through the main gate, a tall, roofed structure with high platforms on either side of the road where villagers gathered to sit and talk during the heat of the summer or in the rainy season, whenever there was no field work. Just inside the gate they found themselves in a small open area with room for perhaps sixty or seventy persons from which several narrow lanes led away to the various parts of the village. These passages were no more than four or five feet wide, unpaved, with a crown in the center to better the chances of adequate footing during the semiannual monsoon. Throughout the village there was little apparent difference in the buildings along these lanes. On each side of the path were *adobe* walls eight to ten feet high, interrupted by double wooden doors leading to individual residences, often the only indication of where one house ended and another began.

Initially the visitors were probably struck by the similarity of all village houses—single story, flat-roofed, *adobe* structures without windows. But the discerning eye might have noted that the doorways were spaced at much greater intervals in some parts of the village than in others, and that in front of a few somewhat larger doorways the path widened perceptibly. In the three main *pattis* near the main gate and in the western and southern parts of the *abadi* where the land was the highest, the doorways were furthest apart—the only overt indication of the large houses and comparative wealth of the Sahotas. Moving down a noticeable incline into the eastern end of the village where the untouchable castes lived—the Weavers, Leatherworkers and Sweepers—the houses were much smaller, with doorways every twenty feet, in many cases. On the edge of this section of the settlement was a large, usually stagnant pond where most of the drainage water of the village collected, and from which clay was taken for making *adobe*.

The contrast between the houses of the Sahotas and those of all others, only suggested from the outside, was immediately apparent upon entering a few homes. In most of the fifty-five Sahota houses, the door opened directly into a large uncovered courtyard. In front of this open area next to the door stood a shed for cattle, and along the back was a long building, equal to the courtyard in width, divided into two or three rooms. Most of the daily household activity took place in the open courtyard. A small fireplace in one corner served as the kitchen, except during the rainy season, and the yard was used for drying maize, wheat, and other produce before its use or storage. In the summer everyone slept outside—men on the roof which could be reached by a ladder, and women and young children in the courtyard below. The rooms were used primarily for storing family belongings and produce, but also for living and sleeping in the winter and during the monsoon. As Table 3 indicates, Sahota domestic groups were neither large (4.5 persons on the average) nor complex (56 percent were single couples with

TABLE 3

RESIDENTIAL GROUPS, 1848

Caste	Houses	Persons	Adult males[a]	Persons per house	Adult males per house	% houses with more than one adult male	% population in houses with more than one adult male
Sahota	55	250	89	4.5	1.6	44	52
Chamar	13	60	17	4.6	1.3	31	21
Brahmin	10	50	16	5.0	1.6	40	63
Julaha	10	40	18	4.0	1.8	50	61
Other Jat[b]	8	37	14	4.6	1.8	63	82
Faqir	5	23	8	4.6	1.6	60	88
Tarkhan	5	19	6	3.8	1.2	20	25
Chiir	3	15	6	5.0	2.5	33	67
Nai	3	12	5	4.0	1.7	67	83
Kumhar	3	19	4	6.3	1.3	33	42
Chuura	2	11	5	5.5	2.5	50	91
Gujjar	2	8	3	4.0	1.5	50	83
Rangeez	1	7	3	7.0	3.0	100	100
Rajput	1	6	1	6.0	1.0	0	0
Mirasi	1	5	1	5.0	1.0	0	0
Sonihar	1	3	1	3.0	1.0	0	0
Total	123	565	197	4.6	1.6	42	51

SOURCE: *Khanna shumari* (household census) 1848, Village Vilyatpur.
[a] Adult males include all men over eighteen.
[b] Other Jats indicates families of several different clans other than Sahota living in the village and cultivating land as tenants.

or without children). To be sure, there were some large ones, one with fourteen members and another with twelve, but this was unusual and there were three consisting of a single man or woman. Joint households—containing more than one adult male—which are generally considered to be the norm in Indian society, accounted for less than half of the Sahota domestic groups (44 percent).[9] Because even the joint domestic groups were small, they contained only half (52 percent) of the Sahotas in the community.

In houses where the domestic group had recently divided, a single doorway and courtyard might contain two *ghars,* with two cowsheds, kitchens, and a division in the use of the rooms as well. In at least three cases the members of the two new *ghars* were still cultivating their lands in common despite the separation in domestic arrangements. In time the original building would be rebuilt by constructing a wall between the two sections and putting in a new door to the street. This was the usual pattern, made possible by the relative ease and inexpensiveness of *adobe* construction, and it meant that an individual's immediate neighbors were usually close relatives, members of the same *khandan.* Thus, not only was everyone in the *patti* a member of the same maximal lineage, but each *patti* consisted of a number of clusters of even closer kinsmen living together in a series of connected, though separate, houses. Only where a *khandan* grew very rapidly in one or two generations was it necessary to move out of immediate contact with kinsmen to another part of the *patti*—perhaps two hundred feet away—for lack of space. But such a development was rare since the population of the village—565 in 1848—had probably been fairly stable for some time.[10] Most *khandans* already had room for expansion. In conducting a census of the village in 1848, the revenue party found twelve

[9] Defining of residential and family groups as joint on the basis only of the number of adult males is unusual, and probably results in a somewhat larger number of joint groups than the conventional definition which includes marriage. See Chapter VI for a complete discussion of family organization.

[10] There is no evidence on the size of the village or the rate of growth in the Sikh period other than in the genealogy of the Sahotas and the pilgrimage records. Neither of these indicate any substantial changes when the entries for the periods 1800 to 1850 and 1850 to 1870 are compared. The population of the village grew slowly, with some fluctuation until 1931 when it reached 687, an increase of a little more than 20 percent over the 1848 figure. This relatively slow rate of change before 1930 enabled me to outline the former layout of the village with the assistance of some older inhabitants.

empty houses and five vacant plots in the three main *pattis,* generally the property of the residents of the adjacent house. These vacant buildings, which probably indicated that a particular family was dying out, would come into use when the *khandan* expanded again in a future generation.

The three houses belonging to Brahmin shopkeepers were located in the main *pattis* amongst the Jats. Their houses were not as large as those of the Sahotas, the main difference was a large room in front of the courtyard with a second door opening into the street. This arrangement enabled customers to make purchases of salt, spices, and a few other necessities, usually in exchange for grain or crude sugar rather than cash, without entering the shop. The houses of the artisans and those who performed a variety of services in the community were the smallest and simplest. With the exception of the five houses belonging to carpenters, located on the edge of the three *pattis* with a shed or extra room attached as a workshop, few of this group had more than a single room opening directly onto the lane with a small courtyard behind used for cooking by day and keeping animals at night. The families providing services—the Brahmins working as priests, the barbers, and the water-carriers— lived throughout the village. The water-carriers' homes were popular, well-known places, particularly with the village children because of the oven in front where the ladies-of-the-house made bread and pop corn for anyone who brought flour or grain and gave them a small amount of it as a fee.

All of the Leatherworkers, Sweepers, and Weavers were clustered together in twenty-five small houses, some without a courtyard, in their own part of the *abadi.* The Potters, the Dyer, the Drummer, and two families of Herdsmen, the only Muslims in the village, lived together between the Sahotas' three *pattis* and the area inhabited by the Chamars and the other low castes. Although in contrast to the houses of the Jats, those occupied by the other castes were much smaller and simpler, there was with a few exceptions almost no difference in the size of the residential groups. The average size of the *ghar* of the non-Jats taken as a group was practically the same as that of the Sahotas, 4.8 persons. There were, however, significant distinctions in the composition of domestic groups. Among the Chamars, a large group who were mostly agricultural laborers, joint *ghars* were relatively infrequent and only a tiny part of the Chamar population lived in them. Most of the castes represented by families living in two to five houses in the village were remarkable for the number of members living in joint residential groups.

In the center of the untouchables' quarter was a small open area around a brick well from which the neighborhood residents drew their water; the rest of the population used the other well located near the main gate. As the revenue officials passed by the Muslim houses in this part of the village, they may have been surprised by the number of livestock around the well—over fifty donkeys belonging to the Potters, and almost thirty milk buffalos and cows owned by the other residents. At first it must have seemed that most of the village's livestock, a sign of wealth, was either owned or kept by the untouchables. In fact, the Sahotas who were less than half of the population, owned eight times as many animals—and probably better ones—but these were tethered inside their courtyards at night and taken out to the wells during the day. Therefore, they were seen only early in the morning or in the evening as they were crowded through the narrow lanes by the young boys in the family on their way to and from the fields. Since the untouchables had nowhere to take their livestock, most of them were tied in front of the houses during the day, and shared the single room with their owners at night.

The preeminence of the Sahotas in Vilyatpur, based on their role as original settlers and owners of the village, and reflected in the location and size of their houses and ownership of livestock, received further confirmation as the revenue officials conducted the house to house census.[11] With 45 percent of the *ghars* and 44 percent of the population, they were by far the largest single caste group in the village (see Table 3). None of the fourteen other castes had even one-fourth as many members. In fact, only three were sufficiently numerous to be of much consequence in the life of the community beyond supplying of goods, services, and labor. But even taken together, these three castes—the Chamars, Brahmins, and

[11] In contrast to the village censuses in the North-West Provinces and the districts of Punjab annexed before 1846, which were calculated by counting the houses and multiplying by a number considered to be the size of a typical household, those in Jullundur were based on an actual enumeration. S. R., 1851, 259.

Weavers—accounted for less than thirty percent of the houses and population. The remaining quarter of the village's population was made up of from one to five houses from each of eleven other castes. The predominance of the Sahotas, therefore, was numerical as well as economic and political; important for the maintenance of their position during moments of political uncertainty in the late Mughal and early Sikh periods, and significant since 1848 because the group which dominated the village included a substantial part of its population and not just a privileged few.

Economic Activity and Organization

Almost all economic activity in the village could be summed up in a single word: agriculture. Cultivation of the soil was almost the only productive activity in Vilyatpur in 1848 since those not directly involved in farming either supplied goods required by agriculturalists in their work, or services necessary in their homes. Almost three men in four, representing nine of the village's fourteen castes, were primarily engaged in farming as owner-cultivators, tenants, agricultural laborers, and field servants in cultivators' households (see Table 4). But the agricultural enterprise was by no means only the work of men. The children of all of these families played an important role, from the daily chore of minding cattle to the more seasonal tasks of assisting their parents in planting, harvesting, threshing, and manufacturing *gur* (crude sugar). In each operation, there were jobs normally done by children, both boys and girls; for example, they dropped wheat and maize seed in the furrow behind the plow, and tended the furnace during the making of sugar. The processing of produce was largely women's work. With the exception of threshing and sugar manufacture that could not be done in the house for lack of space, processing of agricultural products was carried out by women in their courtyards. The processing included the shelling of maize, carding and spinning of cotton, grinding of wheat, and making of various milk products, particularly *ghi* (clarified butter, the principal cooking oil used in the village). Thus, agriculture involved most of Vilyatpur's population. Practically all the rest earned their livelihoods by supplying goods and services to local residents. Only the weavers, the potters, and the goldsmith (12 percent of the adult males) also manufactured goods for sale outside of the village.

TABLE 4

OCCUPATIONAL STRUCTURE, 1848
(adult males only)

Caste	Traditional occupation	Owner-cultivator	Other cultivator	Sepidars	Other artisans (traditional)	Other services (traditional)	Other services	Other agricultural labor
Sahota	agriculturalist	89						
Chamar	leatherworker			(17)[a]				
Brahmin	priest		(7)			5	(4)	
Julaha	weaver				18			
Other Jat	agriculturalist		14					
Faqir	beggar-saint		(4)			4		
Tarkhan	carpenter		(1)	5				
Chiir	watercarrier			4			(2)	
Nai	barber		(3)	2				
Kumhar	potter				4			
Chuura	sweeper		(4)	1				
Gujjar	herdsman					(1)		
Rangeez	dyer					3		(2)
Rajput	?					1		
Mirasi	drummer					1		
Sonihar	goldsmith			1				
Total		89	33	29	23	15	6	2
Percent		45	17	15	12	8	3	1

SOURCE: *Khanna shumari* (household census) 1848, Village Vilyatpur.

[a] Figures in parentheses indicate individuals working outside their "traditional" occupation, 45 adult males in all, 23% of the total.

The central role of agriculture strengthened the Sahota's dominance in the community. Because they controlled the land and its use, they were the focal point of village economic activity and organization. Among the Sahotas, the property-holding group—usually equivalent to the *tabbar,* often including several *ghars*—was the unit of economic activity. Each of these property-holding groups was at the center of a network of dyadic relationships with tenants, laborers, servants, and artisans which, taken together, integrated the

community and formed the organization for most of its economic
activity. These relationships were asymmetrical; the artisans, servants,
and others were always dependent on the Sahota property group for
the purchase of goods and services in exchange for part of their
harvests. All types of goods and services, even rents, were usually
paid for in grain rather than cash. But there were significant differences in the relationships between the Sahotas and the various families of artisans and servants they supported.

The closest and perhaps most important ties were with the
artisans and servants known as the *sepidars*. A family of *sepidars* was
attached to a particular Sahota group, usually over an extended
period of time, to whom the *sepidars* rendered their services in
return for a fixed percentage of the semiannual harvest.[12] Each day,
for instance, the Sahota housewife could expect the water-carrier
to bring two large pitchers of water, one in the morning and another
in the afternoon, for use in the home. If the harvest was on, he
would also take water to the men of the house in the fields. After
the cattle had been taken out to the well, the sweeper would come
to clean the cattle shed, courtyard, and the street in front of the
house, carrying the refuse out to the household compost heap just
outside the village wall. The barber could be expected to make his
rounds about once a week. He would work in the courtyard, or,
more likely, in the open place near the village gate, or, even at one
of the wells in the fields where he would shave and cut the hair and
nails of the men of the family. For their services, the Chiir, Chuura
and Nai each received one-fourth of a *seer* of every *maund* of grain
at the time of harvest, and a small amount of *gur* every year.[13]

The other *sepidars* were concerned directly with the agricultural
enterprise of the property group. The carpenter repaired the plow
and other agricultural implements, and made new ones with materials supplied by his patron in return for half of a *seer* share twice
a year. Because of his important role as an agricultural laborer, the
Chamar received the largest share of all of the *sepidars,* although
his percentage varied according to the amount of work he was ex-

---

[12] This is Punjab's version of the *jajmani* system first reported by W. H. Wiser,
The Hindu Jajmani System (Lucknow: Lucknow Publishing House, 1958), and
the subject of a substantial anthropological literature. For further discussion, see
Chapter V.

[13] There are forty *seers* (2.2 lbs.) in a *maund*.

pected to do. All Chamars supplied their patrons with shoes for everyone in the household, a leather whip and, in return for a token payment, a leather bucket for the well. In addition, a few worked in the fields throughout the year, but generally they helped only during the peak seasons—the harvest and threshing seasons—or while *gur* was being made. The full-time laborer received two and three-quarters *seers* per *maund* per harvest, the part-timer only one *seer*. The *sepidars* were about seventeen percent of the men in the village. They also gave their services to other families in the village, that is, to the Jats, Brahmins, etc. who farmed land as tenants, and even to each other. When the recipient was a cultivator, payment was usually in the form of a percentage of the crop; otherwise, a fixed amount of grain was exchanged.

The supply of goods and services was not the only aspect of the patron-client relationship, nor did the *sepidars'* earnings through the performance of a defined range of tasks represent their only income. The tie between the families of the cultivators and the servants was often long-term and personal, though a clearly dependent one from the *sepidars'* point of view. They played a role in rituals conducted at celebrations in their patron's house. At a marriage, for instance, the Barber in particular, but also the Water-carrier, Chamar, and Sweeper, had specific duties for which they were rewarded. Also, work outside of the customary services was paid for separately. The carpenter was paid, by the job, for making wooden door frames, doors, rafters, or repairing carts, as was the water-carrier for bringing water to make *adobe* and the Chamar for mending the walls or making a new room.

There were other artisans and suppliers of services in Vilyatpur who did not fit into the system of long-term personal ties based on a fixed percentage of the yearly produce. Here the relationship was more like that of the carpenter and his extra work: Payment was made in grain or some other commodity at a rate that had been fixed for some time, although the total depended on the amount of work done. An enduring relationship, if any, depended on the satisfaction of both parties. The Weavers, for instance, always worked to fill specific orders. A Sahota housewife would bring a quantity of thread, made from cotton grown by the family and cleaned and spun by the women of the house. She would give it to the Weaver specifying the type of cloth to be made. Either the cotton would be weighed against an equal amount of grain, which would be the Weaver's compensation for his labor, or he would take part of the cotton thread itself. The Potters, Dyer, Goldsmith, and Drummer were all paid in this manner. Although they were dependent for most of their business on the Sahotas, and certainly required their acquiescence to live and work in the community, these artisans and suppliers of services neither had the close personal connection with particular Sahota families nor were guaranteed a share of the crop every year. They sold their products outside the village, and people came from neighboring villages to obtain their services.[14] Although all of the Weavers and Potters were engaged in their traditional occupations in 1848, none had been forced into agricultural labor by competition of British-made cloth or tinware brought from British territory across the Sutlej River since the turn of the century. With the four Brahmin shopkeepers who exchanged goods for grain and gave small loans, the independent artisans comprised a little more than one-sixth of Vilyatpur's adult male population.

Still another group were the tenants and agricultural laborers, also about one-sixth of the working men in the community, including a number of Jats of other clans, three households each of Brahmins and Faqirs, and some Barbers, Carpenters and Sweepers. Although the Faqirs and Brahmins were granted rent-free land (except for payment of the government tax), in return for religious services, most of the others paid rent in cash and a few, with a share of the crop. But all were dependent on the Sahotas for their land. The Jats and Gujjars also relied on the Sahotas for the opportunity to do casual labor during peak seasons. The Sahotas' dominance and the subordinate position of the other castes was unambiguously clear, but relations with the landowners were distinct from those of the artisans and servants.

The network of relationships with the *sepidars*, independent artisans, and suppliers of services, and various types of tenants, provided the organization according to which the Sahotas cultivated their fields and obtained necessary assistance and services in exchange for some of the property group's production. Agriculture was intensive, based on the heavy use of the twenty-nine permanent

[14] According to their 1848 censuses, six nearby villages had no weavers or potters.

wells made with locally fired brick. A total of 93 percent of the whole area of the village was cultivated in 1848; the other seven percent was taken by the *abadi*, roads to other villages, and paths leading to the wells. Fully one-third of this area was double cropped.

Most of the land was cultivated by the forty-two Sahota property groups; the tenants and others combined farmed a mere twenty-five acres.[15] Each group had a number of fields scattered throughout the village, mostly in the part belonging to their own *patti*, but some in the other areas as well. The individual plots were numerous and some were small—hardly a twentieth of an acre. The property group also had shares in several of the wells in the village, used to irrigate their scattered fields. For example, there was the group made up of Mehtab Singh and Noubta Singh, the only sons of Sultani, who lived together as a single *ghar* with their wives, two daughters, and four sons, one of whom was married, forming the second largest residential and property group in the village. In 1848 Noubta and Mehtab had about thirteen acres of land divided into nine physically separate plots ranging in size from a sixth of an acre to about one and a half acres, irrigated from three different wells. All but two acres were in their own *patti*. Most of the groups with whom they shared the use, maintenance, and perhaps even the construction of their wells, were part of their own or related *khandans,* though the link with at least one was so distant they were not even considered relatives.

All of the implements used in daily agricultural operations were stored in the family house in the *abadi*. Each morning, and very early in the morning from April through September when the heat of the day made an early start crucial, the men of the house went to the plots to be worked that day, with their bullocks and the plow and any other required implements, including even the gear for the well. The livestock and implements were returned to the house every night, and once the crops were ripe, the produce would be brought from all of the family's plots to its working area just outside the village for threshing, etc., before being taken into the house for the final processing, storage, and use. Nothing was ever stored in the fields—neither implements, livestock, seed, nor

---

[15] This does not indicate the extent of tenancy in 1848. In addition, more than one hundred acres were rented by one landowning Sahota property group to another.

produce—and the physically separate fields were worked in sequence, concentrating all of the labor on one until the plowing or
other operations were complete before moving onto the plots in
another part of the village. The wells were used by the share-holders
according to a rotation established at the beginning of each agricultural year.[16]

Most agricultural operations were carried out by family members without the assistance of *sepidars* or other laborers. With three
men in the family and three pairs of bullocks, Mehtab and Noubta
were certainly able to complete the six to eight plowings of each
field before the sowing of crops without outside help. Other property
groups with less labor of their own exchanged workdays with a
neighbor to put two yoke of oxen in a plot at a time. To preserve
as much moisture in the soil as possible, it was necessary to minimize the time between plowing and rolling. The rapid working of
about an acre a day with at least two teams of oxen, and the use of
the *munna*, a simple plow with a straight wooden share which neither
destroyed the level of the field nor disturbed the structure of the
soil, were both designed to this end. Sowing was also generally done
by the men of the family using two teams of oxen; a boy or girl of
the family followed behind the plow, dropping seed into the open
furrow which was then closed by dragging a heavy plank across the
field. The smaller property groups would also need help from neighbors or their Chamar-*sepidar* in the irrigation of their plots. It was
a laborious and time-consuming task requiring at least two yoke of
oxen, three men, and a boy. One man guided each pair of bullocks
in turn down an inclined plane from the mouth of the well, drawing up the large leather bucket of water. A third man on the rim of
the well maneuvered the full bucket over the spill basin, emptying
its contents into the earthen channels that passed through fields belonging to other families, to the plot being irrigated. There a boy
was stationed with a spade to guide the water into the numerous
sections of the field, formed by several earthen dams about six
inches high that had been constructed after the furrows had been
closed following the sowing of the field. Once the section measuring

[16] Ibbetson, *Karnal Settlement Report,* 169. Unfortunately the section on
agriculture in Jullundur's first settlement report is sketchy. In this account I
have drawn on Ibbetson and S. R., 1892, both of which date from the period
1875 to 1885.

about thirty feet by five feet was full, he would close the entrance with a spadeful of earth, diverting the water to the next one. Even working throughout the day, with only a three-hour break at noon, barely half an acre could be irrigated. Each plot was watered immediately after sowing and again three or four times before harvest.

For weeding, an operation important to aid the crops and as a source for greens for the cattle, all but the largest families called on their *sepidars* for assistance. But the harvesting and threshing of wheat demanded the most labor. In May and June most of the village were engaged almost constantly in these tasks, partly because of the amount of work to be done, but primarily because it had to be completed before the arrival of the monsoon which would ruin any wheat not yet cut and threshed. The wheat was reaped with a hand sickle, first by cutting the best plants just below the grain bearing heads for next year's seed.[17] Threshing also required a large number of men and was a slow process.

All of the crop from the family's fields was brought to its work area just outside the village where it was spread on the ground by a post around which oxen were driven continuously. With sugarcane the whole stalk was cut in the fields and then brought into the work area where the leaves were removed and dried for fuel used in the boiling of the liquid extracted from the cane by the sugar mill. The *belna* (sugar press), erected by the *sepidar* carpenter, consisted of two wooden rollers driven by a series of three wooden gears which were purchased outside the village.[18] The cane juice was extracted by feeding cane between the rollers as they were turned by a yoke of oxen. It was then boiled down in a large clay vat made by the potter, cooled, and formed into round lumps about the size of a child's fist. Not every Sahota property group had its own *belna*, boiling pan, and furnace. There were sixteen presses in the village and these were shared, usually by members of the same *khandan*. It was just after the initial processing of the crops—threshing, *gur* manufacture, etc.—in the family's work area that the *sepidars* were given their share of the harvest. The remainder of the produce was then taken to the house in the village for family use and storage.

Land was used with almost equal intensity during each of the two seasons. The *rabi*, or winter crops, were wheat (38 percent of

[17] Ibbetson, *Karnal Settlement Report*, 169.
[18] S. R., 1892, 120.

the total area sown in the year), barley (5 percent), gram (4 percent), and pulses (3 percent); the *kariff* (summer) crops were maize and other grains (3 percent), pulses (9 percent), and fodder (27 percent). Sugarcane, which covered 8 percent of the total area, was a full-year crop. The *rabi* crops were the most important, providing the household with the bulk of its grain for the year, and demanding more labor than those in the summer. The principal crops were sugarcane and wheat, the former because of its high value. Much of the winter months after the wheat was sown—December, January, and February—were devoted to the harvesting of cane and the manufacturing of *gur*. Some *gur* was used in the household, but a substantial part of it was sold in the market town about fifteen miles away, for money to pay the government's revenue which, at least in the late Sikh period, was collected in cash, not in kind.[19] Some wheat crop was also sent to market. Seven carts were used for transporting produce to market in 1848; the two owned by Jat tenants were available on hire. On special payment, the Potters also used their donkeys to carry produce to market.

The returns to individual Sahota property groups from agriculture depended largely on the amount of land they controlled and the amount of labor available within the family itself. The size of holdings varied considerably among the Sahotas, ranging from less than a quarter of an acre to more than forty acres (see Table 5). The average holding was thirteen acres and more than one-third of the forty-two Sahota property groups with land had between ten and fifteen. Exactly half of the groups fell in the ten to twenty acre category that owned 54 percent of the village's agricultural land, indicating a rough equality in the holdings among the landed. But this equality was only approximate in that holdings at the two extremes of the ten to twenty acres category were very different; the larger were almost twice the size of the others. Large holdings did not necessarily bring the greatest returns of grain and produce to the family if it had to engage full-time Chamar *sepidars,* agricultural laborers, or if it had to give some land to tenants for lack of sufficient labor within the family to cultivate it fully. This was necessary for some of the Sahota property groups since they differed considerably in size and composition (see Table 6). Groups with more than

[19] S. R., 1850, 265, 275.

TABLE 5

SIZE OF AGRICULTURAL HOLDINGS, OWNED AND USED, 1848

(number of holdings, and percent of holdings and acreage in holdings of various sizes)

		Holdings, in acres											
		Less than 0.50	0.50–0.99	1.00–1.99	2.00–3.99	4.00–5.99	6.00–7.99	8.00–9.99	10.00–14.99	15.00–19.99	20.00–29.99	30.00–39.99	40.00–49.99	Total
Size of owner's holdings	No. holdings	4			4	3	4		16	5	4		2	42
	% holdings	10			10	7	10		38	12	10		5	
	% acreage	---			2	3	5		37	17	19		17	
Size of farms	No. holdings	11	1		7	5	6	2	20	5	3		1	61
	% holdings	18	2		12	8	10	3	33	8	5		2	
	% acreage	---	---		4	5	7	3	44	16	12		8	

SOURCE: Land file.

TABLE 6

CASTE AND PROPERTY GROUPS, 1848

Caste	Ghars	No. groups	Average size	Composition in percent			
				Single adult male	Father & son or sons	Brothers	Total more than one adult male
Jat[a]	63	55	5.1	49	31	20	51
Chamar	13	13	4.6	69	23	8	31
Brahmin	10	9	5.5	44	22	34	56
Julaha	10	7	5.7	29	14	57	71
Faqir	5	5	4.6	40	40	20	60
Tarkhan	5	5	3.8	80		20	20
Chiir	3	3	5.0	67		33	33
Nai	3	2	6.0			100	100
Kumhar	3	3	6.3	67		33	33
Chuura	2	2	5.5	50	50		50
Gujjar	2	2	4.0	50	50		50
Rangeez	1	1	7.0			100	100
Rajput	1	1	6.0	100			
Mirasi	1	1	3.0	100			
Sonihar	1	1	5.1	100			
Total	123	110	5.1	52	25	23	48

SOURCE: *Khanna shumari* (household census) 1848, Village Vilyatpur.
[a] Includes Jats of all clans.

one adult male were in a slight majority among the Jats. This reflected, in part, the demand for family labor in agriculture given the
size of holdings. There was hardly an abundance of agricultural
labor in Vilyatpur; seventeen Chamar *sepidars,* two full-time agricultural laborers, and eighteen tenants (Jats and Chuuras) who were
free for occasional work—together only thirty-five men, less than
one for each Sahota property group (see Table 4).

The percentage of landed property groups with only one adult
male (49 percent) was inflated by demographic pressures that have
nothing to do with the working of the land. Almost half of the
groups consisting of a couple and their children (24 percent of the
total) were a product of circumstances, not a deliberate decision,
since they had no living relatives e.g. a father, brother, uncle, or

adult son or grandson with whom they could combine into a more complex unit. In all, twenty-two of the Sahota groups were able to cultivate all of their land, but the other twenty found it necessary to rent some out, a few leasing substantial amounts. In eleven cases less than one acre was given, frequently to a Brahmin or Faqir, free of rent. Of the other nine, six (30 percent) were from three to eight acres, and the last three were thirteen, nineteen, and thirty-three acres each. The size of holdings actually cultivated was therefore smaller than the ownership units. In 1848 sixty-one groups cultivated the land in Vilyatpur, and although holdings between ten and twenty acres accounted for some 60 percent of the village's acreage, they represented only 40 percent of the holdings. The average was about nine acres, but eleven property groups cultivated less than half an acre in 1848.

There is no discernible pattern to contrast the size and composition of Jat property groups with those of the other castes except the low incidence of groups with more than one male among the Chamars and the high frequency of this type with the Julahas, particularly where the men were brothers. Among the other castes the contrasts are either difficult to interpret, as with the Brahmins, or the number of property groups is so small that the differences are insignificant. But when the size and composition of groups are compared by occupation rather than caste, a pattern is evident suggesting a relationship between the organization of units engaged in a particular economic activity and the enterprise itself.

TABLE 7

OCCUPATION AND PROPERTY GROUPS, 1848

Occupation	No. groups	Average size	Composition in percent			
			Single adult male	Father & son or sons	Brothers	Total more than one adult male
Cultivator	61	5.4	44	33	23	56
Services	12	5.4	50	25	25	50
Manufacturing	15	5.1	53	6	40	47
Agricultural labor	14	3.3	64	29	7	36

SOURCE: *Khanna shumari* (household census) 1848, Village Vilyatpur.

Land Tenure, Ownership, and Revenue

The principal unit of economic activity in Vilyatpur in 1848, regardless of caste or occupation, was the individual property group.
The ties between agriculturalists and the artisans and suppliers of
services were dyadic, connecting two particular groups. But other
aspects of village organization were structured around the Sahotas
as a caste and kinship group, affecting the others indirectly, if at all.
Chapter I showed how caste structure patterned Vilyatpur's settlement and gave the Sahotas sole control of the land. Therefore, the
questions of how land was held and transmitted, the meaning of
land ownership, and the procedure for sharing the revenue demanded by the government concerned only them.

Baden-Powell, in his comprehensive survey of Indian land tenures,
classifies the great diversity found in the subcontinent into two
basic types: the *zamindari* or joint, and the *ryotwari* or severalty.
In *ryotwari* villages the cultivators as a group had no joint claim
to the village; "each man owns his own holding, which he has
inherited, or bought, or cleared from the original jungle." [20] *Zamindari* villages, in contrast, were characterized by a "strong joint body,
probably descendant (in many cases) from a single head or a single
family." [21] Baden-Powell considers the *ryotwari* village to be the
oldest known form of village community in India, a product of the
period of rule by Hindu *rajas; zamindari* villages are a later development and may have emerged from a variety of historical situations.[22]

The history of Vilyatpur's settlement distinguishes it as a perfect
example of a joint village developing "from the original establishment of special clans and families of associated bands of village
farmers and colonists in comparatively recent times." [23] According
to Baden-Powell, the land belonged to the proprietary body as a
whole in all villages of this kind, but he classifies them further into
three types according to how members divided the land and the
burden of the government's tax.[24] In the subclassification of *zamindari* villages, all land was held either by a single individual or

---

[20] Baden-Powell, *Land Systems*, I, 107.
[21] *Ibid.*   [22] *Ibid.*, I, 107, 129.   [23] *Ibid.*, II, 620.   [24] *Ibid.*, I, 130.

jointly by a small group of closely related members; while in *patti-dari* villages, members' shares were determined by the operation of the law of inheritance; an individual family's holding at any moment was determined by the number of equal divisions between heirs in the preceding generations. *Bhaiachara* villages differed slightly from the *pattidari,* supposedly to insure an equitable division of the land's productive capacity.[25] At the time of settlement the land was divided into lots that were equal in productivity rather than size. After the original division the lots—variously named, but called *hals* (plows) in Vilyatpur and many other parts of the Punjab—were transmitted as in *pattidari* villages by equal division between all heirs in each family.[26] The land was never measured; each property group cultivated its inherited fields while the tax burden was apportioned according to the number of plows it held.[27]

When Vilyatpur was reconstituted into three *pattis* (based on the three maximal lineages) by Mughal revenue officials, the land of the village was divided into twenty-three plows, with nine, eight, and six *hals* in the three village subdivisions. Taking the cultivated area as of 1848, this meant an average of about twenty-one, twenty-four, and thirty acres per plow for the *pattis* respectively. The principle behind the choice of the number of *hals* is not known, but it probably was based on the number of property groups in each of the *pattis* about five generations before 1848. There was a rough equity in the system—shares within each *patti* were apparently equivalent to each other, and although the average size of a *hal* varied from one *patti* to another, those with the largest area paid more revenue because the share for each village subsection was the same. The difference in the average size of the *hals* might also be a function of the number of wells, the primary factor determining the productivity of land because the soil was generally uniform throughout.

But even if at the outset holdings within each *patti* were approximately equal and the share of revenue paid by all property groups was roughly equivalent in the village, the differential growth of individual *tabbars* and *khandans* rendered the holdings progres-

[25] *Ibid.,* II, 131–133, 676.
[26] These plows are not to be confused with actual working plows.
[27] *Ibid.,* II, 132.

sively less equal with the passage of time. The property was sometimes
parcelled out to heirs in each generation resulting in smaller holdings,
while in others there was only a single descendant so the original
patrimony remained intact. This process partially accounts for the
range and distribution of holdings (shown on Table 5) found by
revenue officers when they measured property actually being cultivated by each Sahota group in 1848. To accommodate the differential
redistribution of holdings resulting from the unequal growth of property groups and to still have an easy way to calculate the part of the
revenue which each had to pay, the number of *hals* was progressively
increased. It would have been cumbersome to keep the number
constant for a long period. The shares of property groups in *khandans* that had grown rapidly would be indicated by small fractions,
while those of lone descendants would still be one plow. Instead, the
number of *hals* was increased, but in the process of revaluation, the
relationship—however approximate—between a *hal* share and the
actual amount of land held by the property group was gradually lost.
By 1848 a *hal* represented a group's share of the *pattis'* contribution
to the total revenue levied on the village by the government rather
than the amount of land it controlled.[28] Among the Sahotas there
were a total of sixty-three and a half *hal*. The individual property
group's contribution ranged from one-half to three shares which
correlated only roughly with the amount of land held. As the *hal*
system came to represent shares of the revenue rather than land, it
was also used to indicate the contribution of the cultivators who
were not part of the *bhaiachara*—tenants and others—to the payment of the land tax. An approximate relationship between the

---

[28] Most authorities on land tenure and the village community in the Punjab
have a different explanation of the variation between traditional shares of land
and the amount cultivated by various property groups. It is argued that since
land was plentiful a property group cultivated only as much land as it needed
to satisfy its needs and could easily farm with the labor available in the family
and assistance from *sepidars,* etc. Revenue was paid only on the land cultivated,
a plow share symbolizing the extent of land that a family could potentially claim
rather than either the amount cultivated or its contribution of the tax. Outsiders
were welcomed to cultivate land for a share of the government's tax burden. Ibbetson, *Karnal Settlement Report,* 96; S.R., 1851, 280. Although conditions in Vilyatpur might have been similar at some time in the past, I cannot reconcile this
formulation with the evidence on the late Sikh period, when the land was fully
cultivated; when one Sahota property group rented land to another, and the
plow-share system was applied to tenants not part of the *bhaiachara* to indicate
their share of the tax which was collected in addition to rent (see below).

TABLE 8

TRADITIONAL SHARES, 1848

	Plowshares	0	½	1	2	3
Sahotas	Number	4	2	20	18	2
	Ave. size (acres)	4.2	3.5	12.6	10.8	29.7
	Range (acres)	.1–14	2.6–4.5	.1–51.1	.9–22.8	28.9–30.6
Others	Number		3	11	2	1
	Ave. size (acres)		.1	3.3	8.9	5.1
	Range (acres)		0–.2	.3–10.2	6.1–11.6	5.1

SOURCE: *Khanna shumari* (household census) 1848, Village Vilyatpur.
Sample: All resident landowning/using property groups.

amount of land cultivated and the size of the share is apparent among the non-Sahotas as a group. In contrast to the Sahotas, however, their effective assessment was high, and considering that most of them paid rent as well, the "outsiders" paid dearly for the right to cultivate land in Vilyatpur during the pre-British period.

Although individual property groups in Vilyatpur's *bhaiachara* had holdings that could be transmitted to their descendants and that could be leased either to another Sahota property group or to various kinds of tenants in the pre-British period, they did not own the land in the sense of having "the power of absolute disposal in perpetuity." [29] In many respects the land and the village belonged to the Sahotas of Vilyatpur collectively. A group might transfer all or part of its holding to another Sahota family,[30] but not "to anyone outside the proprietary body." [31] Nor could a shareholder freely adopt an heir from outside the clan. In 1848 there was only one non-Sahota considered to be a member of the *bhaiachara*, a Jat of the Uppal *got* whose father had married a Sahota girl with no brothers; he was allowed by the proprietary body to succeed his father-in-law. If a suitable adoption could not be arranged, then the shareholder's line died out, his land being divided among members of his *khandan*. When a particular property group left the village temporarily, its holdings were kept in trust by the *bhaiachara*

[29] Neale, *Economic Change*, 19.
[30] S. R., 1850, 280; Ibbetson, *Karnal Settlement*, 96.
[31] Ibbetson, *Karnal Settlement*, 96; Punjab Census, 1881, I, 44.

until its return. At least three families lived outside of the village
in 1848, and, although they could not collect rent from those using
the land, their descendants in the next generation were able to claim
it again on their return to the village. The proprietary body as a
whole was also preeminent in the community's relationship to the
government, since payment of the revenue was structured through
the organization of Vilyatpur's three Sahota lineages. The Rajput
zamindars and Sikh revenue officials both dealt with the lineage
muqaddams rather than individual property groups.[32]

But why this continued corporate control over the ultimate title
to the land when the different property groups in the community
used it on a day-to-day basis in a more individualistic manner?
Baden-Powell's explanation is not satisfactory. He attributes the
continued collective control of land in villages like Vilyatpur to a
"strong tribal feeling" which is part of a universal evolutionary
sequence (the "stages of property") where land is first held by the
tribe or clan, then by the joint family, and finally by the individual.[33]
The dynamic that moves a society from one form of property to
another is improvement of the land, making first the family, and
then the individual, seek direct control of a separate holding. Although suggestive because of the emphasis on clan organization and
land control in the village, Baden-Powell's theory misses the significance of the *bhaiachara's* role in the context of Mughal and Sikh
rule because of his preoccupation with an evolutionary theory of
property and ownership. The proprietary body's control of Vilyatpur
was based on its clearing of the land and settlement of the village,
and the *power* to sustain its dominance. The local clan structure of
the Sahotas played an important role in the establishment of the

[32] I am not arguing here that Mughal and Sikh administrations recognized or
enforced the joint responsibility of the *bhaiachara* for the village's revenue. Authorities on the Mughal revenue system find no evidence of joint ownership of
land in the period: Habib, 123; Moreland, 178–179. Similarly, although *bhaiachara*
villages existed in the Punjab in the Sikh period, the administration held the
individual cultivator responsible for payment of the revenue: S. R., 1851, 277, 280.
In normal circumstances, however, revenue collectors used the structure of the
bhaiachara, dealing with its leadership to simplify the task of collecting the
revenue. Records of these administrations often list only the total revenue demanded and collected and never mention the internal distribution of the assessment within the village which, along with local collection, was left to the *muqaddams:* Kohli, 79, 86.

[33] Baden-Powell, *Land Systems,* I, 109–111.

village, and remained vital throughout the Mughal and Sikh periods, meeting any threat to its position by groups like the Rajput *zamindars,* the different *misls,* and perhaps even from the state.[34] In their daily economic activities, Sahota property groups used the land individually, but long-term possession of their holdings necessitated the continued vitality of local clan structure. "Absolute disposal in perpetuity" of any village land was incompatible with the maintenance of the social and political organization provided by the local clan structure of the Sahotas.

Social and Political Organization

There is no detailed information on social and political life in the village in the late Sikh period. But enough data exists to make use of recent anthropological studies of structurally similar villages in independent India to draw conclusions about Vilyatpur in 1848. Even though these observations are based on analogy and are general, they are useful as part of the baseline for highlighting some basic political and social changes that occurred in the British period and since 1947.

There are studies in the recent anthropological literature on villages in which a single numerically large caste group dominates the economic, political, social, and ritual life of the community.[35] These studies have provided a basis for developing the concept of the dominant caste village as a distinctive type of community about

[34] This analysis draws on Nicholas' application of the work of Marshall D. Salhins on segmentary lineages to the political structure of Indian villages. I am extending their position that segmentary lineages generally develop when a tribe moves into an already occupied area, to argue that the lineages also developed and are perpetuated under threat of secondary conquest. Nicholas, *Politics in Villages,* 272.

[35] Cohn, *Notes on Disputes and Law,* 86, suggests that "the recurrence of this kind of village in the literature . . . is in part an artifact of the anthropologist's interest in the caste system and thus his choosing as a research site a situation in which the interaction of a large number of castes can be observed. Whether this is "the typical" village in India may lie open to question but it is the typical village chosen by most anthropologists to study." The presence of a dominant caste was *not* one of the criteria in the selection of a village for this study. For the procedure followed, see Kessinger, "Historical Materials," 491–493. In fact, the dominant caste village is the most common type in the Punjab because of the predominance of *bhaiachara* villages, all of which are *ipso facto* dominant caste villages.

which generalizations can be made concerning the political, legal, and social structure, valid for all such villages. The Sahotas satisfied three of the four criteria in Srinivas' original definition of a dominant caste: numerical and economic preponderance, and relatively high caste status.[36] Their political dominance follows, given the history of the village's settlement, the nature of Mughal and Sikh rural administration, and the fact that, even in contemporary villages, political dominance seems to derive from economic and numerical preponderance.[37]

Two observations about politics in dominant caste villages in anthropological studies are relevant to the study of Vilyatpur in the pre-British period. Srinivas finds that even in contemporary communities only the dominant caste has an "autonomous political existence" in the village.[38] All other groups participate in politics indirectly, through connections with the dominant caste. In villages like Vilyatpur it was inconceivable that the Carpenters or Barbers could participate directly in village politics, but they were incorporated individually through their ties as *sepidars* to particular patrons. As a corollary to this pattern of participation, political conflict in dominant-caste villages is usually structured around factions within the dominant caste rather than between it and any other group in the community.[39] Chapter I shows that the history of Vilyatpur's settlement is full of conflict between the three lineages in the community following this pattern. Closely related to their hegemony in village politics is the dominant caste leaders' role in the settlement

[36] M. N. Srinivas, "The Social System of a Mysore Village," Marriott, *Village India,* 18.

[37] Nicholas, *Politics in Villages,* 273. Nicholas's point represents an important refinement of the concept of the dominant caste. He goes on to argue that "in the ideal model of a village caste system, dominance derives from a superior power alone; numbers play no necessary part in the establishment of a dominant caste . . . There may have been occasions in the past when the numerical size of a caste group was of importance, but, for the most part the legitimacy of the rule of even a small dominant caste was rarely questioned." The emphasis on legitimacy is an important contribution, but at least in Vilyatpur legitimacy is derivative of the processes of settlement and maintenance of control over time, in which numerical strength in the community *and* the *ilaqa* were crucial in the pre-British period.

[38] Srinivas, *Social System,* 217.

[39] Nicholas, *Politics in Villages,* 276.

of disputes involving members of all castes in the village, not simply members of their own group. The only area where they might not become involved is in "matters internal to other castes" which do not relate to village property or to any member of the dominant caste." [40] Given the small number of property groups in any caste but the Sahotas, the *bhaiacharas'* control of all the land used for residential construction, and, their domination of the only productive activity in the village, the jurisdiction of the dominant caste leaders was extensive, including everything but domestic disputes of the other castes.

The studies suggest a few simple conclusions about social and political life in Vilyatpur in the Sikh period. In the context of Sikh administration of rural tracts, the dominant caste's hegemony of village politics and dispute resolution—which is always qualified in studies of present-day communities—was a virtual monopoly. There was no check on the outright use of force by the dominant caste, common even during the British period, and no alternative to justice they dispensed in the village. Law courts did not exist for rural areas,[41] and although application could be made to revenue officials or a relative in the service of the state for arbitration of intractable conflicts,[42] it is unlikely that any but members of the Sahota *bhaiachara* could do this. Political networks existed above the level of the individual community, but only through the clan structure of the dominant caste.[43] This does not mean that there was no alternative for the aggrieved and alienated—it was always possible to leave the village and take up residence elsewhere. But if individuals, families, or caste groups wanted to make a living or even to reside in the community, acceptance of the political and jural power of the Sahotas was an inevitable necessity. The possibility of using institutions *outside* of Vilyatpur to achieve social, economic, and political gains *within* village society existed only for the Sahotas in the Sikh period, and, even for them, only to a limited extent.

[40] Cohn, *Notes on Disputes*, 91.

[41] Chopra, 88.

[42] Kohli, 87.

[43] For an historical account of a particularly well developed clan structure see Pradhan, 94–214.

The Classical View of the Traditional Village

The history of *Jullundur doab* and the settlement of the village emphasized the relationship between Vilyatpur and the world outside—the state, the *zamindars,* other villages, and the mainstream of events in the Punjab—for evaluating the idea of the self-sufficient, isolated, Indian "village republic." With the reconstruction of village organization and life in 1848, we can now also reexamine some generally accepted views of the detailed internal workings of rural communities prior to British annexation.

The picture of Vilyatpur in 1848, which emerges from the census, revenue, land, and agricultural records of the village, and the revenue report for Jullundur district, shows some similarity to the classical view of the traditional village found in standard economic histories. This is at least implicit in anthropological studies of social and economic change. Caste and kinship played a prominent role in the organization of the social, political, and economic life of the community. The corporate character of the local clan structure of the Sahotas (a product of the village's settlement pattern), retained its vitality in the context of eighteenth and early nineteenth century Punjab, forming the core of local society. Vilyatpur was their village, everyone else in the community was in some manner or another dependent upon them. Land was used individually by kin-based property groups, but was ultimately controlled by the *bhaiachara,* emphasizing the land's political as well as economic importance. Customary relationships dominated economic activity in the village. *Sepidars* performed their traditional tasks for patrons with whom they had long-term, personal ties, receiving a percentage of the produce, thereby assuring themselves of support regardless of the size of the harvest. Other artisans and servants were compensated by the job in grain at fixed rates. Sugarcane and wheat were grown for sale in the market as well as for consumption, and the revenue was paid in cash, but custom rather than the market regulated economic activity in the village.

And yet although caste, kinship, and custom were paramount in Vilyatpur in 1848, some qualifications and corrections in the classical view of the traditional village prior to British annexation are needed. Within the village, the *bhaiachara* had ultimate control of the land, but because economic activity involved individual and property groups, some of which controlled large holdings compared to others (Table 5), the *bhaiachara,* though corporate, was hardly egalitarian. It is difficult to reconcile a situation where 5 percent of the property groups control 17 percent of the land at one extreme while 35 percent of the Sahotas had only 10 percent of the acreage at the other with either the idea of "fair shares" within the community,[44] or with a more general notion of an equal distribution of resources and power. Nor is it correct to say that land was only important as a basis for power. Land tenure had a political aspect for the Sahotas as a group, but individual holdings were not usually large enough to provide the property group with a substantial number of dependents who would be supporters. For most of the Sahotas, the land was important for what it produced and not as a source of power over *sepidars,* laborers, or tenants.

A number of misconceptions about village economic organization and life also can now be corrected. The *sepidari* system was a central and vital feature of the village economy. But although most economic relationships were embedded in elaborate personal and ritual ties, and all economic activity was compensated for in grain at customary rates, not all artisans and servants in the village were part of the system and therefore guaranteed a share of the produce (Table 4). The weavers, potters, and Brahmin shopkeepers did not have the same tie to the community as the *sepidars.* In addition, even the *sepidars* were quite mobile, many staying in the village for only one generation. While this is not rapid mobility, neither is it a closed hereditary system reaching back beyond the memory of man. The system of customary relations was stable, not the individuals and families that filled it. There was some correlation between traditional and actual occupations; but it was rough, since almost one man in four worked in a nontraditional type of job (Table 4). These were not artisans forced out of their traditional crafts by competition with cheap British goods, but Leatherworkers, Carpenters, Barbers, Brahmins, Sweepers, and Faqirs, who worked in agriculture primarily as tenants, but also as laborers. Several Brahmins were shopkeepers and moneylenders rather than professional priests.

Agriculture in the village does not conform to the classical view

---

[44] Neale, *Economic Change,* 25–27.

of large unfragmented holdings and available uncultivated waste, implying current abundance and untapped resources for the future.[45] But neither was it neglected and crude as "subsistence agriculture" is so often regarded. Most of the Sahotas' holdings were small, comprised of a number of small fragments. Agriculture, although oriented primarily toward production for consumption, was well-developed and fairly intensive. There was no uncultivated waste, a third of the fields were double cropped, and there was substantial investment in livestock, irrigation channels, and jointly-owned brick wells.

Even the joint family does not deserve the influence in society accorded it by the institution's admirers and critics. In the demographic conditions of the mid-nineteenth century, as many as one-fourth of the Sahota groups were nuclear in structure because of an absence of relatives needed for a more complex farm. About an equal number of groups had only one adult male by choice. Even the joint property groups with more than one adult male were not large, averaging only 5.2 persons per group for the Sahotas and 5.1 for the whole population. Thus, the image of a hoary old man presiding over a large, four-generation family conjured up by most descriptions of the joint family in traditional India was seldom if ever fulfilled in Vilyatpur.[46]

These qualifications and corrections of the classical view of the traditional village in pre-British times, important in themselves, are essential for the rest of the study. The details of the physical layout of the village, the composition of the population, and the nature of economic activity and organization, the distribution of land, and the outlines of social and political life will be used as referents to determine the nature and extent of change over the ensuing period. Thus, as new occupational opportunities led to changes in the occupations of groups and individuals and modifications in family property-group composition and relations, they will be examined against the background of the village in 1848 when

[45] For good summaries of the classical view see, Morris D. Morris, "Economic Change and Agriculture in Nineteenth Century India," *Indian Economic and Social History Review*, III (1966), 185-209; and Dharma Kumar, "Caste and Landlessness in South India," *Comparative Studies in Society and History* IV (1961-1962), 337-363.

[46] Bailey, *Caste and the Economic Frontier* (Manchester University Press, 1957), 10.

one man in four worked outside of his traditional occupation and a similar percentage of property groups were "nuclear" in structure. This kind of statistical analysis[47] is indispensable for the study of social and economic change. The designation of areas where significant variations to prevailing patterns existed in 1848 also provides an insight as to where change will occur as the external political, economic, and administrative environment altered over the next one hundred and twenty years.

The emphasis on 1848 in no way implies that there was no change prior to the baseline year. Chapter I shows there were several important developments before British annexation. The selection of 1848 as a starting point is arbitrary, in this case determined by the availability of information. The baseline is useful for highlighting changes—it says nothing about the preceding period.

The Immediate Effects of British Rule

The remaining chapters are devoted to the examination of the causes and nature of social and economic change in Vilyatpur in British and post-Independence Punjab. Most of these developments resulted from the interplay of several factors and had incremental effects. But certain changes can best be seen as a restructuring of the village through the working-out of policies, procedures, and the formal structure of British rule as it was introduced into Jullundur district. Since these alterations in the administrative context of the village occurred at the very beginning of our period, the restructuring resulting from the immediate effects of British administration form an important addendum to the picture of Vilyatpur in 1848. Though part of the baseline, they warrant separate consideration because they represent a significant departure from conditions in the late Sikh period.

At the time of the annexation of the Punjab, the form and content of British revenue policy was explicitly conservative. "The system," wrote James Thomason, its architect in the Ceded and Northwest Provinces, "professes to alter nothing, but only to place on record what it finds to exist."[48] But the goal of conserving rural

---

[47] Meyer Fortes, *Time and Social Structure,* 58–60.
[48] Quoted in Marriott, *Little Communities,* 184.

society as the revenue officials found it proved difficult to attain
because revenue officials were continuously confronted by complex-
ities which forced them to make a series of decisions that resulted
in innovation and change. The first and most basic innovation was
the decision to make the *mauza* (village) the unit of administration
rather than the *mahal* (estate) used by the Mughals and perhaps the
Sikhs; the latter is a larger unit usually consisting of a number of
villages belonging to a single lineage of *zamindars* or caste group
of cultivators.[49] Even at the time of the first settlement, the implementation of this decision was neither simple nor treated casually:

On selecting a *Parganah* or *Tahsil* for Settlement the first step should be
to draw out a list of *Mauzas,* which *are to be separately marked off* and
surveyed. This requires more care than may at first be supposed. It is
necessary to decide in what cases separate properties in the same *Mauza*
should be separately surveyed and formed into distinct *Mauzas;* and in
what cases *Mauzas* constituting the same property may be surveyed together and formed into one new *Mauza* . . . The names in English of
the villages having thus been fixed should be afterwards maintained both
by the Surveyor and the Settlement Officers.[50]

Considering the importance given to the village community in rural
administration under the British and in the Indian nationalist
view of India's civilization and past, the innovation of selecting the
village as the basic unit and the task of deciding what was and was
not to be a village had profound consequences. The crosscutting of
many of the ties between villages in an *ilaqa* inhabited by branches
of the same clan, like the Sahotas in Vilyatpur, Barapind, and the
other satellite villages, was one result. In addition to weakening the
networks between communities, British policy reshaped the development of village social structure and laid the basis for the Community Development program after independence which, under
Gandhi's influence, sought to make the village the focus for institutional development in the countryside.

There were numerous changes in village social organization that
resulted directly from British land revenue settlement procedures
and policy.[51] Although every effort was made to follow local custom

---

[49] *Ibid.*
[50] D. G. Barkley, *Directions for Revenue Officers in the Punjab* (Lahore: Punjab Government, 1875), 3 (emphasis added).
[51] Cohn, *Notes on Disputes,* 110.

in determining who was liable for the payment of revenue, the discretion of the individual settlement officer was frequently the most important factor, in part because of the multiplicity of rights and claims but also because of an officer's individual predilections. The decision to override the claims of the Muslim Rajput *zamindars* in Jullundur illustrates this nicely. The results of the settlements in the various districts of the Punjab were therefore not uniform simply because they were carried out by different officials.

Individual idiosyncracies and theories of what was best for the country were apt to lead men to disregard or curtail rights which they thought to be antiquated or hurtful, to exalt one class in the community and to depress the status of another. Sympathy with old tribes and families which had been the victims of the political and social convulsions preceeding British rule, led one man to revive dormant rights and sympathy with the actual tillers of the soil and induced another to treat lightly rights which still had a substantial existence.[52]

Another innovation was the decision to make the *bhaiachara* collectively responsible for the collection and payment of revenue. Collective responsibility had not been part of revenue policy in the Sikh period, but the British felt it crucial for maintaining the cohesion of the community, a force that could not "be weakened without altering the whole framework of the community and introducing a new state of society." [53] The decision to assess and collect revenue from the lineages comprising the *bhaiachara*

may have been to strengthen lineage organization among the proprietary castes by giving the lineages legally recorded corporate property in perpetuity. This step contributed to the development of deep lineages, and thereby fostered the system of politics which brings lineage segments into conflict with one another.[54]

The number and composition of Vilyatpur's three lineages was frozen by the act of recording them in the records as joint owners of the village. While the village records note the creation of new lineages in the pre-British period, none have developed since 1848 even though the population of the community has more than doubled, rendering the lineages cumbersome because of size. The emphasis

[52] Douie, 53.
[53] *Ibid.*, 134.
[54] Nicholas, *Politics in Villages*, p. 272; Marriott, *Little Communities*, 185–186.

on the lineages also seems to have acted as a deterrent to the immigration of affinal relatives.[55] Although a non-Sahota succeeding his father-in-law became a member of the proprietary body before 1848, none have done so since, although several achieved this indirectly after 1956 when a change in inheritance laws gave women an equal share with their brothers in the paternal estate.

Lineage organization was reified by settlement policies and procedures which simultaneously led to a substantial decline in the importance of the proprietary body as a whole. Despite the explicitly conservative goal of continuing customary forms and usages, changes occurred because these were viewed as static and formal rather than situational.[56] The consequences of this conception are particularly apparent in relation to land tenure and law. I have argued that land ownership as understood by the British did not exist in the village before 1848 and that the rights of the Sahotas were derived from their settlement and control of the village that, rather than some abstract notion of property, was the basis of their legitimacy. The continued joint "ownership" of the village can only be understood in terms of these two processes. By designating the Sahotas "individually and collectively" as the owners in perpetuity of particular plots of land, the British revenue system fixed village organization as it existed in 1848.[57] The legitimacy of the Sahotas' position was henceforth not to be found in their status as the village's settlers and controllers but in the land revenue records maintained in the district headquarters and enforced in the district courts by government appointed judges.[58] As a result, the rationale for continued joint control of the village and its land no longer existed.

[55] Marriott, *Little Communities,* 185.

[56] This is another manifestation of what Cohn has characterized as the tendency of administrators to think of villages in terms of categories and types. This way of thinking has the advantage of reducing the need for specific knowledge but "latently . . . directed attention away from internal politics in villages and from question of the nature of actual social relations, of the distribution of wealth, of what was happening to agricultural production; in short, the Victorians were not concerned with what the actual conditions of life in the village were but with general theoretical questions derived from social theory of the day." Cohn, *Notes on the History of the Study of Indian Society and Culture,* 21.

[57] Marian W. Smith, "The Misal: A Structural Village-Group of India and Pakistan," *American Anthropologist,* LIV (1952), 49.

[58] Bernard S. Cohn, "From Indian Status to British Contract," *Journal of Economic History,* XXI (1961), 619.

The very notion of the settlement procedure, placing "on record what it finds to exist," produced a number of important changes that weakened the cohesion of the proprietary body. The minute recording of the ownership of every field, with an elaborate procedure for transferring the title, for which a fee was charged, encouraged fragmentation and made any consolidation of fields a difficult task where before the consent of both parties was all that had been required. The record system also created absentee landlords by making it possible for shareholders living outside the village and newcomers who purchased land in the village to profit from their possessions. Before 1848, shareholders outside the village had a claim to the land if they returned but could not profit from it while outside the community, whereas under the British system, absentee ownership became possible.[59] Similarly, the sale of individual fields by members of the *bhaiachara* was now formalized in the records.

In other respects the "freezing" effect of "writing down what existed" led to distortions by formalizing and maintaining customs that became increasingly unharmonious with changing conditions in the late nineteenth and early twentieth centuries. On the basis of earlier experiences elsewhere in India, the British realized by the time the Punjab was annexed that no fixed and generally applicable "Hindu Law" existed in the classical Sanskrit texts[60] and sought instead to record and compile local customary usages which could then be enforced in the courts. An elaborate and detailed questionnaire was developed to collect information systematically from local caste and village leaders on a range of practices: inheritance and adoption, the use of common land, the rights of the proprietors, and even the disposition of the dung of animals belonging to other village residents.[61] But this effort to perpetuate what "actually existed" foundered because British administrators thought of customary law—though unwritten and localized—as something static

[59] Marriott, *Little Communities,* 186.

[60] For a detailed discussion of this problem see Cohn, *Notes on Disputes,* 109–113.

[61] For the original outline of efforts to codify customary law and the actual questionnaire see C. L. Tupper, *Punjab Customary Law* (Calcutta: Superintendant of Government Printing, 1881) 3v., and for a shorter description of the whole enterprise and its place in the development of Punjab's judicial administration see B. H. Baden-Powell, "Tribal Law in the Panjab," *Imperial and Asiatic Quarterly,* 3rd Series, II (1896), 46–60.

and general rather than *processual* and situational.[62] The effect of codification was to fix the usage, thereby depriving it of its flexibility in different situations and, what is more important from a historical point of view, its adaptive qualities. Henry Maine summarized the effects of the system of compilation and administration on customary usage:

The changes . . . arose from the mere establishment of local courts of lowest jurisdiction, and while they effected a revolution, it is a revolution which in the first instance was conservative of the rigidity of native usage. The customs at once altered their character. They are generally collected from the testimony of the village elders; but when these elders are once called upon to give their evidence, they necessarily lose their old position. They are no longer a half-judicial, half-legislative council. That which they have affirmed to be the custom is hence forward to be sought from the decisions of the Courts of Justice, or from official documents which those courts receive as evidence. . . . Usage, once recorded upon evidence given, immediately becomes written and fixed law. Nor is it any longer obeyed as usage. It is henceforth obeyed as the law administered by a British Court and . . . the vague sanctions of customary law disappears.[63]

Through its collection, recording, interpretation, and administration by the court, customary law became static, and the proprietary body lost one of its functions and sources of power and prestige in the community. The growth of institutions like the courts and rural based police outside the village, which could be used for ends within the community, significantly altered the context of village political and social structure. In Vilyatpur the Sahotas took immediate advantage of the new facilities, registering seventeen civil and two criminal cases against each other in the district courts between 1848 and 1851. The first case of an individual of another caste pitted against the Sahotas did not occur until the 1890's. The existence of the courts provided members of the *bhaiachara* with a new arena—outside the community and the local clan structure—to fight their disputes and encouraged litigation, and as a result "loosened the communal tie and weakened the authority exercised by the proprietary body over its individual members . . ."[64]

---

[62] Cohn, *Notes on Disputes*, 111.

[63] Henry Sumner Maine, *Village-Communities in the East and West* (London: John Murray, 1871), 71–72.

[64] Douie, 63.

In making the village the unit of administration, designating village cultivators as the corporate owners of the village, recording in minute detail the proprietorship of every field, and attempting to codify customary law, the intention of British policy in the Punjab was explicitly to preserve rural society as they had found it. Paradoxically, the effort contained within itself the seeds of change because it was not always possible to identify what was customary; the act of *writing down* the distribution of pieces of land and local usages froze them as they existed; and so British rural administration altered the context of the village and its institutions.[65] Although a wealth of ethnographic information was collected on the Punjab in the late nineteenth century, and although the official view of rural society approximated what existed at the time of annexation more closely than had been the case at a comparable stage in Bengal, the Punjab policies were not successful in the long run in preserving society in its pre-British form. Many programs and legislative acts directed toward rural problems in the Punjab, most notably the Punjab Land Alienation Act (1900), the Co-operative Societies Act (1904), and the Pre-Emption Act (1913), are attempts by British administrators to shore-up what in their view was customary village organization because they recognized it was changing rapidly. The alteration, in part, can be attributed to the working of the judicial system, the inflexibility of recorded custom, and the nature of British rural administration. The primary source, however, was the new opportunities opening up to Vilyatpur's residents in the late nineteenth century, mostly outside the village, but within the community as well. How people took advantage of these opportunities and the consequences of their actions for the community will form the subject of the rest of the study.

[65] P.A.R., 1849, 72.

Chapter III

DEMOGRAPHIC CHANGE, 1848–1968

Population—the problem of increased pressure on scarce resources —is an important factor in the quest of independent India for economic development and social justice. The statistics of each Five-Year Plan show that a substantial portion of the economy's growth has been nullified by the rapidly expanding population.[1] And the ramifications of the population problem are not limited to economic development, social welfare, and political stability; the rate of increase, as Cohn recently suggested, has consequences for the form of society in the future.[2] Historically, however, the rapid increase in the population of India is a fairly recent phenomenon. At the aggregate (national and provincial) levels, the nineteenth and early twentieth century census figures show overall growth, but with significant fluctuations. The rate from 1881 to 1921 was 23 precent for the country as a whole.[3] The Punjab record for the same period was 22 percent.

The provincial and national trends set the general context for the village and its inhabitants. Individual families and lineages, however, had histories of growth and contraction which, though related to the aggregate picture, show great contrasts throughout the period from 1848 to 1968. Some families expanded early only to contract more recently, others have pyramided slowly over time, while a number have died out, and the continuity of still another group has been constantly in peril—there being only one male descendant in each generation. The varied demographic histories of particular families have been an important dynamic in changing patterns of behavior— decisions to lease, buy, and sell land, to migrate, and to seek new occupations in an effort to adjust to changing pressure on the family's resources and to take advantage of new opportunities. Demographic change lies behind many modifications in Punjabi villagers' behavior

[1] See *Third Five Year Plan* (Delhi: Manager of Publications, 1961), 25–26.

[2] For an interesting discussion of some of the consequences of demographic trends for social structure and organization see Cohn, *Anthropology of a Civilization,* "Conclusions," 157–164.

[3] Computed from figures in *The Census of India, 1931* (Simla: Government of India Press, 1935), Vol. I, Pt. II, Imperial Table II.

that form the subject of the next three chapters. A look at Vilyatpur's population also reveals some shifts in composition of consequence for all facets of life in the village.

Disease and Population

Table 9 summarizes information on the size, rate of change, and density of population in the village, Jullundur district and the Punjab for the period from 1855 to 1961. An accelerating increase in the size of the population of the district and province has been registered since 1911; the earlier period covered by the census was characterized by a fluctuating rate of growth with an actual decline in absolute size in the decade from 1901 to 1911. At the provincial level a number of factors contributed to the pre-1911 oscillations. Epidemic disease played an important part; major outbreaks of cholera occurred in 1867, 1869, 1872, 1875, 1878–1879, and 1892, of plague in 1897–1898, 1901–1904, and 1907–1908, of smallpox in 1869, and 1879, and of "fever" intermittently throughout the period.[4] Equally important, and often related to the incidence of epidemic disease, were the recurrent famines resulting from a failure of the rains and the lack of adequate transportation facilities to move stocks of grain and fodder into afflicted areas. Famines had been a check on population growth in the pre-British period. Three occurred in the late eighteenth century in 1753 and 1759, and a particularly severe one in 1783 during the political turmoil accompanying the disintegration of Mughal authority in the Punjab and the increased activities of the *misls*. There were six more famines between 1802 and 1837, the worst being the one in 1833.[5] In the last half of the nineteenth century following British annexation, the Punjab experienced severe shortages four times: in 1860, 1868–1869, 1878–1879, and 1898–1899.[6] After 1880, however, scarcity was a local problem that could be relieved by moving grain from surplus areas within the state along newly developed rail networks.[7] After the concurrent expansion of area irrigated by canals in western Punjab, a surplus beyond the

---

[4] *Punjab Census, 1881*, I, 54–56; *Punjab Census, 1931*, I, 15–16.

[5] *Punjab Census, 1881*, I, 49.

[6] *Ibid.*, 54–56; *Punjab Census, 1931*, I, 15–16.

[7] Hugh Kennedy Trevaskis, *The Punjab To-Day: An Economic Survey of the Punjab in Recent Years* (Lahore: Civil and Military Gazette Press, 1931), I, 230.

TABLE 9

POPULATION GROWTH, 1855–1961

	Vilyatpur			Jullundur			Punjab		
	Population	Percent of change	Density [per sq. mile]	Population	Percent of change	Density	Population	Percent of change	Density
1855	565		638	708,728		513	a		
1868	704	24	796	794,764	12	596	a		
1881	714	1	807	789,555[b]	−1	597	20,800,955	7	152
1891	880	23	994	907,583	15	686	22,915,894	10	168
1901	810	−8	915	917,587	1	694	24,367,113	6	178
1911	705	−13	797	801,920	−13	606	23,791,841	−2	174
1921	700	−1	791	822,544	3	622	25,101,514	6	184
1931	687	−2	776	943,721	15	713	28,490,857	14	208
1941	875	27	989	1,129,016	20	845	34,309,861	20	248
1951	1092	25	1234	1,055,600[b]	−7	793	c	26	322
1961	1197	10	1353	1,227,367	16	914	c	65	429
1855–1941		55			59				
1855–1961		111			73				

SOURCE: For Vilyatpur; 1855–1941, Lal Kitab, Village Vilyatpur, 1951–1961, *Jullundur District Census Handbook*; for Jullundur and Punjab, the decennial Census.

[a] Census for this year did not include the Native States.

[b] A slight change in Jullundur's boundaries occurred in this decennium. The figures cannot be adjusted for this change.

[c] Boundary changes accompanying Partition in 1947 render comparison of figures for this year meaningless.

needs of the province was produced annually and the Punjab never again experienced a deficit in food production.

Because of the large area irrigated from wells, Vilyatpur, and Jullundur district in general, never suffered much in famine years despite the density of its population.[8] Jullundur's merchants and cultivators were so accustomed to adequate crops even in the worst years, that they sold everything not needed for immediate consumption during famines to take advantage of the inflated prices in afflicted areas. This caused difficulty in the district when a scarcity extended over several years because there were no reserves for the local nonagricultural population to draw on. But few deaths were ever attributed to famine in Jullundur.[9]

The periodic epidemics took a heavy toll, accounting for much of the fluctuation in the size of the population of the village and the district until 1921. The cholera outbreak was very severe in 1878–1879, producing the variation in the 1868–1881 period. A serious attack of cholera in 1892, coupled with the effects of the plague in 1897–1898, was largely responsible for a decline in Vilyatpur's population in the last decade of the century. In 1903 the *Tehsildar* noted that eighty-six persons had died that year in still another attack of the plague—the Brahmins suffering disproportionately—which, if accurate, represented 11 percent of the 1901 population with still another year of the plague to come! Contagious disease continued to be a problem in the next decade, when an attack of plague in 1915 was followed by three years of "fever" ending in a severe outbreak of influenza in 1918.[10]

After 1918 the Punjab never again experienced an epidemic attack. The disappearance of contagious disease is difficult to explain. Steps were taken to localize outbreaks of cholera and smallpox, the most common killers, but there was no wholesale introduction of Western public health methods in rural Punjab. Perhaps the answer lies in better nutrition brought by the developments in village agriculture which form the subject of the next chapter.[11] Although the

[8] S. R., 1892, 45.

[9] *Ibid.*, 46; *Report on the Famine in the Punjab During 1869–1870* (Lahore: Punjab Printing Co., 1870), 31.

[10] *Punjab Census*, 1951, I-A, 35.

[11] This possibility has been suggested by Professor Morris D. Morris, University of Washington.

cause is not clear, serious epidemics disappeared after 1918, and the population of the district and the province entered a period of accelerating expansion.

The repeated outbreaks of contagious disease contributed to the limitation of growth in the village's population. The short life span in rural Jullundur had pronounced consequences for village social structure. Although the consideration of structural change belongs to a later chapter, two examples will illustrate some effects of insecure life on the village, making the community before 1910 fundamentally different from twentieth-century Vilyatpur. In 1848, 25 percent of the property groups consisted of a single adult male and his dependents "of necessity," that is, he had no sufficiently closely related kinsmen with whom he might combine if he so desired (see Table 10). Through 1910 these groups accounted for at least 22 percent of the property groups in Vilyatpur; afterwards their proportion declined steadily. The break between 1910 and the following periods is even sharper if the nonresident members who had migrated tem-

TABLE 10

EFFECTS OF INSECURITY OF LIFE, 1848–1968

	Percent property groups with one male "of necessity"		Age of new head of property group at the time of succession on death of the former head				
Year	Resident members only	Including non-residents	Percent 20 years old or less	Percent 25 years old or less	Percent 30 years old or less	Number of cases	Percent of total cases
1848	25	25					
1884	26	26	39	57	74	32	26
1898	22	22	24	48	67	29	35
1910	22	21	36	49	69	72	74
1922	18	16	7	18	32	45	76
1934	19	16	22	27	36	75	74
1946	15	15	15	27	40	90	70
1958	11	11	8	17	33	49	70
1968	10	9	10	19	27	97	85

SOURCE: Family biographies.
Sample: All property-groups, resident and nonresident.

porarily, but still shared property with groups in Vilyatpur, are included. With this adjustment groups composed of a single-adult-male and his dependents with no other adult male relatives are only 16 percent of all groups for 1922.

The meaning of pre-1922 mortality rates for the average man is more vividly illustrated by the age at which heads of property groups inherited their positions. The results in Table 10 for the years 1884 and 1898 are not conclusive because the percentage of all cases of succession in the two time periods (1848–1884 and 1884–1898) on which the data are complete is quite small (32 percent and 29 percent). But from 1898 to 1910 the information on age is complete enough to indicate a marked contrast between that interval and the rest of the present century.[12] In more than one-third of the cases of succession between 1898 and 1910, the heir was twenty years old or less, and one in eight was fifteen or less. Therafter, more people lived longer, bringing a sharp rise in the age at the time of succession so that by 1968 four men in five were over twenty-five when they inherited the group's property, and almost three out of four were over thirty. The 1910 figures of 69 percent under thirty and 36 percent under twenty are striking in that they refer not only to succession from father to son, but from all members of the property group in a superordinate generation to a kinsman in a succeeding one.

The incidence of epidemic disease before 1910 made it significantly more difficult for men in Vilyatpur to belong to joint property groups than became possible later. When joint groups did exist in the late nineteenth century, they were less long-lived than after 1910. The meaning of these facts for relations within the family and for continuity between generations will be explored in detail in the chapter on family and kinship organization.

Migration and Population

After disease, migration has been a major factor in Vilyatpur's population history. Since 1848 only a handful of individuals have settled in the village for extended periods of time. With the exception of a few shopkeepers who came after the Partition of 1947, several Carpenters who stayed in Vilyatpur for a short period of time, and a

[12] Data on ages are unavailable for a number of cases in the last few years because some individuals living outside the village could not be interviewed.

Chamar who married a local girl and decided to live in the village, the pattern shows people left the village rather than settle in it. Emigration, permanent or for long periods of time, has long been a common practice in Vilyatpur. In 1848 at least nine men from the village were living elsewhere with their families. All were Sahotas, with a claim to land in the community, who had taken up residence in other villages where they obtained the use of some land, in most cases through their wives' families. One Sada Singh had already been outside the village for thirty years in 1848, and neither he nor any others ever returned to the village, although their descendants, with one exception, did come to live in Vilyatpur claiming the family's share of the land.

Migration from the village increased toward the end of the nineteenth century and has remained important ever since. At present there are few *khandans* in Vilyatpur without a member in the last two generations who has lived outside the village for an extended period of time. But the rate of migration has not been constant throughout the period. There were several years of great activity, the effects of which are evident in the figures on the size and rate of change of Vilyatpur's population. Movement from the village to other communities in Jullundur district was gradual and an individual affair, but most of the other migration was characterized by group movements to particular places over a limited span of time. The stimulus to migrate, the use of money earned outside the village, and the type of work done by emigrants will be discussed in a later chapter. Here the focus will be on the timing and extent of migration—questions important for the history of population growth in Vilyatpur and Jullundur district.

One indication of the timing, volume, and geographical distribution of migration from Vilyatpur is the residence of migrants at each of the reference dates. Table 11 shows the net number of emigrants in various places or areas at each point in time. The first group movements occurred in the 1890's when forty-one men left in two groups of about equal size for the canal colonies in western Punjab and for Australia. Although next in significance to mortality from epidemics in the decade, the numbers in these movements were large enough to have an impact on the population and they set a pattern which held as the volume increased later. In 1892 large tracts in western Punjab

TABLE 11

LOCATION OF MIGRANTS FROM VILYATPUR, 1848–1968
(males of all ages)

	Other Jullundur District	Canal colonies	Other Punjab	Kota	Ahmedabad	Other India	Abroad	Total
1848	8					1		9
1884	36					1		37
1898	19	20	3			3	21	66
1910	17	20				2	30	69
1922	22	46	7			5	33	103
1934	22	73	12	3	3	4	24	141
1946	30	82	19	3	5	18	20	177
1958	63		65		8	30	37	203
1968	73		64		10	33	79	259

SOURCE: Family biographies.
Sample: All males born in the village living elsewhere.

that had formerly been arid and sparsely populated were opened for settlement upon the completion of an extensive system of perennial canals. The government organized an elaborate program for selecting colonists to settle in these tracts; its objective was twofold:

To relieve the pressure of population upon the land in those districts of the Province where the agricultural population has already reached, or is fast approaching the limit which the land available for agriculture can support.

To colonize the area in question with well-to-do yeomen of the best class of agriculturists, who will cultivate their own holdings with the aid of their families and of the usual menials, but as much as possible without the aid of tenants, and will constitute healthy agricultural communities of the best Punjab type.[13]

In practice every effort was made to emulate the process by which villages like Vilyatpur had originally been settled. Colonists from a group of neighboring villages who were already landowners and experienced agriculturalists and, if possible, "connected by common

[13] *Chenab Colony Gazetteer,* 29.

descent," were selected to form the core of a new community in the canal colony.[14]

As the most densely populated district in the state, Jullundur certainly was qualified to send colonists, and by 1901 had provided over 56,000 settlers.[15] In 1894 a group was recruited from the Sahota villages in the district, which included three property groups from Vilyatpur, to found a new community in the colony which the settlers named Atti, after the Sahota village immediately southwest to Vilyatpur. Each property group was granted one "square," of 22 to 27 acres, as tenants-at-will for five years after which permanent occupancy rights were awarded with the option of actual purchase after another five years.[16] The Sahotas migrated to the new village with their families, and also induced some *sepidars* and artisans to accompany them, to work there as they had in Vilyatpur, much as in the original settlement process. Sixteen Chamars and one Weaver migrated to Atti in the 1890's. The emigration to Australia, at about the same time and in contrast to the colonization of Atti, was the product of the initiative of the villagers themselves. Early in the 1890's a "few adventurous spirits" returned to Jullundur district "from Australia with substantial proof of the fact that money could be made there." [17] It then became common for villagers from Jullundur district in particular to go to Australia in search of their fortunes. Vilyatpur had a substantial share in this movement. In 1903 the *Tehsildar* noted in his inspection of the village that about thirty-five men had gone to Australia from Vilyatpur, a figure equal to one-third of the working men in the community in 1898!

There was little new migration in the first decade of the present century. Four or five men went to Canada, but their numbers were offset by those returning from Australia. No new emigration to Australia took place because of the inauguration of a White Australia policy from 1901.[18] Thereafter all persons immigrating into the country had to be able to pass a fifty word dictation test in English, an obstacle that no one from Vilyatpur, and few persons from rural

[14] *Punjab Colony Manual* (Lahore: Civil and Military Gazette Press, 1926), I, 38.

[15] *Chenab Colony Gazetteer,* 36.

[16] P. A. R., 1921, I, 174–5.

[17] D. G., 1904, 52.

[18] C. Kondapi, *Indians Overseas, 1838–1949* (London: Oxford University Press, 1951), 195.

Jullundur, could overcome in 1901.[19] In the next two periods—1910 to 1922 and 1922 to 1934, however, there was a marked increase in the movement from the village, and migration became a factor in determining the size and rate of growth of Vilyatpur's population. Twelve Julahas and three Jats took advantage of the expansion of the army during the First World War to join the military; the Weavers all entered a single regiment of sappers and miners that saw service in the ill-fated Mesopotamian campaign. But most migration occurred between the two reference periods when in 1921–1922 another new canal development was opened for colonization. Three men from the village were given grants in lieu of pensions for their military service—two Weavers, and one Jat—and two other Sahota property groups received allotments according to the regular procedure for distribution. Once again the colonists recruited artisans and *sepidars* from the village, a large number of Chamars, three Weavers, a Water-carrier and even a Brahmin shopkeeper accompanied them to the new village. In addition to the substantial group of migrants to the canal colonies in this period, one night in 1928 twelve men left the village for Calcutta and from there to wherever their fortunes took them. Their motive for migration was different: a fight and a murder. They settled in different countries, including Malaya, the United States, Brazil, Panama, and Fiji.

Migration therefore became a factor in the course of Vilyatpur's population history as the significance of epidemic disease began to decline. Movement from the village contributed along with the outbreaks of plague in 1915 and influenza in 1918 to bring about a slight decrease in the population in the decade from 1911 to 1921. The rapid growth of migration following the opening of the new canal colony in 1922 was largely responsible for a further decline in the size of Vilyatpur between 1921 and 1931, when Jullundur district and the province had already entered into a period of steady growth (see Table 9).

The next substantial movement occurred as the result of the Partition of the Punjab in 1947 when the province was divided between India and Pakistan. Except for one man too sick to travel, his wife and infant son, all Muslims in the village left for Pakistan: eight Potter families and three of Gujjars, amounting to more than sev-

[19] *Ibid.*, 193.

enty persons. In Vilyatpur's case this loss was offset by the return of
fifty-six refugees, mostly Chamars and Weavers, who had been in the
canal colonies, now on the Pakistani side of the border. The Sahotas
returned as well, but only until they were allotted land that had belonged to Muslims who had fled elsewhere in the district. Jullundur
district suffered a net loss in the exchange of population in the decade
as well. The rest of the period from 1946 to 1958 and the last period
saw a pronounced increase in migration. A substantial expansion occurred in the number of persons settling elsewhere in Jullundur district, in other parts of the Punjab, and, to a lesser extent, in other
Indian states. Most represent a redistribution of the refugees from
the canal colonies. The new development in the late fifties and early
sixties was heavy migration overseas—primarily to England—of Vilyatpur's residents. In 1968 seventy-nine men and boys from the village were living abroad. For the first time in the history of overseas
migration from Vilyatpur, whole families went to settle in the new
country, bringing a decline in the village's growth rate.

Caste Composition of the Village

During the period from 1848 to 1968 a shift occurred in the caste
composition of the village owing to differences in the incidence of
disease, responses to opportunities for migration, and perhaps a differential survival rate from one caste group to another.[20] Whatever
the combination of responsible factors, each large caste group had a
distinctive history of growth within the village with consequences for
Vilyatpur as a whole. Table 12 shows the proportion of each caste to
the total number of adult males in the village for each reference
year, and also indicates in the vertical column the direction of change
in the absolute numbers of men in each caste from year to year.

The numerical position of the four largest groups in the village in
1848—the Jats, Julahas, Chamars, and Brahmins—shows a distinctive pattern of change over the ensuing one hundred and twenty
years. The case of the Chamars is the most dramatic; they increased
steadily in numbers and, except for 1922, as group percentage of the

[20] "Survival rate" refers to the number of male offspring who reach adulthood.
I use the concept rather than fertility or birthrate because the only data on the
past come from genealogies and do not usually include infants or boys who die
before reaching adulthood.

TABLE 12

VILYATPUR'S CASTE COMPOSITION, 1848–1968
(percentage[a] of working adult males)

[+, −] indicate change in absolute number

Year	Jat	Chamar	Julaha	Brahmin	Nai	Chitr	Tarkhan	Faqir	Chuura	Sonihar	Gujar	Kumhar	Rajput	Rangrez	Mirasi	Arora	Number of castes
1848	52	9	9	8	3	3	3	4	3	1	2	2	1	2	1		15
1884	64+	12+	5−	5−	2−	1−	2−	6+	1−	...	2	1−	1−	...	...		b
1898	62+	13+	5+	5	2	1	1−	6+	1−		2+	2+	1−				12
1910	61+	16+	8+	1−	1−	3+	3+	4−	1+		1−	1−					11
1922	63+	15+	7−	1−	4+	1−	2−	3−	1−		1−	4+					11
1934	58−	18+	9+	1	3−	1+	1−	3+	1−		1	4+					11
1946	55+	20+	8+	1+	4+	1+	2+	3+	1+		1+	4+					11
1958	51+	28+	8+	2+	3−	1+	2+	2−	1+			1−			1	1	12
1968	45+	30+	7+	2+	5+	2+	2+	3+	1+			1+			1	1+	12
1848–1968	+	+	+	+	+	+	+	+	+							+	

SOURCE: Family biographies.

Sample: All resident property groups.

a The total exceeds 100% frequently since all figures less than 1% are entered as 1% to indicate the presence of the caste in that year.

b The Goldsmith, Dyer, and Drummer left the village in the late nineteenth century; I was unable to find out from the pilgrimage records or my informants when they departed.

Explanation of symbols for all tables: ... = not available (unknown)

                  --- = negligible.

community. From the third largest caste group in Vilyatpur—one more adult than the Brahmins, one fewer than the Julahas, and far smaller than the predominant Sahotas—the Chamars grew to an unchallenged second place in the village with 30 percent of the adult males. The change, in part, can be accounted for by different patterns of migration: The Brahmins, and more recently the Jats, have found it easier to move into new occupations outside the village than the Chamars; the canal colonies provided the Chamars with opportunities for migration from 1892 to 1947 but after the creation of Pakistan most of them returned to the village; and the Chamars' proportionate growth in the community is the result of a greater number of off-spring in each generation than in other castes. The Brahmins had the opposite experience, declining both in absolute numbers and as a portion of the total until 1946 when a small expansion reversed the trend, though it still left them as one of the smallest groups in Vilyatpur. The Sahotas' pattern of growth provides still another variation; with the exception of one year they increased constantly in absolute size, but at the same time became a smaller part of the whole after a high point in 1884. The Julahas held about the same percentage of the community throughout the period.

Vilyatpur shows several developments of consequence for life in the village at different points in time. The smaller groups, whose members were mostly engaged in the supply of goods and services, declined in the nineteenth century. By 1910 there were only eleven castes in Vilyatpur and the three largest—the Sahotas, Chamars and Julahas—accounted for 85 percent of adult males. The structure of the community became progressively simpler with the decline in the number of caste groups and the proportion of most small ones. But the rapid growth of the Chamars, coupled with the decline in the percentage of the Sahotas, had the opposite effect. Although the numerical preponderance of the Jats continues to this day, after 1946 the Chamars developed into a numerical block of secondary importance in the community that, together with the Julahas (another untouchable caste to whom the Chamars are related historically), accounted for almost 40 percent of the village population since 1958.[21] Had the political and economic environment of Vilyatpur in the late

[21] Punjab Census, 1881, I, 323. Several Chamars and Jullahas consider that this connection exists, pointing out that the two groups have many *got* names in common.

nineteenth century remained unchanged, the shift would have been less significant. In the context of expanding economic opportunity which freed the Chamars from economic dependence on the Jats, and democratic politics in independent India, in which large numbers means more votes, the relative increase in the number of Chamars in the community is an important development.

The Differential Growth of Individual Families

The differential rate of growth of individual lineages and *khandans* in Vilyatpur is of greater consequence. Change in the caste composition of the village through varying rates of mortality and migration is reflected in the basic structure and social relations of the community. The rapid growth of some *khandans* coupled with the varying fortunes of others is equally significant for village politics. Growth in numbers means growth in influence. Through the history of various *khandans* and lineages we can observe the patterns of land management and acquisition, occupational change, migration, and the values that motivate them. Therefore I will not confine myself to the size of the groups remaining in the village as in the discussion of changes in caste composition. Wherever possible, I will include family members who left the village to examine the growth of different groups in order to lay the groundwork for the later analysis of choices to migrate or to stay.

As a technique for illustrating the different histories of growth, I have individually considered each property-group resident in 1848 as the starting point, and then traced his descendants over the next one hundred and twenty years. This is somewhat artificial because the individual property groups making up the village at the time of annexation were part of an existing framework of kinship ties that was very important. But the isolation of baseline families (each separate property group in 1848 and all of its descendants), which was indispensable as a framework for ordering and analyzing the data reveals contrasting histories of growth of different families. The baseline family represents the collection of property groups who, over time, shared the inheritance of the property belonging to its progenitor in 1848.

In all there are five different patterns of growth among the baseline families traced from the one hundred and ten property groups in

Vilyatpur in 1848 and the eight that owned land there, but lived elsewhere.

1. *Terminal.* By 1900 a large number of the original property groups were no longer represented in Vilyatpur. Seventeen Sahota groups, five Chamars, two Julahas, eight Brahmins, and twenty-one groups from other castes (including non-Sahota Jats) had either died out or migrated from the village without leaving a trace. Those that might have migrated rather than died out include all non-Sahota Jats, some Carpenters, the Rajput family, and the Goldsmith. All other missing Sahotas, Brahmins, and Weavers had died out, as had most Chamars no longer in the village by 1900. The bulk of groups disappeared in the thirty-six year interval from 1848 to 1884. Another fourteen died out or left between 1884 and 1898, and four have done so since. The decline in the termination rate is influenced by the use of baseline families and is not an accurate indicator of changes in fertility, mortality, etc. By definition each baseline family was represented by only one property group in 1848; the chances of it dying out between 1848 and 1884 were greater than later when most families included a number of property groups. Baseline families that died out freed resources for those that expanded. The Sahota groups that died out had controlled one hundred and ten acres of land in Vilyatpur in 1848. The land was redistributed as they disappeared.

2. *Straight-line.* Several baseline families—five Sahotas and one Chamar—had but one property group in each of the reference years. In most cases there was only one adult male in each generation, both inside the village and out. I found the heads of the property group in straight-line families were particularly well aware of this characteristic in their genealogy. The families continued to exist but with almost no increase in size.

3. *Gradual pyramid.* The second most common history of growth was a kind of gradual pyramid where the number of men and property groups increased slowly over time. In all, twenty-five baseline families exhibited this pattern, thirteen of which were Jat Sahotas. A good example of the gradual pyramid is the baseline family of Birbal, a Sahota land owner. Birbal, an eight-year-old minor, was entrusted to his maternal grandfather in 1848. By 1884 he was married and had four sons who through 1898 remained together, forming the baseline family's only property group. After Birbal's death, three sur-

viving sons split into the three new property groups which represented the baseline family from 1910 through 1958. In 1968 a fourth
group was created when two of Birbal's grandsons, who had succeeded
their father in 1934, divided their household and property. The expansion of one property group including one male in 1848 to four
with nine males in 1968, stayed ahead of the aggregate growth of the
village population.

4. *Diamond*. A few families started like gradual pyramids, adding
slowly to their numbers over time until a number of the constituent
property groups failed to produce male heirs and died out; that
brought about a contraction in the baseline family as a whole. Five
Sahotas and three others followed this pattern. For example, sometime before 1884 Khushal Singh was succeeded by his three grandsons, who established three separate property groups, only one of
which produced a male heir. By 1934 only one of the grandsons,
Narang Singh, and the one great-grandson, Waryam Singh, remained,
each holding property separately. When Narang Singh died child-
less in 1942, only Waryam Singh was left in the baseline family. He
has three adult sons so a new expansion is possible in the near future.
The diamond type baseline families probably stayed abreast of the
general growth of the population as long as they continued to grow,
but fell behind at the end of the period.

5. *Rapid pyramid*. Whereas the terminal and straight-line baseline families had growth rates much below that for the village as a
whole, and the gradual pyramids and diamond families either kept
ahead or fell slightly behind the aggregate rate, the rapid pyramids
expanded to such a degree that they accounted for most of the growth
of Vilyatpur's population from 1848 to 1968. Fourteen Sahota, seven
Chamar, two Julaha, and one Nai family followed the rapid pyramid
pattern, significantly representing the caste groups with the best over-
all growth rates in Vilyatpur (Table 12). In twelve of the twenty-four
cases the rapid expansion clearly occurred after 1922, the last reference year in the period of population decline indicated in the census
data. The baseline family of Bagh Singh, a Sahota landowner, is the
most striking example of rapid pyramid expansion. Bagh Singh had
three sons, two of whom were alive in 1884, forming one property
group. The three sons of the third son constituted a second group.
All five men produced male offspring who lived to inherit part
of the land so that there were six property groups in the baseline

family by 1922, eleven by 1946, and twelve by 1968. In one hundred
and twenty years the descendants of Bagh Singh, who had eleven
acres of land in 1848, grew from one property group with six men
and boys, to twelve groups with sixty-one males—an expansion of
roughly 1000 percent. A Chamar family was a close second in terms
of expansion. From one group with two males, the baseline family
grew to fifteen separate property groups with fifty men and boys.

The Consequences of Demographic Change

Population growth has increased pressure on Vilyatpur's resources
over the one hundred and twenty years from 1848 to 1968. The increase has not been constant because of the impact of disease and
migration; there were several decades when the man/land ratio improved. But the classical view of increasing rural poverty through the
British period resulting from population growth, the repeated subdivision of holdings, and the redundance of labor on the land does
not hold. Demographic change at the level of the baseline families
and property groups has provided an important dynamic for other
developments in the village that have meant a rising standard of living for its residents.

Added together the five patterns of expansion and contraction produced a history of growth for the village, which saw modest expansion
from 1855 to 1891, then fluctuation from 1891 to 1931, followed by
a period of rapid increase. But individual property groups found
themselves in different circumstances in terms of the pressure of numbers on their resources. The varying histories of growth reflect the
contradictory nature of values regarding family size in the village.
The principal consideration is continuity, enough offspring should
be produced to ensure the continuity of the male line. But there has
been a conflict between that and other attitudes toward the size of the
group. In the short run a large family has generally meant influence
and position in the community. But over time, a large number of
sons meant division of the baseline family's patrimony. The absolute
size and changes in the size of Vilyatpur's total population was a factor in the choices the members of rapidly expanding families made
between ways to adjust their numbers to available resources. In periods of relatively slow population growth or decline more land was
available for purchase or lease in the village than later, when Vil-

yatpur was growing. The pattern of growth of individual baseline families, and, in some cases, of their constituent property groups, influenced the way in which families responded to opportunities inside the village and out.

The classical view holds agricultural technology and hence productivity at a constant in the British period, and either ignores migration from the village or considers it a bad development—the forcing of people off the land. Although population growth meant increased pressure on the land, agriculture in Vilyatpur did not involute as did Indonesian rice farming according to Geertz.[22] There was no "shared poverty" resulting from the addition of more and more labor to the technologically stable, consumption oriented, farming of smaller and smaller holdings. Chapters VI and V trace developments which enabled agriculture to absorb an increase of 110 percent in population in a district which was already considered to be overpopulated and closely farmed in 1848. Migration, as a source of capital and ideas, and as a means for rapidly growing families to adjust labor supply to existing resources figures prominently in the process.

[22] Clifford Geertz, *Agricultural Involution* (Berkeley: University of California Press, 1966).

Chapter IV

ECONOMIC CHANGE, 1848–1968: AGRICULTURE

Introduction

Historical accounts of rural India in the British period have generally focussed on the significance of land control, and the changes in social and political structure resulting from modifications in the pattern of control during British rule.[1] In most cases change occurred because of the procedures and policies followed at the time of annexation,[2] while in others expanding occupational opportunities, a by-product of the arrival of the new administration, were the principal cause.[3] The emphasis has been fruitful for understanding rural social and political structure and the importance of government policy in shaping it. But the concentration on land tenure and official policy has diverted attention from the history of the use of land and its produce, Indian agriculture generally being treated as a kind of residual category of little significance. Rural people farm only if none of the new occupations are open to them, and agriculture itself simply goes along, changing slowly if at all.

The form and history of land control was of importance for Vilyatpur. Socially and politically the community was organized around the dominant Sahotas, who owned the village. As part of the proprietary body, individual Sahota property groups had influence and esteem in the community based on their share of the land, which allowed them to support some part-time dependents (*sepidars,* tenants, laborers, and the like) through the network of patron-client relationships. But the use of land was of equal importance to the people of Vilyatpur. Agriculture remained the principal economic activity throughout the period 1848–1968. As late as 1958, three men in four were directly engaged in farming as owner cultivators, ten-

[1] See in particular the essays collected in Robert E. Frykenberg (ed.), *Land Control and Social Structure in Indian History* (Madison: University of Wisconsin Press, 1969).

[2] For references see Chapter I, footnote 69.

[3] For instance, Bailey, *Caste and the Economic Frontier.*

ants, and agricultural laborers. Even in 1968, these activities accounted for 64 percent of the working men in the community. Knowledge of agricultural practices has always been highly valued in rural Punjab. Jats consider themselves to be good farmers, and look up to anyone possessing particular ability in cultivation.[4] Along with an admiration of physical strength, a fondness of carousing and drinking, a sense of independence, and a tendency toward violence—particularly where honor is involved—the Jat self-definition of manliness includes an ability with livestock and skill in farming. Unlike some dominant land-owning castes in North India, most notably the Rajputs, Jats take great pride in working with their hands. There are no agricultural tasks that a Jat will not do himself. The value placed on agriculture by the owner cultivators, who are also the dominant element in rural society, is an important factor in the history of agricultural development in the Punjab.

Many aspects of agriculture in Vilyatpur show remarkable stability throughout the period 1848–1968. It has remained the principal occupation of the overwhelming majority of village inhabitants. No new crops have been introduced; wheat and sugarcane retain their 1848 position as the two most important ones. There has been little change in the pattern of land ownership. The Sahotas continue to own almost all land and their holdings are still cultivated primarily with family labor. Yet within the stability of the basic occupational structure, cropping, and land ownership, numerous changes in village agriculture have taken place through the interplay of several developments. Improved technology, better marketing facilities, an increase in the total capital devoted to agriculture, an expansion of double cropping, and an intensification of labor, have brought a gradual increase in village production. A marked change in the organization of agricultural labor also occurred owing to a combination of demographic, technological, and occupational factors.

The increase in agricultural production has made it possible for the village economy to absorb effectively the most problematical change of all, the increased pressure on resources resulting from the expansion of the population. There have been two periods of population growth: between 1855 and 1891, and again at an accelerated rate since 1931. A proportionate share of the new workers took to

[4] S. R., 1892, 73.

agriculture—which consistently provided the livelihood for about
75 percent of the men until very recently—leading to a decline in
the size of holdings owned and cultivated, and an increase in the supply of agricultural labor available. Increases in production have been
sufficient not only to sustain village agriculture in the face of this
pressure, but to yield a rising standard of living for most residents.
Farming continues to be a valued economic activity despite the small
size of holdings.

Punjab Agriculture, 1860–1968

Information on agriculture in the Punjab before the 1880's is scarce
because the government, the only source of data on the subject at the
provincial level, took time to develop a well-defined interest in cropping, production, and the procedures for collecting detailed and
reliable information. Statistics on the area and the yield of various
crops in the districts were published in the annual *Administration
Report of the Punjab* since 1866. But the data are notoriously un-
reliable; the author of the report for one year admitted that the
figures "are so manifestly erroneous, that it has been thought advis-
able to omit the return on the present occasion." [5] During the revenue
survey of each district, the settlement officer and his staff collected a
wealth of information on village agriculture which formed the basis
of the assessment. But thereafter the responsibility for up-dating the
figures on cropping was left to the local revenue staff, which was too
small and untrained to do an adequate job.[6] The detailed information on village crops—the description of different varieties, their
properties and extent of cultivation contained in the various settlement reports—did not receive any general consideration and was
never systematically compiled for the whole province.[7] The government's only interest in agriculture, beyond its study as part of the
revenue surveys and the annual reporting of statistics on cropping
before the 1880's, was in the introduction of new cash crops like
tea, American cotton, and flax.[8] The most successful project was a

---

[5] P. A. R., 1868–1869, 96.

[6] Trevaskis, *Five Rivers,* 269.

[7] For example including local names for different varieties see Ibbetson,
Karnal Settlement, 189; Walker, *Ludhiana Settlement,* 113.

[8] P. A. R., 1860–1861, 86; 1862–1863, 140, 157.

tea plantation in the Kangra hills which provided seed and training for British and Indian tea planters who purchased land in the area.[9] Individual British officers made some scattered efforts to introduce new types of common crops and were also instrumental in the spread of a few improved implements—particularly a more efficient sugar-cane press.[10] There was, however, no department concerned with village agriculture. The only efforts to study and develop new methods, crops, and implements were made by the Agri-Horticultural Society of Lahore, a semi-official body whose members were government officials and large land-owners. The society received a government subsidy and maintained an experimental garden in Lahore from 1863 to 1883, after which it was taken over by the Punjab Government.[11]

The idea of creating a separate department responsible for village agriculture arose not from the considerations of general development—as was the case for railway and canal construction—but as part of the effort to avert, or at least alleviate, the effects of repeated famine. The proposal was first made by the Bengal and Orissa Famine Commission in 1866. A central department was created in 1871, but was terminated in 1878 for without provincial counterparts it proved ineffective.[12] But the severity of the famine of 1877–1878 caused some rethinking in official circles about the role of government in village agriculture. The Famine Commission of 1880 recommended the establishment of departments in each province under a director of agriculture, whose duties would be:

1) Agricultural Enquiry—the collection of agricultural information to keep the authorities informed of the approach of famine.

2) Agricultural Improvement—with a view to the prevention of famine in the future.

3) Famine Relief—to take charge of operations in the campaign against actual famines.[13]

[9] *Ibid.*, 1861–1862, 21.

[10] *Ibid.*, 1880–1881, 145.

[11] *Ibid.*, 1872–1873, 82; 1881–1882, 94; 1882–1883, 85; *The Select Papers of the Agri-Horticultural Society of the Punjab* (Lahore: Lahore Chronicle Press, 1868), iii.

[12] John A. Voelcker, *Report on the Improvement of Indian Agriculture* (London: Eyre and Spottiswoode, 1893), 1.

[13] *Ibid.*, 2.

Punjab's new Department of Land Records and Agriculture was created in 1885. Initially its activities, reflecting the department's origin, were directed toward improving the collection of statistical information on agriculture to lay the basis for effective measures against famine, and to simplify future revenue settlement surveys by making up-to-date information available to revenue officials.[14] The impact of officially sponsored research into improved seeds and practices was not felt until after 1905–1906 when the Department of Agriculture was separated from the Department of Land Records.

Although information on the period 1860–1880 is imperfect, agriculture in the Punjab certainly received a stimulus from the fairly rapid development in railway and road networks and the construction of several large irrigation canals. The development of an adequate transportation system facilitated the marketing of crops, making it possible to export agricultural commodities—particularly wheat, sugar and *ghee*—to other parts of India in the 1860's. In contrast, during the Sikh period this had been difficult because of the "badness, the insecurity of the roads, and the levy of vexatious transit and customs. . . ."[15] The result was an increase in prices for agricultural produce, a welcome development to cultivators in irrigated tracts like Jullundur, where continuous surpluses without

TABLE 13

DEVELOPMENT OF PUBLIC WORKS, 1868–1892
(Punjab and North-West Frontier Provinces)

	Cultivated area (mill. acre)	Miles of		
		Canals	Railroads	Paved roads
1867–68	18.0	1569	. . .	1,147
1872–73	18.8	2744	410	1,036
1877–78	22.6	. . .	530	1,423
1882–83	23.4	4583	1,186	1,467
1887–88	25.7	. . .	1,312	1,757
1892–93	26.7	12,368	1,725	2,142

Source: H. Calvert, *The Wealth and Welfare of the Punjab* (Lahore: Civil and Military Gazette Press, 1922), 54; P. A. R., "statistical appendices" for years indicated.

[14] Trevaskis, *Five Rivers*, 273.
[15] P. A. R., 1865–1866, 92.

a satisfactory outlet had tended to depress prices in the past.[16] The construction of large scale canal projects since 1859 also contributed to the development of agriculture in the Punjab, increasing the productivity of land already under cultivation and bringing substantial areas under the plow for the first time.

The contention that the development of public works had a substantial impact on agriculture between 1860 and 1885 is supported by the continuing role of railways and canals in the subsequent development of agriculture in the Punjab for which more adequate information is available. Blyn's study of agricultural output and productivity in India between 1891 and 1947 makes it possible to summarize the important features in the history of agricultural production in the region. For the period 1891–1947, Blyn finds that total production of food grains and other crops increased substantially in the Punjab and North-West Frontier Provinces. The expansion of food grains was about equal to the average rate of population growth in the region,[17] and nonfoods increased at a significantly faster pace.[18] In Punjab, as for India in general, expansion in acreage of crops was the most important source of increased output.[19] But in Punjab this was accomplished primarily by a continued development of irrigation in previously uncultivated tracts,[20] rather than by an intensification of present acreage through double cropping as occurred elsewhere.[21]

Although the total cultivated area continued to expand in "Greater Punjab" throughout the period studied by Blyn, the rate of increase slowed noticeably after 1921 when the last of the large canal projects was completed.[22] Thereafter increases in yield per acre became the more important factor for food grains and other crops, the trend for both increases toward the end of the period covered in Blyn's work.[23] His study of yields shows that irrigation played the predominant role in increasing production from 1901 to 1911.[24] In the next decade the development and use of new seed varieties took first place. The percentage of the total area under improved varieties in the Punjab and North-West Frontier Provinces was 6 percent in 1922–1923 and reached 33 percent in 1938–1939.[25] Increases in yields were most dramatic for the nonfood crops of sugarcane and cotton, but also

---

[16] P. A. R., 1860–1861, 85.   [17] Blyn, 98.   [18] Ibid., 111.
[19] Ibid., 127.   [20] Ibid., 191.   [21] Ibid., 128, 131.
[22] Ibid., 132.   [23] Ibid., 165–166.   [24] Ibid., 188.
[25] Ibid., 200.

in a few food crops, particularly wheat.[26] Blyn concludes that the combination of the substantial increase in yields of nonfoods and a moderate one in food grains, together with the allocation of an ever increasing proportion of the cultivated acreage to nonfood crops in the Punjab, produced "the most favorable all-crop yield-per-acre trend of all the regions, one with sustained moderate increase." [27]

The isolation of indigenous varieties of high quality and the development of new types suited to the conditions in Punjab villages was the outcome of the research efforts of the Department of Agriculture. The initial step, in 1884, was to send a questionnaire to all districts to collect systematic information on local wheats in different parts of the province.[28] This laid the groundwork for Sir Albert Howard's scientific classification between 1906–1910 of indigenous wheats grown in the Punjab, and the selection of the best varieties from the point of view of yield, durability, and price in the local and export markets. The propagation of pure seed on government farms and its distribution to village cultivators followed soon after. The department made its first recommended wheat variety, Punjab 11, available for distribution in 1913, and by 1920–1921 it was sown in more than 600,000 acres.[29] Punjab 11 was slowly displaced by another type introduced in 1919 that was planted over more than 1.3 million acres by 1927–1928.[30] Both varieties yielded from 16 to 33 percent more per acre than the unrefined types used earlier.[31]

The department's success with the acclimatization of American cotton was even more dramatic than in the case of wheat. Experiments started in 1908, and in 1913 the first type was distributed.[32] In contrast to the new wheats, American cotton was valued not so much for its additional yield, as for the premium it fetched in the local and export markets. It was suitable for use in standard textile mills for

[26] *Ibid.*, 167–168.

[27] *Ibid.*, 168.

[28] *Punjab Wheat: Its Varieties, Distribution and Husbandry* (Lahore: Punjab Government, 1884), 1–2.

[29] *Report on the Marketing of Wheat in the Punjab* (Lahore: Superintendent, Government Printing, Punjab, 1940), 282–283.

[30] *Ibid.*, 283.

[31] William Roberts and Kartar Singh, *A Text Book of Punjab Agriculture* (Lahore: Civil and Military Gazette Press, 1951), 220.

[32] *Ibid.*, 434.

weaving fine cloth,[33] whereas the short-staple local cottons could only be used for making cheap coarse cloth and guncotton.[34] The American cottons caught on quickly. Over 700,000 acres were planted by 1921 (primarily in the canal colonies) and they continued to spread despite a few setbacks (the seed deteriorated after several years of use).[35] Improved types of indigenous cotton were soon isolated and distributed around the province.[36] The other significant development before Independence and Partition in 1947 was the introduction of high yielding varieties of sugarcane, leading to substantial increases in the output of this valuable crop. Several types developed in South India were brought to the Punjab in 1918 and their use spread rapidly in the 1920's and 1930's. By 1937–1938, improved varieties yielding 80 percent more sugar per acre than the usual Punjab types covered about three-fifths of the acreage sown to cane.[37]

From its inception as an independent department in 1905–1906 until 1947, the Department of Agriculture's mode of operation changed little. Its emphasis was on the development and propagation of improved seed types, the distribution of improved implements, and the upgrading of village agriculture.[38] The department maintained seed farms in seven different districts of the province (primarily where agriculture was most developed), the canal colonies, and the central districts including Jullundur. "District work," the combined activities of propagating seed, selling it to village cultivators, and running demonstrations of new and correct methods for the cultivation of improved varieties on government farms, was concentrated in the central districts.[39] The work of the department was carried out by a single agricultural inspector and a small staff on the government farm.

Although by contemporary standards the spread of the new seeds may not seem rapid, taking a number of years to cover more than half of the acreage devoted to a particular crop, it must be remem-

[33] *Report of the Operations of the Department of Agriculture, 1915–16* (Lahore: Civil and Military Gazette Press, 1916), 2.

[34] W. Roberts and O. T. Faulkner, *A Text Book of Punjab Agriculture* (Lahore: Civil and Military Gazette Press, 1921), 134.

[35] Roberts and Singh, 436.

[36] *Department of Agriculture, 1934–1935, 50.*

[37] *Ibid.,* 1937–1938, 70; Roberts and Singh, 308.

[38] *Ibid.,* 1914–1915, 7.

[39] *Ibid.,* 5.

bered that before 1947 the department depended on word of mouth communication in rural areas. There was no staff for village extension work in any district. Given the oft-mentioned conservatism of village farmers in India, it is surprising that the government's development efforts met with such success. In fact, local people not only made use of improved seeds, but worked to propagate and distribute them as well. Large landowners, under the department's supervision, in a number of places, raised wheat and cotton for seed. The government then purchased, at a premium, these seeds for redistribution under a guarantee of purity.[40] A number of cultivators were in business for themselves. They sold seed without the assistance or certification of the department, which made it difficult to determine from year to year the quantity of improved varieties actually available.[41] The department commissioned grain dealers in many market towns to sell certified varieties of wheat and cotton.[42] Artisans in small towns and cities responded to the opportunities created by changing agricultural technology. Some implements introduced by the department that proved particularly popular and effective were quickly copied by blacksmiths and carpenters—particularly a simple iron plow, the hand driven fodder chopper, and an improved sugarcane press.[43] Though rough in finish, the local copies worked well and were considerably cheaper than the tools imported or fabricated by the department.[44]

Since 1947 government efforts to develop village agriculture have increased dramatically. Many programs have followed earlier patterns on an expanded scale: intensive research in new high yielding varieties, increases in cultivated areas and double cropping through the construction of irrigation works, and replacement of low value crops with more valuable ones.[45] The Bhakra Nangal Project provided canal irrigation to a vast area in the southern portion of the state, most of which is now in Haryana. Research efforts in India and abroad have produced a hybrid maize suited to local conditions which

[40] *Ibid.*, 1913–1914, 3, 11.
[41] *Ibid.*, 1917–1918, Appendix, III.
[42] *Ibid.*, 1916–1917, 8.
[43] *Ibid.*, 1914–1915, 8.
[44] *Ibid.*, 1934–1935, 62.
[45] *Draft Outline, Fourth Five Year Plan, Punjab State* (Chandigarh: Punjab Government, n.d.), 12–16.

yields 150 percent more than the type previously used.[46] New Mexican wheats, with increases of over 100 percent are producing a "green revolution" by bringing a large increment to agricultural incomes. The Department of Agriculture has also been successful in encouraging the cultivation of groundnut (peanuts) and grapes, and the use of chemical fertilizers on a large scale.

A major change, since 1947, came with the implementation of the Community Development Program and the National Extension Service in 1952–1953. It was designed to bring information about agricultural improvements and development to the villages instead of relying on the informal networks within the district as it was done before 1947.[47] The program has a large staff. There is a development worker for every ten villages in the state, backed by a number of specialists at the block (a unit of development administration) and district levels; these guide the village-level-workers with particular problems and look after special projects. The Community Development Program has many critics; its greatest shortcoming is at the administrative and bureaucratic levels where its objectives are seen as a series of positions to be filled and programs to be implemented—rather than concentrating on "mass mobilization" and self-generating processes of development.[48] Whatever its defects, for the first time there exists in Punjab a branch of the government solely concerned with rural problems.

Perhaps the most significant development since Independence is the efforts and abilities of village residents themselves to institute some basic changes in the countryside. Political processes, the estab-

[46] *Ibid.*, 20.

[47] Community Development has a historical precedent in the Punjab in the efforts and writings of F. L. Brayne, author of *Better Villages* (Bombay: Oxford University Press, 1937), and many other books on "rural uplift." As deputy commissioner in several districts in Punjab, Brayne used the power of his office to implement schemes for rural uplift, including the construction of manure pits, latrines, chimneys on fireplaces, and the like. Brayne considered villagers lazy and unenlightened and sought to motivate them to self improvement through propaganda and strict supervision. Malcolm Lyall Darling, another British civil servant familiar with rural conditions, was critical of Brayne's characterization of villagers and his methods because he did not involve local residents in his schemes, a criticism that parallels Kothari's critique of the current Community Development Program (see below). Malcolm Lyall Darling, *Wisdom and Waste in the Punjab Village* (New York: Oxford University Press, 1934), 39.

[48] Rajni Kothari, *Politics in India* (Boston: Little, Brown, 1970), 133.

lishment of parliamentary democracy based on a universal adult fran-
chise, and the inauguration of the *Panchayati Raj* (local government)
system, have played an essential role. We will consider these developments when we examine the changing administrative and political
context of the village. The initiative of village cultivators in obtain-
ing and employing inputs in agriculture is the important point. Punjabi farmers have been sensitive to the value of good seed since the
turn of the century, and probably long before British annexation.[49]
The heavy investment in chemical fertilizers and privately constructed and owned electric or diesel-powered irrigation wells represents a new step. The timing of this shift may in part reflect the
economics of the situation including prices for agricultural produce
and the availability of appropriately priced inputs. The striking feature is the ability and sophistication demonstrated by village farmers
in dealing with urban merchants and government officials to obtain
electric connections, motors, bricks, cement, and contracts for bor-
ing[50]—all scarce commodities—sufficient to add over 20,000 new
power driven wells to the Punjab[51] between 1964 and 1967.[52] These
capabilities contrast sharply with the view of the villagers' character
held by even the most sympathetic of government officials in the
twenties and thirties. Officials generally saw them as "ignorant, im-
provident and unbusinesslike," easily cheated by merchants and
moneylenders, and generally in need of a paternal government to
look after their affairs.[53]

Farming in Vilyatpur

Vilyatpur's residents profited from the construction of public works
and the Department of Agriculture's development of new, higher
yielding varieties of common village crops. The first paved road and
the first railway line constructed in the Punjab ran through Jullun-

[49] Ibbetson, *Karnal Settlement,* 169.

[50] McKim Marriott, "The New Farmer in Kishan Garhi," paper presented at
the University of Chicago Conference on Occupational Cultures in Changing
South Asia, April 1970.

[51] *Statistical Abstract of Punjab, 1967,* 107. This figure refers to Punjab as
reorganized in 1965.

[52] "Report on the Survey of Minor Irrigation Works in the Punjab," mimeo,
issued by the Economic and Statistical Organization, Punjab, n.d. (1969), 6.

[53] Darling, *Punjab Peasant,* 154, 234–235, 248.

dur District; the road was about six miles from the village and the nearest railway station was about eleven miles away in the market town used by the villagers. Cultivators in Vilyatpur used the new seeds as soon as they were available for general distribution. People still remember that Samund Singh, in 1914, brought some wheat seed from the canal colonies in Lyallpur, where he had visited his relatives who had been granted land there. But we do not have the information necessary to measure the full impact of these developments for Vilyatpur:[54] the per-acre yield of the different crops grown from 1910–1968 (to determine the increases from improved seeds, better irrigation, and more intensive cultivation), and the proportion of the crop that was marketed from year to year as opposed to that consumed (to follow changes in income).[55] To my knowledge no one in Vilyatpur kept records of their agricultural activities in the nineteenth and early twentieth centuries, and only a few of the larger landowners have done so in the recent past. Enough general information is available to follow the broad outlines of the effects of increases in the population, changes in agricultural technology, and some of the methods and motives in farm management. The means of expansion in total agricultural output was achieved in Punjab between 1848 and 1968 by the cultivation of waste land; this was not possible in Vilyatpur, even in 1848. Therefore, changes in the village are particularly relevant now that there is little additional acreage in the state.

A per-capita decline in agricultural land and the amount of land owned by individual property groups was a direct consequence of the growth of Vilyatpur's population. The size of holdings declined dur-

[54] I doubt the information is available for any village of small, family-farming, cultivators like Vilyatpur or the majority of Punjab villages. The nature of rural Punjabi society and the goals of the farming enterprise explain the absence of records (see Kessinger in Jones, *Sources for Punjab History*). It is possible, however, that price and yield data are available on some of the large estates owned by various prominent families. Metcalf suggests this might be the case for the *talukdars* in the United Provinces. Thomas R. Metcalf, "Estate Management and Estate Records in Oudh." *The Indian Economic and Social History Review*, IV (1967), 99–108.

[55] For this reason I have omitted discussion of prices and their impact on cropping patterns, although a substantial literature indicates the responsiveness of Punjabi cultivators to price incentives. For a summary and references see Theodore W. Schultz, *Transforming Traditional Agriculture* (New Haven: Yale University Press, 1964), 164.

ing the period covered in the study (see Table 14). The sharpest contrast is between the figures for the first reference year, 1848 and all of the others. In the year of the first revenue survey, two-thirds of the holdings in Vilyatpur, more than 90 percent of the agricultural land, were larger than ten acres. By 1884 the proportion in this category fell to just about one-fifth of the holdings and 45 percent of the area, and, except for a slight increase in 1898, continued to shrink to the present. Since 1884, the units over five acres form the bulk of the holdings, accounting for more than half through 1898 and over a third of the total through 1946. For the entire period more than half of the village acreage was owned in holdings of five acres or more. But very small holdings have also been common in Vilyatpur for a long time. Since 1910—well before the rapid growth of the popula-

TABLE 14

SIZE OF AGRICULTURAL HOLDINGS (OWNERSHIP), 1848–1968

Size in acres

	Number of holdings						Percent in holdings					Percent of total in holdings				
	.10–1.99	2–4.99	5–9.99	10–19.99	20 plus	Total	.10–1.99	2–4.99	5–9.99	10–19.99	20 plus	.10–1.99	2–4.99	5–9.99	10–19.99	20 plus
1848	3	7	4	21	6	41	7	17	10	51	15	—	4	5	54	36
1884	7	20	28	10	4	69	10	29	40	15	6	2	13	38	25	22
1898	15	17	24	13	4	73	21	23	32	18	5	4	11	34	32	22
1910	21	31	17	10	5	84	25	37	20	12	6	4	22	25	25	23
1922	18	28	30	7	3	86	21	33	35	8	3	4	20	43	20	14
1934	33	36	32	7	2	110	30	33	29	6	2	6	23	41	17	13
1946	49	49	32	6		136	36	36	24	4		9	35	42	14	
1958	62	49	28	4		143	43	34	20	3		12	35	40	13	
1968	64	51	27	4		146	44	34	20	2		12	36	40	13	

SOURCE: Land File.
Sample: All landowning property groups.

tion in the village and the province—holdings under five acres have been the most common type. Since 1958 holdings under two acres account for more than half of the total. Very small holdings, however, have only recently come to comprise a substantial part of the agricultural land of Vilyatpur.

The size of holdings neither indicates the relationship of population to land over time, nor does it tell how the land was farmed and managed by individual property groups. Whereas the size of holdings declined generally between 1848 and 1968, Vilyatpur's population, after increasing substantially from 1855 to 1891, declined for forty years until 1931 when it increased once again. The consequences of this pattern are illustrated in the three distinct trends in the amount of per-capita land from 1855 to 1968 (see Table 15). The fluctuation had little impact on the size of holdings because much of the decrease in the population resulted from migration to the canal colonies and abroad. These migrants retained their ownership of land and received a share of the family land when it was divided on the death of the head of the property group even if they were nonresidents. The change in the size of different property groups holdings is crucial for understanding the pattern and goals of migration from the village (to be discussed in Chapter V). For agricultural activity, however, the size and management of actual operating units rather than units of ownership is the important factor.[56]

TABLE 15

CULTIVATED LAND, PER-CAPITA, IN VILYATPUR, 1855–1968
(acres)

I		II		III	
1848	.95	1901	.64	1941	.59
1868	.76	1911	.73	1951	.46
1881	.74	1921	.73	1961	.43
1891	.59	1931	.75	1968	.36

SOURCE: Acreage figures for the years indicated from the annual statistics in the *Lal Kitab* (village notebook), Village Vilyatpur. Population figures from Table 9. The 1968 population figure is from my own census of the village, checked against that of the malaria eradication program's survey of the community that year.

[56] Hugh Calvert recognized the importance of the distinction between ownership units and actual operating farms in the Punjab in two publications in the 1920's. *The Size and Distribution of Agricultural Holdings in the Punjab,* The

TABLE 16

SIZE OF FARMS (OPERATING UNITS), 1848–1968

Size in acres

	Number of farms						Percent of farms					Percent of total in farms				
	.10–1.99	2–4.99	5–9.99	10–19.99	20 plus	Total	.10–1.99	2–4.99	5–9.99	10–19.99	20 plus	.10–1.99	2–4.99	5–9.99	10–19.99	20 plus
1848	12	8	12	25	4	61	20	13	20	41	7	1	5	14	61	20
1884	27	17	29	12	3	88	31	19	33	14	3	3	10	38	33	16
1898	41	19	22	15	3	100	41	19	22	15	3	4	13	31	39	12
1910	41	16	18	17	3	95	43	17	19	18	3	4	11	25	48	12
1922	44	19	26	14	2	105	42	18	24	13	2	5	13	37	38	8
1934	60	23	30	12	1	126	47	19	24	10	1	6	15	42	30	6
1946	66	19	27	15		127	51	15	21	12		8	14	38	39	
1958	68	20	23	14	1	126	54	16	18	11	1	9	14	34	38	5
1968	69	21	22	14	1	127	54	17	17	14	1	9	15	33	38	5

SOURCE: Land file.
Sample: All landowning/using property groups.

The size of operating units, following the same fluctuation as the population (Table 16), in Vilyatpur declined between 1848 and 1968. As with the ownership units, there is a sharp contrast between the first year, when nearly half of the holdings farmed were over ten

Board of Economic Inquiry, Punjab, Rural Section Publication-4 (Lahore: Civil and Military Gazette Press, 1926) deals with ownership units while *The Size and Distribution of Cultivators' Holdings in the Punjab,* The Board of Economic Inquiry, Punjab, Rural Section Publication-11 (Lahore: Civil and Military Gazette Press, 1928) is concerned with how land is farmed by combining ownership with various tenancy arrangements. The following discussion necessitates a clear verbal distinction between how land was owned and how it was used. Therefore I will employ the term "holdings" to refer to ownership units, and speak of "farms" to discuss the units in which land was actually used.

acres and accounted for 81 percent of the cultivated area, and all of
the years since. By 1884 the biggest category was five to ten acres—
although just under half of the area was still cultivated in holdings
over ten acres in size. But after a further decrease between 1884 and
1898, the reference periods of 1898, 1910, and 1922 show a stability in
the size of farms which was caused by the decline of the population
between the late 1890's and the late 1920's. In the interval of some
thirty years over 80 percent of the cultivated area was farmed in holdings larger than five acres and about half in units of ten acres or
more. By 1934 the beginnings of a new period of decline became
evident, a trend which continues through 1968. The number of small
holdings is indeed striking. As early as 1898 those less than five acres
were consistently near 60 percent of the total and from 1946 50 percent was under two acres. Yet as late as 1958 more than three-fourths
of the agricultural land in Vilyatpur was used in units larger than
five acres and about 40 percent in holdings of ten acres or more.

Two important features can be traced by the size of operating units
over time. With a declining population for a forty-year period, the
village experienced a stability in the size of farms at the time when
the first improved crop varieties were introduced in the district, factors which created the potential for significant increases in per-capita
output. Although the data is imperfect, information on cropping
patterns and investment in agriculture and indications of an increased
orientation toward the market suggest that this potential was at least
in some measure realized. The nature and extent of change, however,
was conditioned by the land use and management practices of individual property groups. The contrasting findings of a steady increase
in both the total number of farms and units of small size, and the
continued cultivation of a substantial number of comparatively large
holdings, points to some questions about land management that will
be considered in the next section.

There have been few changes in cropping in Vilyatpur over the
past one hundred and twenty years. With the exception of several
contrasts between the year 1848–49 and the quinquennial average of
the allocation of acreage to different crops from 1880 to 1884 (since
then a continuous record is available), no new crops have been added
to those grown in the nineteenth century other than a few acres of
different kinds of vegetables. Several crops important in the late
nineteenth and early twentieth centuries were not grown in the vil-

lage in the year of the initial revenue survey: cotton, *jowar* (a millet), hemp, and several types of oil seeds. This is surprising, for all are considered "necessities" and occupied close to one hundred acres a year in the nineteenth century and about fifty acres for much of this century. I cannot account for the absence of cotton and oil seeds, both of which were grown elsewhere in Jullundur district in 1848.[57] Hemp is not mentioned as one of the crops in the district, but may be lumped into the miscellaneous category of the crop return in the settlement report. *Jowar* is the one crop that may have been added to those grown in the village after 1848. It was cultivated in the district that year, but in very small quantities on primarily unirrigated land; it amounted to less than one percent of the district's acreage.[58] By 1893 however, *jowar* accounted for 11 percent of the crops grown in Jullundur.[59]

Change in the cropping pattern came through the disappearance of crops that had been cultivated in the nineteenth century rather than with the introduction of new ones. Between 1885–1895 the crops grown numbered as many as twenty. After 1915 there were never more than fourteen, if vegetables and fruits are omitted. The abandonment of the cultivation of several pulses, a food that still forms an important part of the daily diet of Vilyatpur residents, accounts for most of this change. Five different pulses were raised before the turn of the century. After 1905 only *mash* was cultivated, and that in progressively smaller amounts. *Jowar* and barley, both important grain crops covering almost one hundred acres before 1895, declined since then and vanished finally in the 1940's. The gradual disappearance of these crops, particularly the pulses which still form an important part of villagers' diet, is indicative of a growing orientation toward the market. The available land went for expanded cultivation of wheat, sugarcane, and maize (corn) for consumption and sale, and pulses were purchased in the market.

Increases in total production through the extension of double cropping and the use of improved varieties were more important in the development of village agriculture than changes in cropping. Table 17 illustrates the impact of increases in the intensity of land

[57] S. R., 1851, "Produce Statement II."
[58] *Ibid.*
[59] P. A. R., 1893, Appendix No. 42.

TABLE 17

INCREASES IN AGRICULTURAL PRODUCTION, 1848–1968
(quinquennial averages of area equivalents)

	I	II	III	IV	V
	Percent agricultural land double cropped	Percent increase from double cropping (base 1880–84)	Percent increase from improved seeds (base 1880–84)	Index of increase in production (base 1880–84)	Index of increase in population (base 1881)
1848–49[a]	31	4		104	84
1880–84	31			100	100
1885–89	36	4		104	
1890–94	41	8		108	123
1895–99	35	3		103	
1900–04	37	4		104	113
1905–09	35	3		103	
1910–14	55	18		118	99
1915–19	32	0	3	103	
1920–24	36	3	8	111	97
1925–29	41	8	8	115	
1930–34	43	9	8	117	96
1935–39	49	12	15	128	
1940–44	b	b	b	b	123
1945–49	61	20	18	138	
1950–54	54	16	16	131	153
1955–59	71	32	19	150	
1960–64	61	21	20	141	167
1965–68[c]	71	22	69	191	190

SOURCE: Computed from the annual figures on cropping in the *Lal Kitab* (village notebook), Village Vilyatpur. Population computed from figures in Table 9.

[a] Figures for only one year.

[b] Acreage figures for the quinquennium 1940–1944 were missing in the *Lal Kitab*.

[c] Three year average.

use and improved seeds on total village production.[60] Column I shows how intensively village cultivators used available land by the ratio of the acres of crops sown each year in a quinquennium over the cultivated area. In 1848 almost one-third of the area was double

[60] The measures I have used to follow change in agricultural production are very rough. This is inevitable from the available data for the period 1848 to

cropped. This grew with some fluctuation (always declining during periods of epidemics, 1895–1899, 1905–1909, 1915–1919) throughout the following period. The ratio indicates the extent to which cultivators used available resources rather than increases in total output through the addition of acreage after 1848 by double cropping. The cultivated area itself fell by almost 5 percent after 1848 as the number of houses in the village grew to accommodate an increasing population and changing tastes in domestic structures. The growth of production through double cropping is indicated in column II as a percentage increase in acres cultivated taking the quinquennium 1880–1884 as a base. This period rather than the 1848–1849 data forms the base because the latter are only for one year and there is no indication of the method of their collection, whereas from 1880 the procedure was well established. Unfortunately, data on the period 1850–1879, when much of the transportation facilities in Jullundur were constructed, no longer exist. Column III shows the increases from the use of improved seeds in the form of additions to the cropped area with 1880–1884 as a base, that is, I converted the reported increment in yield into an equivalent number of additional acres to roughly approximate the role of higher yields in increased output.[61] Thus, assuming an increase of 25 percent for wheat intro-

---

1968. Neale has argued that even in current synchronic surveys of village economies usable data are only available where a count is necessary because of the organization and knowledge of agriculture in rural India (see below). But even with a rough counting, major changes in housing, cattle, and cropping pattern can be established. Walter C. Neale, "The Limitations of Indian Village Survey Data," *Journal of Asian Studies*, XVII (1957), 293–298. The measures I have used indicate the direction of change and give at least a rough sense of its magnitude.

[61] The standard method for evaluating changes in cropping patterns and measuring change is to compare the total value of all crops grown in the village at various points in time. Price figures for a nearby market town are available for the period which would make this possible. But, as should be clear from the following discussion, because the goal of the family farm in Vilyatpur is the maximization of output of a range of versatile crops per-capita of family labor, and not maximization of profit calculated according to conventional accounting methods (cost of labor and other inputs, market value of produce, depreciation of equipment, etc.), I have attempted to estimate increases in the volume of physical product. Village cultivators are influenced by prevailing prices for their crops. Raj Krishna, for instance, found a high level of responsiveness to cotton prices among Punjabi farmers. ("Acreage Response Functions for Some Punjab Crops," *Economic Journal*, LXXIII (1963), 477–487). But the responsiveness for wheat, the staple crop, is very low (*Ibid.*) because of the nature of the family farm.

duced in 1915 and of 75 percent for sugarcane from the 1930's, for every four acres of improved wheat another acre was added to the area cropped for that year, and for every four of sugarcane three were added to the total. For the three year period, 1965–1968, I have assumed a 75 percent increment for the Mexican wheats over the previous "improved" varieties, and a 100 percent increase over the pre-1915 unrefined types. The increments to the village acreage from both new seeds and increased double cropping added together form an "index of increase" showing the growth in total output. The measure, though crude, does indicate that from a more intensive use of land and better seeds an expansion in total production was achieved in Vilyatpur by 1920, and an expansion of significant proportions by 1934 that more or less kept pace with the growth in population. The computation is a conservative estimate of gains from practices relating to cropping alone. It neither takes account of shifts from crops in which no improvements occurred into wheat and sugarcane (the acreage of which grew in both absolute size and as a percentage of the yearly crop after 1930), nor of improvements in irrigation and other forms of investment in agriculture.

The number of wells has always been the most important factor determining the productivity of land. Even in 1848 Vilyatpur was highly developed in this respect, possessing thirty wells lined with bricks made in the village. Until recently there has been little change, the number of wells in working order fluctuating between thirty and thirty-eight. But there have been two periods of important changes in the second form of investment in irrigation—the apparatus for lifting water. Until 1933–1934 all wells were worked with a *charsa* identical to that found in Vilyatpur in 1848 as described in chapter II. In 1933 Partap Singh, the *surpanch* (headman) of the village, built the first Persian wheel. This mechanism was by no means new in the Jullundur district, but it had not been used in Vilyatpur before. The general rise of the water table in the area made its use possible. It could be worked with fewer men and animals, and with far greater control of the discharge of water than the *charsa*, which made it desirable even though a number of factors complicated its adoption. It required an initial investment ten times the cost of the *charsa*. The all-iron mechanism had to be purchased outside the village while the wood and leather *charsa* was made by the *sepidar*-carpenter; also the Persian wheel was more expensive to maintain.

TABLE 18

CAPITAL IN AGRICULTURE, 1848–1968

		Maximum number reported in the decade			
	Average number of operating wells	Power driven tube wells	Carts	Sugarcane presses	Threshers
1848–49	30		7	3	
1880–89	28		20	16	
1890–99	36		22	...	
1900–09	37		25	...	
1910–19	36		23	19	
1920–29	32		25	...	
1930–39	33		26	35	
1940–49	37	1	28	37	
1950–59	37	3	53	46	2
1960–68	41	13	73	62	9

SOURCE: *Lal Kitab* (village notebook), Vilyatpur.

While I cannot estimate the increment to production from this shift, authorities on Punjab agriculture generally see the existence of the Persian wheel as coinciding with the careful and intensive use of the land.[62] The substantial growth in the intensity of cultivation and increase in double cropping from 1935 to 1939 (Table 17) probably reflects the impact of this change.

By 1940 all wells in Vilyatpur were fitted with Persian wheels. In 1944 Partap Singh drilled the first deep well, which he operated with a diesel engine. When the first electric line was constructed in 1957, the diesel engine was replaced with an electric motor and two more farmers installed tube wells. Since 1965 ten more tube wells have been bored, bringing the total to thirteen. All other forms of investment in agriculture show two periods of increase (see Table 18). The number of carts and sugarcane presses increased substantially in the late nineteenth century. The increase was probably an indication of greater marketing of crops in response to the development of roads and railways. Like the growth in outlays for irrigation apparatus, the number of sugarcane presses and carts has grown since the 1930's. Much new equipment was of an improved type as well—more effi-

---

[62] S. R., 1892, 104–105; Roberts and Singh, 142–145, 160–161.

cient presses fitted with a series of iron rollers, and larger carts with inflated rubber tires instead of wood wheels. In 1968 there were two tractors and nine power driven threshers. One tractor belongs to a farmer cultivating more than thirty acres, and the other to a village carpenter who does custom threshing and hauls produce to market on hire.

Labor, the last input of importance for yields and productivity, changed in cost and supply over the last one hundred and twenty years. Throughout the period most labor was contributed by members of the property groups engaged in farming, while outside labor —hired, or as part of the *sepidar* system—was strictly supplemental except in occasional and extraordinary circumstances. Leaving the question of additions to family labor for the discussion of the family farm, the changes in compensation and organization of nonfamily labor suggest both an increase in productivity and the growth of the influence of the market in the village economy.

Agricultural laborers formed 10 percent of the working men in 1848 and grew slowly in numbers and as a proportion of the work force through 1922 when they represented 14 percent.[63] Throughout the period the *sepidar* system remained intact. Although the compensation for full-time *sepidars* increased from 7 percent of the annual crop to 10 percent in 1884, the rates for part-time assistance, the most common type of *sepidar*-agricultural labor, remained unchanged at 2.5 percent.[64] Since the nineteen twenties, however, the *sepidar* system (for agricultural labor) has slowly disintegrated; the compensation for labor has gradually risen. The practice of a particular *sepidar* working with the same property group for a number of years has been replaced by annual agreements on the amount of work expected and the rate of compensation received: 2.5 percent for harvesting

[63] By 1968 the agricultural laborers were 20 percent. Although the number of laborers and their proportion in the community increased steadily from 1848–1968, the increase was not the result of a decline in rural handicrafts pushing artisans into agricultural labor, indebtedness, or any other cause which might drive anyone from a family that had once held land into the ranks of the landless. In 1968 all but one agricultural laborer in Vilyatpur were Chamars whose ancestors had been *sepidar*-laborers before them.

[64] The rates of compensation for the nineteenth century are taken from the the revenue records and are normative statements rather than an average of all the cases in the year. See Lewis, pp. 346–347. If available, actual wage data would be preferable. In their absence, information on changing norms must suffice.

alone, 5 percent for weeding, harvesting and threshing, and 10 percent for full-time assistance in the field and home. By 1947 the last vestiges of the system had disappeared for agricultural labor, the yearly contracts giving way to daily arrangements at cash rates for certain jobs and piece-work rates for others. I failed to inquire about the level of wages and compensation in the 1950's, but by 1968 they had reached Rs. 5 per day for casual labor and a 5 percent share for harvesting or making *gur*. These rates generally prevail. During the wheat harvest laborers gather daily at one corner of the village near the Chamar-*basta;* when cultivators arrive to get the workers they need for the day, the bargaining begins. If the wheat crop is particularly dry and liable to be damaged by winds, or if rains appear to be near, the reapers enjoy the advantage and may earn more than 6.5 percent (as on the best day during the wheat harvest of 1969 in Vilyatpur) or 8.5 percent in the neighboring village, where laborers from Vilyatpur regularly go to work. Mechanical threshers, recently introduced, have not undermined the earning power of the agricultural laborers. The machine in use in the Punjab (a large fanlike contraption inside a metal hood that chews the wheat and the straw, blowing the straw further than the grain) requires four to five men to work effectively. It is a dusty job that pays quite well. With substantially increased crops to be harvested, greater demands for laborers for their transportation, and the development of a variety of off-season occupations for semi-skilled and general labor (the subject of the next chapter), more Chamar-agricultural laborers are fully employed at better rates of pay than ever before. Indeed, only in interviews among this caste and occupational group informants did not begin with an idealized account of "the good old days." Others remembered something which made the past better—"people used to give surplus milk away instead of selling it," "sons were obedient," "vegetables tasted better because no one used fertilizers," etc.; the Chamar-agricultural laborers' income and place in society have so much improved that they find the present better than the past without exception or qualification.[65]

[65] I think that this suggests some difficulties for the critics of the "green revolution." For instance, see Francine Frankel, "India's New Strategy of Agricultural Development: Political Costs of Agrarian Modernization," *Journal of Asian Studies*, XXVIII (1969), 693–710. The new technological package is by no means indivisible and the use of machines like the locally constructed

The finding that there was no change in agricultural labors' organization and compensation before the 1920's when the district experienced general development and the village population declined, and that rates of payment and employment increased in the period when the supply of labor expanded quite rapidly, contains an apparent contradiction which must be explained. The latter phenomenon is the product of the growth in agricultural investment, the use of improved practices, and the cultivation of improved varieties, all of which effectively absorbed additional labor. As productivity increased, wages rose and changes took place in the organization of labor. The *sepidar* system was replaced first by a series of yearly contracts and then by daily bargaining over the wage to be paid. There was a steady increase in part-time rural employment which supplemented agricultural labor as a source of livelihood for the unskilled laborer. Work in brick kilns, housing construction, whitewashing, painting (as the number of brick houses grew), and, more recently, rural-based industries have provided supplemental work outside agriculture. The expansion of the canal colonies in the 1920's presented laborers from Vilyatpur and neighboring villages with an opportunity for seasonal migration during the wheat harvest.[66] In fact, it was the departure of a substantial number of Chamars and village grantees to the canal colonies in the 1920's that irreparably disrupted the traditional *sepidar* system. The web of relationships never recovered from the sudden departure of a large number of its participants.

So much for developments after 1920. But what of the stability in compensation and the *sepidar* system in the earlier period? The first wave of migration to the canal colonies in the 1890's did not have any disruptive effect. Did existing production techniques make labor redundant in Vilyatpur before the developments of the 1920's? If not, why was there no increase in compensation if there was some growth owing to better marketing facilities? Schultz argues that the marginal value product of labor in traditional agriculture, like that in the Punjab before the 1920's, is not zero. He cites the effects of

---

thresher will not have the dire consequences predicted, at least in the wheat growing areas. A combine that efficiently harvests and threshes the whole crop of the village in a matter of days is, of course, quite another matter.

[66] Anchal Dass, and Hugh Calvert, *An Economic Survey of Tehong: A Village in the Jullundur District*, The Board of Economic Inquiry, Punjab, Punjab Village Surveys—3 (Lahore: Civil and Military Gazette Press, 1931), 15.

the 1918 influenza epidemic in India to prove his point. Had labor
been redundant, he argues, the sudden contraction in the work force
because of deaths in the epidemic would have had no effect on the
area sown with crops, "the best proxy for agricultural production." [67]
But cropping in the year following the attack registered a 3.8 percent
decline throughout India.[68] The influenza epidemic had the same
effect in Vilyatpur. The cropped acreage contracted so much between
1918 and 1920 that the average for the quinquennium 1915–1919
dipped to the base year average for the only time in the period covered in the study. The other two five-year periods when the intensity
of cropping declined, 1895–1899 and 1905–1909, occurred during the
two epidemics of plague that took so many lives in Vilyatpur.

Labor in Vilyatpur was not at zero value before the increased investment in agriculture, improved technology, and more complete
use of available resources. Rather, village political organization accounts for the absence of change in the organization and compensation for agricultural labor. Before 1848 the Chamars, and all non-
Sahotas were dependent on the proprietors for the right to earn a
living and reside in the community. No one lived in the village who
did not work there. Such an arrangement conflicted with the basic
structure of village society in the Punjab, as described in Chapters
I and II, and was impossible at any rate since the kind of work that
required commuting was nonexistent.[69] The entire village, including
the residential site, belonged to the Sahotas, and no one else had a
permanent right to any part of it. The Chamars' time was at the disposal of the Sahotas; they were required to do *begar* (forced labor)
for the Jats without payment. Compensation for agricultural labor
was regulated by custom and enforced by the Sahotas through their
ability to use sanctions which ranged from physical violence to an
arbitrary change of wages, and not by any kind of market mechanism.[70] The conservative nature of revenue policy in British Punjab

[67] Schultz, 65.

[68] *Ibid.*, 67.

[69] This of course was not the case in villages near cities. Residents in communities like Vilyatpur, however, would find little variety in occupational opportunities within twenty miles, an impossible distance for regular commuting
before the proliferation of bicycles after 1950.

[70] Examples of these sanctions are the arbitrary reduction of wages, restrictions
on grazing cattle on village land, prohibition on the gathering of firewood, de-
nial of access to wells, and the immediate foreclosure of all outstanding debts.

and the codification of customary usages translated this state of affairs into written law:

> The customary law as to the inhabited site in villages may be readily understood if Sir Meredyth Plowden's *dicta* as to the presupposition of a grant be applied to it. The village *abadi* belongs to the proprietary body of the village and the custom assumes that nonproprietors have settled under grants from that body.[71]
>
> I think the true foundation of the agreement is this, that in return for the privilege of being allowed to reside in the village the *kamin* agrees to perform certain tasks, and the proprietor makes certain allowances to him for his work. The performance of the tasks is an incidence of the residence and not a personal liability of the *kamin* and the *kamin* could free himself at any time by leaving the village.[72]

Before 1898 not one of the non-Sahotas lived in Vilyatpur and worked elsewhere, not even in a neighboring Sahota village. But the growth of occupational opportunities outside the village, particularly since the late nineteenth century, repeatedly raised problems about the status of nonproprietors and their families in the community, and two cases were taken to the courts. In both instances (a Chamar in 1898 wanted to leave his family in the village to take up service with the railway company, and the Weavers resisted the Sahotas' attempt to reduce the rate of payment for weaving cloth in 1910), the law was on the side of the Sahotas, but the district commissioner declined to make a judgment because in his mind injustices would have resulted. Instead, both cases were referred to the honorary magistrate in Phillaur, the *tehsil* headquarters, for arbitration. They were resolved in essentially the same way; the judge cajoled the Sahotas into selling housing plots to any nonproprietors who wanted to pay the price, thereby freeing them to come and go as they pleased. From 1898 ownership of housing plots became a highly valued sign of success and independence among the nonlanded. This was particularly true among the untouchables, and remained so even after the 1920's when no further efforts were made to restrict residents from working

---

Miriam Young, *Seen and Heard in a Punjab Village* (London: Student Christian Movement Press, 1931), 135, 152–153.

[71] H. A. Rose, *A Compendium of the Punjab Customary Law* (Lahore: Civil and Military Gazette Press, 1911), 217.

[72] T. Gordon Walker, *Punjab Customary Law of the Ludhiana District* (Calcutta Central Press, 1885), 90.

in neighboring villages, or, in the case of the Weavers, from setting their own rates. As long as occupational opportunities outside the village were small in number and the instances where untouchable agricultural laborers and artisans attempted to take advantage of them while still living in Vilyatpur infrequent, the Sahotas' successfully retained their monopolistic control on the supply and cost of local labor. After 1920, however, when the number of new jobs multiplied rapidly, continued Sahota interference even without the decision of the honorary magistrate was impossible. The amount of coming and going increased, undermining the *sepidar* system, and the compensation and supply of labor progressively came under the influence of a wider rural labor market.[73] The importance of the growth of opportunities in rural Punjab, particularly after the turn of the century, for all Vilyatpur residents will be taken up in detail in the following chapter.

Numerous changes have taken place in Vilyatpur agriculture since 1848. The general decline in the agricultural per-capita land occurred, with a period of fluctuation, from the mid-1890's through the mid-1920's when the size of farms became more or less stable. Before the 1920's production expanded slowly through an extension of double cropping; village cultivators probably profited through better marketing facilities. The growth of capital in the form of carts and sugarcane presses seems to indicate an increased orientation toward the market. But the extent of change was limited. The cropping pattern remained similar to that of 1848 during the first revenue survey, and the organization and compensation of agricultural labor remained unaffected by the increased involvement in the market. At the turn of the century a number of developments took place which together brought some important changes. With the opening of the canal colonies opportunities for work outside the village began to grow. By the 1920's these opportunities were so many that the tradi-

---

[73] I could not find any particular trace of the various movements among the Chamars in the Punjab in the 1920–1930's which have been reported elsewhere. Neither the efforts of the Arya Samaj to better the position of the untouchables (Lewis, 73–75); the Christian missionaries (Miriam Young, 135–136); nor the Adharmi movement (*Punjab Census*, 1931, I, 289, 310) seem to have had a direct role in the mobilization of the Chamars to bring about change in conditions of work in Vilyatpur, although the contribution to self-awareness and personal esteem was very real, particularly with regard to the Adharmis. All Chamars in Vilyatpur identified themselves as Adharmis in the 1931 census.

tional system could not withstand the combined effects of another large migration to the canal colonies, the increasing market orientation of village agriculture that was part of the use of improved seed types, and new investment in agricultural appliances. Agricultural labor freed itself of the domination of the landowners, wages rose first perhaps as an adjustment to the new freedom and then because village production and the productivity of labor increased. Additions to village production from the use of improved varieties and double cropping alone kept up with the growth of population. I have made no effort to estimate the impact of better irrigation facilities, the growth in the intensity and productivity of labor, the more careful and intensive cultivation of better crops, and, after 1958–1959, the use of chemical fertilizers. After the 1920's agricultural activity entered a transitional phase between the traditional form of organization common in the nineteenth century and that found after 1947, when market considerations play a predominant role. The extent of change in this transitional phase and even at present, has been conditioned by the organization of the family farm and the goals and motives of Vilyatpur cultivators.

The Family Farm

In his study of social and economic change following the 1855 British annexation of Orissa, Bailey examines the incomes and expenditures of several cultivators in the 1950's to discover why land is sold in Bisipara. By showing that income is just about sufficient to meet the basic expenses of the family throughout the year, he establishes as the basis for the sale of land the meeting of extraordinary expenses caused by social obligations, such as the celebrations connected with marriages and deaths and by economic causes such as the death of a plow animal or a poor harvest.[74] Bailey goes on to demonstrate how recent immigrants into the village have used wealth acquired in trade and other nonagricultural pursuits to purchase the land sold by the original owners, the Warriors, which leads to some basic social and political changes in the community.

We will now turn to the consideration of some basic aspects of farm management by working at the level of individual operating

---

[74] Bailey, *Caste and the Economic Frontier,* 50–93.

units in a manner similar to Bailey. For lack of historical data on incomes and expenditures of particular families, I can add little to what Bailey and the authorities on agricultural indebtedness[75] in Punjab have written about the circumstances leading to the need for a substantial amount of cash at a moment in time among village cultivators. But by concentrating on the family farm over an extended period it is possible to examine attitudes and practices regarding land acquisition and sale, the place of the mortgage, the basis of the high rents and prices paid for land, and the importance of family size, family labor, and tenancy in farm management. Within this framework it will then be possible to account for certain characteristics of village agriculture in the Punjab, including the fragmentation of holdings and the practice of polyculture—the growing of a range of crops rather than concentration on one or two of the most profitable ones. In conclusion, the importance of the Vilyatpur agricultural organization for the adoption of the changes outlined in the two previous sections will be considered and some speculations offered about the future.

Ownership, Mortgages and Sales

At least since the late Sikh period farming in Vilyatpur has been primarily a family concern. Property groups value land as a source of prestige in the community and as a means to support the family. To own a large holding in the village meant influence, earned envy, and enabled one to provide for the family so that no member should have to be dependent as a laborer or tenant on any other property group. There would also be abundant land for each son and sufficient jewelry for each daughter at the time of her marriage, essentials if they were to obtain good matches and evoke favorable comment from everyone at the marriage ceremony. Land is the crucial ingredient in this complex, and is acquired whenever possible and sold only in extreme circumstances. After the amount of land owned by various property groups, the second measure of prestige depends upon whether or not a particular group is a "buyer" or a "seller." Everyone watches the latter to see if the problem is short term or indicative of a period of decline. "Sellers," for instance, find it much more difficult

[75] See the numerous books by Malcolm Lyall Darling, and the studies of Hugh Calvert and S. S. Thorburn.

to obtain satisfactory matches for the marriage of sons and daughters. But, if the amount of land owned may be taken as the index of prestige among the Sahotas, then it is the local community and its range of holdings that sets the scale. The reference group for measuring success in Vilyatpur is the community, not society in general, or any more abstract notion of class. The standing of one group vis-à-vis another is the important factor for valuating and motivating achievement between 1848 and 1968.

The principle means of acquiring land was and is through inheritance. As we shall see, most groups purchase some land at one time or another, but, with few exceptions, the bulk of their holdings are inherited. In aggregate, holdings in Vilyatpur declined slowly over time as the village's population grew. But as the discussion of the differential growth of various families and lineages in Chapter III revealed, some groups grew more rapidly than others and therefore suffered a greater fractionalization of their patrimony because of the practice of equal division between all coparceners. Holdings in large families declined markedly in a few generations, while those in small ones changed comparatively little. All property groups availed of every opportunity to add to their holdings. This task was slow and painful in all cases, particularly difficult if the inherited property was small and did not provide much basis to work from, or if the family was so small that hired hands and tenants had to be employed to work part of the land. The numerous studies of circumstances leading to the sale of land emphasize the urgent need for cash, a need which brings families to the unhappy position of having to sell land —borrowing for marriages, the replacement of draught animals, fighting court cases, and the like. To understand the forces at work in rural Punjab, however, we must also look at the buyers, their source of wealth, and their motives for the purchase of land.

A market for land, and the practice of buying and selling land, has existed in Vilyatpur at least since 1848. The distribution of the size of holdings found in 1848 suggests that transfers among the Sahotas occurred before British annexation as well. The first recorded sale took place in 1851, three years after annexation. By 1965 four hundred and nine permanent transfers had been completed. Although from 1848 to 1900 there were no legal restrictions of any sort on land sales, the land market remained highly localized. Since the total area sold in a year averaged less than two acres and the average sale was only for a little over an acre of land (divided in most cases into from two to five plots), there were few buyers outside of Vilyatpur. Unless an outsider was ready to go to the extreme of appointing an agent to look after his new acquisition the small plots typically offered for sale only attracted Vilyatpur residents, or, if the land was particularly desirable, someone from the contiguous villages. Practical problems aside, land outside of one's own village could bring little prestige to its owner in his home community unless the holding was substantial enough to be an important source of wealth, such as a grant in the canal colonies. Between 1848 and 1900, while land sales were unrestricted, only two outsiders purchased land in Vilyatpur. One man from a neighboring village and another, who took some land in default of a loan, together acquired a total of seven acres. After 1900 two pieces of legislation restricted the freedom of transfer: the Punjab Land Alienation Act (1900) and the Punjab Pre-Emption Act (1913). The first removed a substantial portion of the population from the market for agricultural land by limiting the right of purchase to members of officially designated "agricultural tribes." The purpose of the act was political, an effort to prevent the transfer of land from groups historically dominant in rural areas to village and urban based moneylenders. The Pre-Emption Act, aimed at preserving the integrity of the *bhaiachara* common to most of Punjab's villages, reinforced the local character of the land market by stipulating that members of the community had first option to purchase all land offered for sale before it could be transferred to an outsider. It is unlikely, given the characteristics of land offered for sale in Vilyatpur (at best a few acres divided into a number of plots), that either of these measures made much difference.[76]

The combination of the necessity of raising cash to meet social obligations and economic crises and an ever present demand for land in the village produced an active market involving substantial amounts of money (see Table 19). The usual approach to the data presented in this table is to point to the number of sales and mort-

---

[76] The existence of the Pre-Emption Act has probably inflated the prices of land reported in official documents, since prices higher than those actually received were often quoted to the *patwari* to enable sellers of land to dispose of it to outsiders if they liked. This has not been a factor in Vilyatpur, since 95 percent of the land was sold to village residents and all of the holdings are already well under the ceiling.

TABLE 19

LAND SALES AND MORTGAGES, 1885–1966

	New mortgages				Mortgages redeemed				Sales			
	Number	Area (acres)	Rs. per acre	Total value (Rs.)	Number	Area	Rs. per acre	Total value	Number	Area	Rs. per acre	Total value
1885–89	10	27	90	2,427	11	23	69	1,591	19	15	200	2,998
1890–94	24	42	116	4,860	7	26	25	638	7	3	237	716
1895–99	9	27	81	2,211	20	33	58	1,911	5	4	284	1,135
1900–04	8	13	157	2,045	8	7	548	3,839	10	19	299	5,690
1905–09	14	27	190	5,128	16	21	146	3,070	6	6	524	3,145
1910–14	17	22	426	9,375	16	40	179	7,144	26	29	310	9,003
1915–19	10	27	370	10,000	7	7	250	1,750	7	5	280[a]	1,398[a]
1920–24	10	11	1,066	11,728	4	8	550	4,400	4	10	1,290	12,900
1925–29	37	31	625	19,372	8	12	688	8,250	18	6	1,215	7,287
1930–34	31	32	542	17,352	11	11	220	4,850	22	17	1,164	19,791
1935–39	23	21	369	7,752	12	16	544	8,700	51	17	1,372	23,232
1940–44	21	15	535	8,023	51	38	544	21,053	42	25	1,474	36,854
1945–49	62	50	598	29,915	60	53	815	43,199	51	14	2,553	35,744
1950–54	41	39	2,822	110,055	46	14	1,475	20,655	17	21	3,690	77,500
1955–59	21	21	1,366	28,696	37	35	1,585	55,466	49	35	3,045	106,587
1960–64	28	20	1,349	26,980	76	59	1,406	82,953	59	60	2,894	173,649
1965–66	3	..	..	5,500	2	1	1,600	1,600	18	4	9,300	37,500

SOURCE: The annual statistics in the *Lal Kitab* (village notebook) Village Vilyatpur.

[a] The price for one year in the 1915–1919 quinquennium is missing, depressing the average and the total. If the average is computed only for transactions with complete data it becomes Rs. 465 per acre.

gages over time as a kind of barometer recording the state of the rural
economy, and the ratio of new mortgages to those redeemed, to distinguish periods of prosperity from periods of deficit. To do so is not
altogether fruitless, and some interesting features are brought to
light. The more or less constant increase in the price of land, even
with the general decline in the value of the *rupee* is an important
development. These fluctuations in the price of land in Vilyatpur
reflect the course of change in land prices throughout the province.[77]
Prices grew secularly through the late nineteenth and early twentieth
century, showing a sharper increase in World War I.[78] The war was
followed by a period of inflation reflected in the price of land in
both the village and the province. Then a decline, starting in the
late twenties, continued through the Depression. From the late thirties until Partition and Independence both series move upward; both
also show a decline in the price of land from the early fifties. In fact,
the similarity in the movement of prices in the village and the province indicates that although land markets in the Punjab are highly
localized for both buyers and sellers, the village market is subject
to the same general economic influences as the provincial economy.[79] The only striking differences between Mukerji's findings in
his study of "Land Prices in Punjab" and the figures from village
records for Vilyatpur is that the price paid for land in the latter is
consistently two or three times above the average for cultivated
land in the province, a reflection of Jullundur's prosperity and productivity. The one divergence, a sharp rise in the price of land in the
village in the quinquennium 1905–1909, resulted from the return
of a few Australian migrants who possessed substantial amounts of
cash, an influx which forced prices up in Vilyatpur.

Several distinct periods of expansion and contraction in the num-

[77] Karunamoy Mukerji, "Land Prices in Punjab," M. K. Chaudhuri (ed.),
Trends of Socio-Economic Change in India (Simla: Indian Institute of Advanced
Studies, 1969), 529–546.

[78] *Ibid.*, table 6, 538.

[79] Bailey, in his fascinating account of the local nature of the land market in
Bisipara, argues that because everyone knows of the circumstances forcing the
seller to put land up for sale, it is difficult for him to obtain the land's "market
price." Bailey, *Caste and the Economic Frontier*, 59–60. I found no indication
that the land market in Vilyatpur was or is a "buyer's market" as such, the demand for land being general enough that there is usually some competition for
its purchase. Sellers are generally able to predict the prevailing rate well enough
to sell just enough land to obtain the needed amount of cash.

ber of new mortgages are evident between 1885 and 1965.[80] The total value of mortgages redeemed outweighed new mortgages in only six of seventeen quinquennia, all but one of which came after 1935. The question is how to interpret the information. Does the very existence of debt, and the increase in its volume signify poverty and indicate an imbalance in the rural economy in general, or is it some other phenomenon? [81] To some extent the answer depends on the ideas and attitudes of the investigator. The two greatest authorities on rural indebtedness in the Punjab are S. S. Thorburn, who wrote in the late nineteenth century, and M. L. Darling, who studied the question intimately for over thirty years from 1917. They agree that the cause of aggravated indebtedness can be found in the creation of the right to alienate land in perpetuity inaugurated under British rule. Formerly the extent of credit had been limited by the scarcity of assets to act as security. The right of outright sale brought about a rise in land prices and gave landowners unused to participation in the market a substantial base for credit which they could not manage.[82] An excessive amount of debt was incurred that could not be repaid, particularly because much was spent on "unproductive" social obligations which in no way contributed to the production of income to repay the debt. Loans at high rates of interest led to mortgages of land and eventually to sale. Men who had previously been landowners entered the ranks of sharecropping tenants and agricultural laborers. This sequence, established in the nineteenth century, was then aggravated in the current one by the rapid increase in population which generally meant "less to go around." [83]

Darling's greatest contribution is his demonstration that debt did not reflect poverty. In his survey he found that indebtedness was

[80] Mortgages were legal transactions officially entered in the *intiqal* (mutation) register maintained by the Patwari, in contrast to unsecured loans based on a verbal agreement.

[81] The following discussion of indebtedness is limited to mortgage debt, the only aspect of the question for which historical information is available. Darling estimate the mortgage debt to be about 50 percent of all debt in Jullundur district in 1917, a ratio which he considers to be "good" in that the higher the proportion of secured loans the more sophisticated the borrowers. Jullundur ranked among the districts with the highest ratio of mortgages to general loans. Darling, *Punjab Peasant*, 6.

[82] *Ibid.*, 210, 216–217; Thorburn, 49–52. For an analysis by an economist who follows the same line of reasoning see Neale, 87–88.

[83] Darling, *Punjab Peasant*, 17.

greatest in Punjab's most prosperous districts, and that larger landowners generally owed more than those with smaller holdings.
Prosperity provided an expanded basis for credit[84] and stimulated
increases in expenditures—as indicated by the much larger outlays
on ceremonial occasions, rural Punjab's most valued form of con-
spicuous consumption.[85] But because Darling conceives of debt as
something bad and generally unnecessary,[86] if care were taken, and
because he does not pay attention to purchasers of land, I think that
he misses an important part of the picture which relates to the study
of the management of the family farm, and the motives of village
landowners and cultivators.

Darling correctly observes that despite its prevalence, people looked
down on debt in rural Punjab. He suggests that unsecured loans are
preferred even at very high interest rates because they need never
become public, secured loans bringing a loss of prestige to the
debtor.[87] In practice land is mortgaged only when it proves impossible to obtain needed cash either from a relative or through an unsecured loan. A mortgage is definitely preferred to a sale, and most
of the land transferred in Vilyatpur is first mortgaged and sold only
when it proves impossible to repay the loan or an additional need for
cash arises. A hand count of the sales records since 1885 shows that in
the years 1885 to 1914 only three cases of outright sales occurred,
whereas forty-nine took place from 1915 to 1944, an increase of about
400 percent after adjusting for the larger number of transactions.
After 1947 outright sales grew continuously and by 1960 almost half
of the permanent transfers took place without prior mortgage.[88]

[84] *Ibid.*, 210–211.

[85] *Ibid.*, 215–217.

[86] *Ibid.*, 222. Darling considers that, in part, the problem was out of the cultivator's control because the small size and fragmentation of holdings was as important in causing indebtedness as the cultivator's improvidence. But I take issue
with his general analysis because Darling failed to understand or sympathize with
the probably long standing practice of borrowing well beyond yearly income for
heavy expenditure on socially valued ceremonies like marriages. Darling considered it irresponsible to borrow for such an expense, while a Sahota would
find the idea of spending only what one had saved on such a function to be
equally irresponsible.

[87] *Ibid.*, 7.

[88] In these calculations I did not consider it necessary for the same physical
piece of land to be mortgaged and then sold. Outright sales were defined as all
cases where a cultivator sold a piece of land and either had no land mortgaged,
or did not redeem the mortgage on the piece sold or any other piece of land at
the time of the transaction.

Mortgage is preferred to sale, partly from the point of view of the mortgagee's reputation, but primarily because it preserves the mortgagee's title to the land. Although the most common form of mortgage in rural Punjab requires the mortgagee to surrender the use of the property to the mortgagor in lieu of interest payments, meaning that the borrower loses the potential production of the land for the duration of the mortgage; it reverts to him upon repayment. It may appear to be more rational to sell a smaller piece of land, obtain its full value (a mortgage generally yields about half of the sale price), and then save to repurchase an equivalent piece at some future date. There is never any assurance that land will then be available, however, or that the new piece will be as advantageously located as the one sold. In a recent case for which I have most of the details, Mihan Singh mortgaged two and a half acres of irrigated land in 1942 for Rs. 1400 to finance some business interests outside the village. For the next thirteen years Mihan Singh and his sons worked as tenants on their own land, paying the mortgagor half the produce as rent. In 1955, after Mihan Singh's death, his sons repaid the loan and took possession of the land again. From the point of view of Mihan Singh this process was not altogether unsatisfactory, although his family lost half of their income from the two and a half acres for an extended period of time. Had the land been sold, there would have been a blemish on the family's name, while in addition the transaction at average prices would have cost them almost four thousand rupees (plus the portion of the produce they received for working their own land as sharecroppers). Even if the mortgagor had cultivated the land himself, depriving Mihan Singh and sons of all profit from it, they would only have lost its use for thirteen years but not the land itself, a far more important factor in the mind and experience of village cultivators.

This strong desire to retain land even at considerable cost, correlates with the rationale behind efforts of property groups to add to their holdings whenever possible. Land is purchased at every opportunity, often at prices which exceed its productive value in strict economic terms and absorb most of the family's savings. Thus there is little left for investment to increase the land's productivity. Land serves as a kind of investment that can, in the event of a need for liquid capital, be mortgaged and, if necessary, sold. The importance of land purchase as a form of investment and savings and not poverty or irrational, irresponsible management of the family's economic affairs accounts for the large volume of mortgages and sales in Table

19. The prevalence of the practice is readily apparent in the fluctuations in the amount of land owned by individual property groups at twelve year intervals during the course of their existence. Changes, both additions and losses, occur with considerable frequency, and many more are probably lost in my analysis since the data is drawn from every third *jamabandi*. To a significant extent, then, transactions in land in prosperous areas like Jullundur are better seen as part of a credit-savings mechanism for meeting necessary expenditures, "productive and unproductive," rather than as an index of the general state of the rural economy. Until very recently there have been no institutional alternatives for rural finance suited to villagers' needs and attitudes toward land. With the growth of village co-operative credit societies, the movement of commercial banks into agricultural finance, and the emergence of alternative forms of investment, these attitudes and needs are beginning to change, and the number of outright sales are increasing.

Management and Use

While land is important for its investment and savings potential and its role in determining a family's standing in the local community, village cultivators value land primarily as a means to provide for the property group. I have already noted the role of the local community as a referent group in measuring individual and family standing and success throughout most of the period. A related value, at least through 1947, is the definite preference for providing for all members of the family at an adequate standard of living from the property group's holding in the village, rather than family members migrating in search of work. The only exception was migration overseas, always a special case in Vilyatpur. But the emphasis here is on the word "preference," and, as already indicated, migration from the village has been quite common since the late 1890's. I have little information on the use of land by individual cultivators in the past—cropping, adopting of improvements, and investing to raise productivity—that would add to the aggregate picture of the province and the village presented in the first two sections of the chapter. But the examination of how the various groups managed their holdings—the importance of family size and the role of tenancy—underscores the influence of the organization of the family farm on the general character of village agriculture and the course of change since 1848.

Most farm labor in the village, while the *sepidar* system was still intact and afterwards, was provided by members of the property groups using the land. Family members working in agriculture have always outnumbered full-time agricultural laborers by a wide margin. In 1968, when the latter assumed their greatest proportion, they were still less than one-third of the adult males working in agriculture. Nonfamily labor is used only when a given task must be completed quickly; weeding between irrigations, making *gur*, harvesting, and threshing. But families expand and contract in size. The normal cycle of birth, maturation, and death, in the history of each separate property group and the fluctuations from generation to generation in the lineage cause variation over time. These changes make it difficult to adjust the supply of family labor to the size of the group's holding, necessitating adjustments that take a variety of different forms. Groups with more land than can be farmed with family labor at the existing level of technology do not sell it, given its long-term economic and prestige value. They either lease some land to tenants, or, when possible, make innovations, either technological or organizational, to allow available labor to manage the holding. Larger families with relatively small holdings either rent land in the village or send members outside to find work. Migrants are supplied with foodstuffs from the farm and are expected to acquire wealth for the purchase of additional property in Vilyatpur, thereby adding to the group's resource base as well as its standing in the community. The history of emigrants' occupations and the use of earnings from outside Vilyatpur belongs to the next chapter. Here I will focus on the relationship of family size and composition to the size of holdings to demonstrate the role of tenancy as an adaptive mechanism in villages like Vilyatpur, and establish the motive for migration and occupational change.

The primary factor influencing the decision of how to use the family's land appears to have been the size and composition of the group itself. Of course the ideal size of the farm depended not only on the amount of land and family labor at hand, but these as well as on the prevalent or available technology. Still another factor that must have entered into calculations was a decision as to the amount of produce/income, or, in other terms, the standard of living, the

family wanted from its holding and other activities. Recent surveys
by agricultural economists show one reason why owners of larger
holdings in rural India use less labor and capital per acre (and get
lower yields per acre) than those with smaller holdings is that, with
the larger area, they can obtain a moderate income without the extra
effort of hiring nonfamily labor and investing in new inputs required
of the others to earn the same amount.[89] I have no detailed information on the preference map of village cultivators for the present, much
less for the past. But I do want to emphasize that the amount of land
necessary to yield a given standard of living has not been constant
over the period under study, given the rise in value of village produce in the nineteenth century and the increases in the productivity
of land after 1920. However, abundant evidence of increased investment and consumption in the village is shown, in the village's
agricultural implements and equipment, larger expenditures on marriages, and steady improvement in the number and size of village
houses (from a single brick house in 1901 to 194 at present).

The practice of renting land in Vilyatpur dates back at least one
hundred and twenty years. In 1848 21 percent of the land leased out
through one-year verbal agreements dating from the beginning
(April–May) of the local (vikram) calendar, primarily (82%) on a
share-crop basis (half the crop). By 1884 the figure reached 30 percent, and since 1898 it has consistently hovered around 40 percent.[90]
But with the exception of a few widows living alone who had the use
of their husband's property for the rest of their lives, there were no
rentiers in Vilyatpur as such. Entire holdings have been rented from
time to time, but only when their owners were not in the village for
an extended period of time; a handful of cases in one hundred
twenty years. But neither was there any group of tenants, completely
dependent on securing land for cultivation on lease. Some land was
rented to landless Chamar and Nai households, and a little given
rent-free to support Brahmins and Faqirs, but the bulk of the land

[89] Morton Paglin, " 'Surplus' Agricultural Labor and Development: Facts and
Theories," The American Economic Review, LV (1965), 828.

[90] I think that the increase in the amount of land rented out between 1848
and 1898 is largely a product of the working of the records system described in
the addendum to Chapter 2. The minute recording of holdings enabled widows
and minors to own their own land which was usually rented, and allowed village
land owners who took advantage of new occupational opportunities outside the
community to retain title to their land and profit from it by leasing it to others.

not owner-cultivated was leased by one Sahota property group to another.

Comparing the size of agricultural holdings to those actually farmed reveals several patterns and trends. Table 20 shows the number and percentage of farms, and the percentage of land in farms of different sizes relative to ownership units for the period 1848 to 1968 (derived from Tables 14 and 16). While farms are generally more numerous and smaller in size than holdings because owners commonly rented some of their land to others for cultivation, there is considerable variation for farms of different sizes. A consistent, though at first glance, curious pattern is the excess of farms relative to holdings of the smallest (.01–1.99) and the second to largest sizes (10.00–19.99). That owners of the largest holdings in Vilyatpur (20 acres and more) leased some of their land to those with smaller holdings or without any land seems reasonable. The practice of taking very small amounts of land on lease, as a source of food stuffs, by individuals engaged in agricultural labor, traditional services, and more recently in new manufacturing and construction industries

TABLE 20

RELATIVE SIZE OF FARMS TO HOLDINGS, 1848–1968
(L larger, s smaller, — no difference)

| | | Size in acres | | | | | | | | | | | | | | | |
| | Number of units | | | | | | Percent in units | | | | | Percent of total in units | | | | |
	.01–1.99	2–4.99	5–9.99	10–19.99	20 plus	Total	.01–1.99	2–4.99	5–9.99	10–19.99	20 plus	.01–1.99	2–4.99	5–9.99	10–19.99	20 plus
1848	L	L	L	L	s	L	L	s	L	s	s	L	L	s	L	L
1884	L	s	L	L	s	L	L	s	s	s	s	L	s	L	s	s
1898	L	L	s	L	s	L	L	s	s	s	s	—	L	s	L	s
1910	L	s	L	L	s	L	L	s	s	L	s	—	s	—	L	s
1922	L	s	s	L	s	L	L	s	s	L	s	L	s	s	L	s
1934	L	s	s	L	s	L	L	L	s	L	s	—	s	L	L	s
1946	L	s	s	L	L	s	L	s	s	L		s	s	s	L	
1958	L	s	s	L	L	s	L	s	s	L	L	s	s	s	L	L
1968	L	s	s	L	—	s	L	s	s	L	—	s	s	s	L	—

SOURCE: Derived from Tables 14 and 16.
Sample: Property groups owning/using agricultural land.

(to be discussed in the following chapter) accounts for the consistent pattern in the .01–1.99 category. But to understand the reason why 10–19.99 acre farms are always more numerous than holdings of that size and, since 1910, have accounted for a large percentage of farms than holdings we must look to family size and structure. The supply of family labor also explains why farms in the 2–4.99 and 5–9.99 range are relatively less common than holdings of that size numerically and as a percentage.

TABLE 21

PROPERTY GROUP SIZE AND COMPOSITION,
AND LAND USE, 1848–1968
(acres)

		Percent with single adult male					Percent of total property groups
		.01–1.99	2–4.99	5–9.99	10–19.99	20 plus	
1848	holdings	100	96	75	43	17	48
	farms	40	75	50	28	0	41
1884	holdings	71	50	60	22	50	53
	farms	67	57	57	30	0	53
1898	holdings	59	42	50	54	75	53
	farms	58	33	45	40	100	54
1910	holdings	64	62	79	60	20	62
	farms	69	67	59	47	33	62
1922	holdings	67	80	58	17	0	60
	farms	79	77	52	0	0	59
1934	holdings	65	65	73	83	0	65
	farms	66	76	64	36	0	63
1946	holdings	67	61	65	50		64
	farms	73	47	42	40		62
1958	holdings	51	52	62	40		51
	farms	57	56	43	21	0	51
1968	holdings	50	53	60	42		52
	farms	58	55	46	38	0	53

SOURCE: Family biographies.
Sample: Resident landowning/using property groups.

Table 21 shows the size of holdings and farms belonging to property groups with a single adult male. The figures are the percentage of units in each size category that single-adult-male groups own or use. The balance in each case is owned/farmed by larger and more complex groups (Table 22). The table shows a consistent pattern of adjustment between family labor and available land. A relationship is evident even between the amount of land *owned* and the property

TABLE 22

PROPERTY GROUP SIZE AND COMPOSITION,
AND LAND USE, 1848–1968
(acres)

		Percent more than one adult male					Percent of total property groups
		.01–1.99	2–4.99	5–9.99	10–19.99	20 plus	
1848	holdings	0	4	25	57	83	52
	farms	60	25	50	72	100	59
1884	holdings	29	50	40	78	50	47
	farms	33	43	43	70	100	47
1898	holdings	41	58	50	46	25	47
	farms	42	67	55	60	0	46
1910	holdings	46	38	21	40	80	38
	farms	31	33	41	53	67	38
1922	holdings	23	20	42	83	100	40
	farms	21	23	48	100	100	41
1934	holdings	35	35	27	17	100	35
	farms	34	24	36	64	100	37
1946	holdings	33	39	35	50		36
	farms	27	53	48	60		38
1958	holdings	49	48	62	60		49
	farms	43	44	57	79	100	49
1968	holdings	50	47	40	58		48
	farms	42	45	54	62	100	47

SOURCE: Family biographies.
Sample: Resident landowning/using property groups.

groups' size and composition. With only three exceptions (two in 1898 and one in 1934) single-adult-male groups had less than their percentage (right-hand column) of holdings ten acres and larger in size. From 1848 through 1968, except for three cases, the smaller property groups were consistently underrepresented in the two largest categories and over represented in the rest. Table 22 illustrates the reverse, that is, with the same exceptions the larger property groups owned more than their "share" of the larger holdings and fewer of the smaller ones. This suggests that division of the groups' land and a change in family organization might itself be a type of adjustment to existing resources and new opportunities, a possibility that is explored in Chapter 6.

An even closer relationship exists between the size of farms and the composition of the cultivating group. Reading Tables 21 and 22 for farms shows only one deviation from the relationship between property groups size and land use. Except in 1898 in the 20 acres plus category, single-adult-male groups always farmed less than their percentage of operating units ten acres and more because of a shortage of family labor. After 1898, probably because of the intensification of cultivation, groups in the 5–9.99 class even found it necessary to lease out land more frequently. Reading the tables another way underscores the consistent pattern of adjustment. Comparing the percentage of holdings to farms in each size category for each year (45 pairs in each table) shows that single-adult-male groups generally farm less land than they own (27 pairs to 14, inapplicable in 4 cases). The fact that six of the exceptions to the pattern occur among the smallest class of holdings, and five more in the range 2–4.99 acres just confirms the relationship. Conversely, larger property groups generally farmed more land than they owned (30 pairs to 14, one inapplicable case) with the exceptions occurring primarily (10 pairs) among owners of units smaller than five acres who apparently found their holdings so small that they rented them out and looked to other sources of income.

The amount of land rented out by different types of groups confirms the relationship between family labor and the use of land owned by the group. In all reference years there was a direct relationship between group size and composition, and the amount of land put out to rent (Table 23). Unfortunately, Table 23 can only

TABLE 23

PROPERTY-GROUP SIZE AND COMPOSITION, AND THE
AMOUNT OF LAND PUT OUT ON RENT, 1848–1968

	Percent of different size holdings rented out by property groups with a single adult male				
	.01–1.99	2–4.99	5–9.99	10–19.99	20 plus
1848	36	0	40	0	100
1884	71	0	75	100	0
1898	37	40	69	100	
1910	46	63	55	75	
1922	39	53	80	33	
1934	53	76	78	100	0
1946	69	87	64	100	
1958	50	45	75		
1968	54	49	76		

SOURCE: Family biographies.
Sample: All resident and nonresident landowners.

be taken as a general reflection of actual arrangements. It does not take into account that some groups rented as much land of others as they leased out of their own, a mechanism used to exchange inconveniently located pieces of land for fields near the bulk of one's holding. But I believe that the pattern expressed in the table is substantially correct. Groups with only one male account for an increasing share of the renters as the amount of land involved increases since they did not have family labor enough to cultivate the entire holding.

Another means of adjusting the amount of labor in the family to land available to the property group was migration. Adult males who could not be accommodated satisfactorily on the family holding or secure additional acreage to cultivate by sharecropping or rent, and who could not find suitable work outside of agriculture in or near the village, often migrated to find productive employment elsewhere. Throughout the period men from groups owning more than ten acres clearly migrated with less frequency than others. The other interesting feature brought out by Table 24 is that men from families with middle range holdings (5 to 10 acres) left Vilyatpur in almost the same proportion as those who owned less than five acres, or who

TABLE 24

MIGRATION AND LAND OWNERSHIP, 1848–1968

	Landless	.01–1.99	2–4.99	5–9.99	10–19.99	20 plus
	Percent of adult males in property groups with different size holdings who have migrated					
1848	4	0	0	14	0	0
1884	14	0	19	11	7	0
1898	22	23	14	18	5	0
1910	15	23	21	30	13	4
1922	29	30	33	17	0	4
1934	28	25	40	18	19	0
1946	33	30	25	29	0	
1958	22	25	30	26	9	
1968	27	26	32	24	9	0

SOURCE: Family biographies.
Sample: All resident and nonresident adult males.

were landless. The finding is important, and will be taken up in some detail in the next chapter which discusses migration, new occupations, and the use of wealth earned outside Vilyatpur.

Family Farming and Change in Agriculture

Agriculture was the most important economic activity in Vilyatpur from 1848 to 1968. Until 1958, when a measure of industrial development in the area began to attract some village residents, over 70 percent of the working men were directly engaged in farming as owner cultivators, tenants, and laborers even though the population of the community more than doubled in size. Agriculture not only *absorbed* these additional laborers and *supported* a rapidly growing population, but for several reasons it remained a valued occupation. As in most rural areas around the world, farmers considered working the land a respectable and wholesome vocation—the Jats deem ability in cultivation a sign of manliness. Membership in village society was also an important consideration. But rural Punjabis respect other occupations and money earned from other types of work—particularly in the form of salaries that come regularly every month—has its own attraction. Agriculture retained its attraction because, by all indications, it yielded a rising standard of living to the landowners in Vilyatpur. Improvements in transportation and marketing facilities after the 1860's raised the value of village produce, and Vilyatpur residents purchased additional equipment—bullock carts and sugarcane presses—to take advantage of the developments in public works. From the mid-1890's through the mid-1920's, the village experienced a decline in population due to the combined effects of epidemic disease and migration overseas and to the canal colonies—factors which eased pressure on agricultural resources. Just prior to the renewed expansion of the population, higher yielding varieties of common village crops (a product of the Department of Agriculture's research efforts) were introduced. Since the 1920's the gains from the use of improved types of wheat and sugarcane, and from an increase in double cropping alone, added enough to the village's total production to keep abreast of population growth. The increment from improved irrigation facilities, dating from the thirties, and the more intensive cultivation of existing acreage through the use of additional labor were also substantial, although I have no way of estimating their exact magnitude. They were certainly sufficient to make agriculture a profitable as well as a prestigious occupation.

Numerous indicators point to the increasingly important role of the market as a mechanism for allocating resources in village agriculture since British annexation. In the Sikh period the government tax was paid in cash, and Vilyatpur cultivators were accustomed to marketing wheat and *gur,* although in small quantities. In spite of the monetization and the practice of selling at least some of the year's surplus production, in 1848 custom and not the market regulated economic life in the village. After annexation, the development first of the roads and railroads and then of the canal colonies brought an increased integration of the village into the economy of the province. The rise in the value of land in Vilyatpur, following the creation of a private marketable right in land, is just one indication of this integration. The development of public works, particularly the canal colonies, created new occupational opportunities in the Punjab, stimulating both short- and long-term migration.

The first indications of a decline in the role of custom in the governing of economic relations came only at the turn of the century. Two disputes over the right of the Sahotas to control the labor of all village residents and set the prices for all goods and services indicate substantial changes. After 1920, following a second large migration of cultivators and laborers to the canal colonies, the organization and compensation of agricultural labor began a dramatic change, which has continued to this day. Two factors contributed to the change from "custom-bound" to "market-related" labor relationships. Expanded opportunities, including many that made short-term migration attractive, gave agricultural laborers an alternative to year-round dependence on Vilyatpur landowners. Of equal importance were the many changes in village agriculture which necessitated an increased involvement in the commercial economy of the province. Sugarcane presses and bullock carts, both of which were purchased in increased numbers in the late nineteenth century, were never made in the village and could therefore not be "bought" like other agricultural implements from the *sepidar*-carpenter in exchange for part of the year's produce. New seed varieties also had to be bought for cash outside the village, and changes in irrigation technology (such as the Persian wheel and the power driven pumps which came later) all were brought from market towns. Changes in consumption also increased participation in the regional economy. The slow but steady growth in the number of brick houses necessitated purchases of bricks and mortar from a kiln started in the late 1890's near the *tehsil* headquarters. These developments were marked changes. Expanding occupational opportunities for the residents of the village and their increased participation in market towns as *buyers* (they had always been sellers) made the market a more important factor in allocating resources in Vilyatpur. Although the change was very gradual, taking perhaps fifty years, it was dramatic, and has accelerated since the First World War.

The organization of the family farm has been the principle factor determining the nature and extent of change in agriculture, accounting for the slow rate and limits of the process of transformation. Focusing on the family farm makes comprehensible the behavior of villagers with regard to tenancy, mortgages, and sales, as noticed in the literature on the Punjab. There was no permanent group of *rentiers* and leasees in Vilyatpur. Tenancy was just one means used to adjust the supply of family labor to the amount of land owned. Given the cyclical character of this process over time, much of the concern for the evils of tenant cultivation (carelessness, lack of investments, and no concern for the long-term productivity of the soil, etc.), appears irrelevant for villages like Vilyatpur. Sales and mortgages were very frequent because they were part of a credit-investment system of providing money for important occasions and emergencies. I think that much of the fragmentation of holdings in Vilyatpur was a product of the large number of sales rather than the system of inheritance. But as long as no form of heavy investment in the land was practical, it is doubtful that the fragmentation retarded productivity. The existence of numerous shareholders did not prevent the construction and use of brick irrigation wells before 1848 and throughout the nineteenth century. Since irrigation by flooding requires that the fields be divided and worked in small units which could be leveled, the size of individual plots had no important consequences beyond the inconvenience of carrying equipment from one place to another.[91] It is only the possibility of using power driven wells that seems to require consolidation and individual investment. The Punjab Government consolidated holdings in the province beginning in 1936 in an effort to eliminate what was seen as one of the principal causes of rural poverty and indebtedness.[92] Holdings in Vilyatpur were consolidated twice, once in 1938 and again in 1962. Little trace of the first consolidation remained ten years later. But the installation of numerous pumping sets following the second consolidation seems to have impeded fractionalization. But there has not been any increase in the area available for cultivation—one of the supposed benefits of consolidation achieved through the elimination of so many pathways leading to the numerous small plots—because the construction of the wells also stimulated the construction of sheds for animals (and, in three cases, of houses in the middle of the fields), leading to a decline in the total cultivated area of the village.

I feel that the concept of the family farm also sheds light on why certain changes have occurred without much difficulty, while other transformations which might be expected with the growth of the market's influence have been slower to occur. Agriculture is always difficult to study because it is impossible to separate agriculture as

[91] See B. H. Farmer, "On Not Controlling Subdivision in Paddy Lands," *Transactions and Papers,* Institute of British Geographers, 1960, 225–235.

[92] Government efforts to consolidate holdings in the Punjab date from the Co-operative Societies Act, 1904 which provided official supervision for voluntary consolidation. Little progress was achieved, however, until 1936 when the Punjab Consolidation of Holdings Act was passed allowing government compulsion in the consolidation of holdings. Darling, *Punjab Peasant,* 252.

a profession from agriculture as a way of life, and distinguish the economics of the farm from the domestic economy of the farmer and his family except in large-scale specialized farms found in some parts of the United States. The family farm typifies this lack of separation in its most extreme form. Village cultivators make no effort to distinguish the income from their profession from the expenses of running a household.[93] The very accounting system used by the Sahotas to reckon their "profits" illustrates the nature and logic of the family farm. The records and accounting system that was followed for a long time and is still used in most cases, can best be understood in terms of a hypothetical iron chest.[94] After the harvest, when the reapers and threshers have been paid in grain (or, in the past, after the *sepidars* received their dues) and enough grain has been put away for family consumption for the six months until the next harvest, the balance is sold and the cash placed in the chest. Incidental expenses for the next six months—money for a trip, a lawyer's fee, school books, a day laborer's pay—is taken from the chest. Cash is never spent lightly; only important items deserve the expenditure of money. Tea, vegetables, and other necessities are generally acquired by exchanging some of the grain stored for consumption at the village shop or with an itinerant salesman. At the end of six months, the money left in the iron chest is considered the "profit" from that season, and, together with that left after the second harvest, constitutes the property group's "income" for the year. Well-to-do families are distinguished by having cash in the chest at the end of season. By being able to refrain from selling all of the surplus production just at the time of the harvest, they can hold some back for a better price. Cash accumulated can then be invested in mortgages or purchases of land or jewelry. This system of accounting renders it almost impossible to determine accurately either gross production costs or net profits.[95] Most labor is contributed by family members in un-

[93] For this discussion I am heavily indebted to A. V. Chayanov, *The Theory of Peasant Economy*, Daniel Thorner, Basile Kerblay, and R. E. F. Smith (eds.) (Homewood, Illinois: American Economics Association, 1966) for ideas and inspiration, although I have made no effort rigorously to follow or test Chayanov's theory.

[94] Most villagers use an iron strong box for storing cash and valuables. The iron chest system, however, refers to the cluster of values and practices for allocating family resources and determining profits rather than the container itself.

[95] These are the features Neale emphasizes when he argues that the very organization of village agriculture renders conventional survey techniques useless. Neale, *Limitations of Survey Data*, 293.

measured amounts—a problem in cost-accounting with all farmers—and nonfamily labor is paid before the total production is ever counted. Food for the family is deducted from the remaining produce before "profits" are determined. But while the iron chest system might distract an economist, it has an internal logic which accounts for many of the characteristics of family farming.

Along with the complex of values attached to family farming—to acquire land in the village whenever possible and sell it only if absolutely necessary, to provide work and sustenance for all members of the group on the family's holding if possible, to minimize dependence on outside labor, and the view of agriculture as a way of life over an extended period and not just from one year to the next—the system of determining the profitability of each season has certain consequences. It facilitates some types of technological change and renders others more difficult. Because of the emphasis on providing foodstuffs for the family and for sale, and fodder for its livestock, family farming is biased in favor of polyculture (rather than the cultivation of the single most profitable crop in the economist sense of market value less cost of all inputs). Crops that can be both consumed and marketed like wheat and sugarcane, are clearly preferred.[96] Since they are easily marketable and valued for consumption they allow the cultivator to store and use surpluses when the market is bad. Polyculture has the advantage, as many have pointed out, of diversifying risks of crop failure, an important consideration where rainfall is unpredictable and irrigation impossible, but not much of a factor in areas like Vilyatpur.

The practice of minimizing cash outlays has other consequences for the selection of crops. It favors changes that require little or non-repetitive cash expenditures and complicates those requiring the continual purchases of inputs. Seed is an excellent illustration of the type of change that "fits" with the iron chest system. Village cultivators have long been sensitive to the importance of good seed and to the purchase of new varieties which were then propagated in the village to be used year after year. The development of higher yielding varieties by the Department of Agriculture was followed quickly by their adoption, since they could be purchased once and used repeatedly. Except for hybrid maize developed in the 1950's (which as a

---

[96] Smith observes this tendency among Japanese peasants who well into the 1950's continued to devote part of their acreage to rice. Thomas C. Smith, *The Agrarian Origins of Modern Japan* (Stanford University Press, 1959), 207–208.

hybrid requires fresh seed every year), the improved varieties of wheat and sugarcane, including the Mexican wheat, can be reused for a number of years before a decline in yield occurs. It is no co-incidence that all of the acreage sown to wheat and sugarcane in 1968 was under improved varieties while hybrid maize accounted for less than 20 percent of the corn grown. Even additions to the stock of agricultural appliances and improvements in irrigation facilities, though requiring cash payments to nonvillage artisans and merchants and bringing the cultivator increasingly into the provincial economy as a buyer, did not conflict with the iron chest system since repetitive expenditure was unnecessary. The regular purchase and use of chem-ical fertilizers, a common practice since the late 1950's, represents a significant change, since an annual outlay of cash is necessary for every crop. Power driven wells, starting with Partap Singh's diesel engine in 1944 and growing slowly in numbers until very recently, when many more were constructed, also departs from the iron chest system in its pure form (given the amount of the initial expenditure and the need for constant payments for fuel).

The system of accounting also favors the maximization of per-capita output for family labor rather than the maximization of profits per acre. Land is often purchased and leased at rates that exceed its productive value in strictly economic terms. This occurs since in-creased production that uses available family labor is valued even if the cost of that additional output is very high.[97] Sharecropping, generally seen as indicative of a lack of development in contrast to cash rents, fits into the system nicely providing an increment to the total production for both lessor and lessee.[98] Cultivators in Vilyatpur consider sharecropping a preferable form of rent because it provides an opportunity for the landowner to enter into the management of the land by sharing in the provision of inputs, and encouraging care-ful cultivation.[99] Cash rents are usual, either when the landowner

[97] For a similar phenomenon in the construction of terraces for rice cultivation in the hills of Burma see Edmund Leach, The Political Systems of Highland Burma (Boston: Beacon Press, 1954), 27–28.

[98] For a reexamination of the significance of sharecropping in areas like Vilyat-pur, see C. H. Hanumantha Rao, "Uncertainty, Entrepreneurship, and Share-cropping in India," Journal of Political Economy, LXXIX (1971), 578–595. Rao finds that sharecropping exists in areas of relative economic certainty where there is little scope for entrepreneurial decision making.

[99] For an economist who takes this view see Morton Paglin, "Surplus Agricul-tural Labor and Development—Facts and Theories: Reply," American Economic Review, LVII (1967), 204.

cannot supervise cultivation or is not interested in bothering. Since more than 90 percent of all rented land has always been cultivated by other landowning property groups, this increment represents another means to adjust profitably (in the villager's sense) the supply of family labor to its own holding.

The iron chest system of accounting which is at least substantively logical, explains much behavior of village cultivators regarding agriculture. But the amount of land owned and the size of property group is the predominant factor which governs the cultivator's seeking of opportunities to adjust labor to resources. Three different means were open to village residents for making the adjustment: the division of the holding and change in family organization, renting land, and migration from the village. But there was no automatic mechanism that determined which of these choices were followed by particular families at a given moment in time. Individuals and families confronted a series of alternative and basically rational means of providing for a living at a standard deemed adequate. The choice made was influenced by a combination of the perception of the opportunities, the values on keeping the family together, and achievement vis-à-vis the local community. In the next chapter the opportunities outside agriculture will be explored, revealing the basis for a change in some of the values paralleling the departures from the iron chest system of accounting associated with the use of chemical fertilizers and power driven pumping sets in Vilyatpur.

Chapter V

ECONOMIC CHANGE, 1848–1968:
NEW OPPORTUNITIES AND THE USE
OF NEW INCOMES

So far we have discussed the developments in agriculture that added to total village production, and the ways in which property groups farmed and used agriculture as a means for adjusting the supply of family labor to the group's resources. The alternatives open to Vilyatpur residents were not limited to farming, renting, buying, and selling land. Other possibilities for productive employment existed for landowners and landless alike. As the construction of public works contributed to the development of agriculture, growth in agriculture and public works together brought an increase in the number and types of occupational opportunities in rural Punjab. Like other changes in agriculture, the expansion was slow but had an incremental effect on the economy of the village and the province. During the period studied, the economic developments yielded several changes: One, a mild shift in village occupational structure, even though it is still an almost totally agricultural community; another, the decline of the village as a discrete economic unit where a sizable portion of residents work. The change parallels the "liberation" of agricultural laborers noted in Chapter IV. The complex of social, religious, political, and economic ties that characterized village society in 1848 gradually disappears, pointing to the growing importance of the market as an allocative mechanism. Another development is the movement of village residents and emigrants into jobs requiring higher levels of skills and investment.

The emphasis on the growth of new occupations in modern India has centered on urban jobs for the graduates of the schools and colleges that increased in the nineteenth century.[1] A few men from

---

[1] See B. B. Misra, *The Indian Middle Classes* (Bombay: Oxford University Press, 1961), and Ellen MacDonald Gumperz "Social Change in Late Nineteenth Century Maharashtra: The Regional Perspective," paper presented at the Annual Meetings of the American Historical Association, December 1970. The new occupations of our concern are briefly described in D. H. Buchanan, *The Development of Capitalistic Enterprise in India* (New York: Macmillan, 1934), 75–97.

Vilyatpur followed this pattern in the twentieth century, becoming government officials and clerks, railroad employees, school teachers, a newspaper editor, an engineer, and employees of large urban business firms. But jobs requiring little education have been the more important source of employment outside agriculture for Vilyatpur residents and emigrants, both Sahota landowners, and others. New types of work (industrial labor, truck driving, construction, and the like) and modifications of existing trades (carpentry, tailoring, and handloom and powerloom weaving) provided them with new opportunities.

Among the Sahotas, new and modified occupations provided alternative means to adjust the supply of family labor to resources. In some instances these opportunities even provided sources of wealth for investment in additional land, new inputs, and improved housing in the village. The biggest source of new wealth was income from overseas migration. From the 1890's, when villagers started to emigrate to foreign countries, one of their principal goals has been the acquisition of wealth to purchase land in Vilyatpur and, more recently, new inputs like power-driven wells. Most migrants were drawn from property groups with several adult males that had recently experienced a substantial reduction in the amount of inherited land because of the large number of coparceners. Migration was a means of reversing the downward trend in a family's fortunes and raising the position of the property group in the community by adding to its holdings. The goal of repatriating funds for the purchase of land in the village has given overseas migration from Vilyatpur a definite pattern and character.

The other property groups in the village have also benefited from the growth of new and modified occupations in rural Punjab, although with significant differences from the Sahotas. As landowners, the Sahotas were in a better position to muster the resources necessary for overseas travel. This factor explains why they always accounted for 95 percent of overseas migrants. When a Sahota left the village he retained his share in the land, could expect to be supplied with foodstuffs from the farm, and would provide cash for improvements in it. In contrast, the nonlanded had little more than a share in the house in common with the members of the property group remaining in the village—there was no focus for investment and no source of supply. The absence of land also meant that property-group members who left the village often became completely independent. For the nonlanded, new opportunities, therefore, have been important primarily as an outlet for individuals and groups not satisfied with prospects in the village. Even for them Vilyatpur remained a place with which to identify and to go in times of adversity.

Village Occupations

Looking at the broad outlines of the occupational structure of the village, little change is apparent from 1848 through 1934 (Table 25). A slight shift took place in the relative proportion of owner cultivators and agricultural laborers, but the two, together, were more or less constant, ranging from 73 to 79 percent of the total. If anything, there was a slight tendency for the relative number of male workers directly in agriculture to increase in comparison with other occupations. Yet, neither the increase in the percentage of agricultural laborers nor of those directly in agriculture was indicative of the so-called process of "ruralization" that resulted from the destruction of rural industries because of an inability to compete

TABLE 25

OCCUPATIONAL STRUCTURE, 1848–1968

(percent)

	Owner cultivator	Ag. labor (sepidar)	Ag. labor (wage)	General labor	Industrial labor	Manufacture (sepidar)	Manufacture (general)	Trade	Services	Professions
1848	63	10				3	10	3	9	5
1884	67	12				3	6	4	6	4
1898	65	13				2	8	4	5	4
1910	62	14				1	10	3	5	2
1922	65	14				3	12	3	3	2
1934	60	14	3			2	15	4	2	1
1946	56	1	16	...		2	16	4	4	1
1958	52	1	23	2	3	2	10	4	3	1
1968	44	...	20	3	9	2	11	5	2	2

SOURCE: Family biographies.
Sample: Resident adult males.

with the products of British factories in the nineteenth century. The increase followed established caste/occupational patterns. Villagers in that category, in 1934, were descendants of Chamar *sepidar*-laborers, and all but two were descendants of families that had been in the village in 1848. The increase in agricultural labor was largely at the expense of "services" and "professions," which fell from a combined total of 14 percent in 1848 to 3 percent in 1934. In part, the decline was real, since the Drummer and Dyers either left the village or died out before 1884, and the number of Brahmins collecting *birt* (an annual share of the crops in return for religious services) fell sharply after the 1903 plague epidemic. But the decrease also reflects that the number of Water-carriers, Barbers, and Sweepers who stayed in the village remained constant, even though the population and the work force grew. The numbers and proportion engaged in rural handicraft production (handloom weavers, potters, and, from 1934, two full-time leatherworkers) grew after 1884.

Within the apparent stability of the period 1848 to 1934, some rather dramatic changes occurred that do not appear either in the table or the census because of the categories employed. To catch these changes, the system of classification must include the basis of compensation and conditions of work as well as the type of work. An example of this kind of transformation has already been discussed in the account of the shift of agricultural laborers from the *sepidar* system, through a kind of transitional phase based on yearly agreements, to the daily cash piece-work system now in vogue. The census misses this transition, lumping it into "agricultural labor." A similar distinction is necessary for the category "manufacturing (general)" in Table 25. The account of the village in 1848 showed a difference between craftsmen like the carpenters who received an annual share of the crop in return for fabricating and repairing the tools for patrons as part of the *sepidar* system, and the weavers and potters, who, though paid in grain at rates that had been constant for some time, were compensated by the piece. They worked for anyone in need of their products, and were not part of the system of ritual duties and exchanges associated with the *sepidars*. After 1910, a number of developments necessitate a further distinction.

The handloom weavers experienced the most dramatic transformation in the organization of work after 1910. The weavers continued to function as they had in 1848 until the turn of the cen-

tury, when the Sahotas attempted to force a reduction in the rate
of compensation (reportedly because they felt the weavers were doing too well). This resulted, as with the Chamars a little earlier, in
the intervention of the Honorary Magistrate. Once the dispute was
resolved, the weavers of the village were free to charge whatever
they felt was appropriate and to take as much work from outside the
village as they liked. This served as a kind of transitional phase
similar to the one that occurred in agricultural labor. About 1945,
a weaver, Prem Singh, found that a merchant in Amritsar (a major
city about 65 miles away) would take as many *khes* (a course 4′ x 6′
cloth used as a wrap and as a part of bedding) as he could produce.
Prem Singh went into production and now has six looms operated
by family members and some young men from the village, who are
paid on a piece work basis. Every three to four days he takes the
completed *khes* on cycle to the railway station six miles away to
ship them to Amritsar. Prem Singh popularized the *japani* (fly-
shuttle) loom in Vilyatpur. The fly-shuttle loom had been introduced
into the Punjab by the Department of Industries about the time
of the First World War but it made little progress in replacing the
old throw-shuttle loom used in the village.[2] The opening up of a
new market with an emphasis on speed, single item production, and
volume, brought a rapid changeover from the old throw-shuttle to
the fly-shuttle loom, which doubled a man's daily production.

All Julahas still working as weavers have followed Prem Singh's
lead and now specialize in particular items that can be wholesaled
in urban markets. Most produce *khes* for the same merchant in
Amritsar, but a few weave on commission for the Khadi Bhavan, a
government-sponsored marketing co-operative, organized to encour-
age handloom weaving. Two Julahas earn a living as retailers of
handwoven and mill-made cloth, which they sell by traveling on
cycles from village to village. As a side line, they purchase handspun
thread for sale to Vilyatpur's weavers, who use it for the woof in
the *khes*. Machine-made thread purchased in the city forms the
warp. Some Sahota housewives also sell surplus thread to the weavers.
The rest of the thread is given to some of the Chamars, who now do
all custom weaving formerly done by the Julahas, for payment in

[2] Punjab Census, 1921, I, 368–369. A survey conducted in 1926 revealed that
less than 2 percent of the looms operating in Punjab were improved *japani*
types. *Bulletin of the Joint Development Board, Punjab*, n.p., n.d., (1925), 40.

cash and grain. In all respects, handloom weaving in Vilyatpur as it has existed since 1946 (with specialized production for sale in the city and the village simply a place where the weavers live and work) is a far cry from its nineteenth century predecessor.

The carpenters' mode of operation has also changed, although not to the same extent because the process of transformation has been very gradual. In 1848, the bulk of the carpenters' work and income came through their *sepidar* relationships. However, in addition they received small amounts for special jobs: the construction of doorframes and furniture, for instance. After 1900, when the first brick house was built income from special tasks began to increase relative to that from the *sepidar* relationship with the cultivators. Most brick houses, which grew steadily in number, were built by two brothers, who were *sepidar* carpenters and the fathers of two of the Carpenters now in the village. While carpenters earned more and more from special jobs, there was a decreasing demand for the implements that they used to make from materials supplied by their patrons. The new implements, which grew in numbers and use in the late nineteenth and early twentieth centuries were iron sugarcane presses, bullock carts, the iron tip for the old wooden plow, and the iron Persian wheel. All came from the city where they were fabricated in workshops specializing in particular items. Village cultivators had to obtain some of their implements from the city, and so were in town more frequently to purchase them and to sell growing surpluses. This led to the practice of buying all implements in town, even the ones that could still be produced in the village. By the 1930's the carpenter's role had changed from fabricator repairman to installer repairman. He would, for instance, make the wooden parts for the plows and then fit the iron tip the cultivator had brought from the city. Or he would supervise the installation of the Persian wheel after supplying the wooden parts.

The Carpenters in Vilyatpur continued to work as maintenance men through the *sepidar* system (doing a substantial amount of housing construction on the side) until 1957 when the village was electrified. Then two Carpenters, the cousins Darshan Singh and Pritim Singh, who separated after their fathers' deaths, bought electrically powered flour mills. Until the 1920's all flour used for making *chapattis* (the flat, unleavened bread of wheat, millet, or corn that is the staple of the Punjabi diet) was ground at home in a

stone hand mill—a long, tiring, laborious task. In the 1920's Darshan
Singh's grandfather installed a bullock-driven mill, which displaced
most handmills. The new electric mills quickly rendered all predecessors obsolete. The two Carpenters ground all the flour for Vilyatpur
and at least two nearby villages, in return for either a percentage of
the grain processed or cash payment. Both men also installed small
cotton gins for cleaning cotton grown in the village for domestic
consumption. In addition, Darshan Singh bought a large bandsaw
(for cutting trees into rafters for houses), a circular saw, and a wood
lathe. In the early 1960's he also acquired a welding set so that he
can make repairs on the iron implements used in increasing numbers, and a "second-hand" tractor (which he keeps running as only
a Punjabi mechanic can) that he uses with a thresher to do custom
work on a commission basis and to haul produce to market. Darshan
Singh continues to collect grain from about half of the Sahota
property groups in Vilyatpur. For repairing implements, however,
he now gets a fixed amount rather than a percentage of the crop.
He receives a cash payment for the installation of new equipment.
Pritim Singh concentrates on the operation of his mill and gin. One
carpenter has started coming to the village from a neighboring community to do repair work. About half of his trade is paid for with
semi-annual grain payments. For the other half, a growing number
of village cultivators (about one-fourth of the total), who no longer
have a permanent relationship with any carpenter, compensate him
by the job. They prefer to handle simple repairs themselves—a new
departure—and pay for help only when necessary.

The emergence of full-time leatherworkers in Vilyatpur provides
still another variation in the pattern of change within the category
of general manufacture. While the *sepidar* system for agricultural
labor was still intact, all Chamars made shoes, whips, and other
leather goods for their patrons as part of their duties. With the
change to yearly agreements in the 1920's, this practice began to
decline. Some Chamars continued to supply leather goods, but
others did not. This change created a demand for shoes which was
in part met by purchasing in the city, and also led two Chamars to
take to shoe manufacture in the village on a full-time basis. The
full-time production of leather goods received further stimulus
when, with the disappearance of the *sepidar* system, the Chamars
doing agricultural labor, stopped making any leather goods at all,

a task which they feel, along with *begar* (forced labor), epitomizes their low status. The Chamars engaged in the full-time manufacture of shoes are aware that the performance of their "traditional" occupation carried a stigma, but they find the shoe business profitable enough to compensate for it. Indeed, the most important and influential man in the Chamar *basta* is a full-time cobbler.

The experiences of the weavers, carpenters, and leatherworkers indicate that, despite the stability of the occupational structure through 1934, several important changes occurred, dating from the 1920's. In general, the movement was from economic relations embedded in a complex of social, political, and ritual ties, and a system of compensation governed by customary and complicated exchanges for tasks that were diversified, to those involving an isolated exchange paid for upon completion without any other duties attached. An increase in the number of residents working outside the community (part-time and full-time) was part of the transformation. In 1848 only the weavers and the potters did business in neighboring villages and in Vilyatpur (Table 26). From 1910 through 1934 an increasingly larger percentage of the work force worked outside the village, with a slight decrease in 1922 at the time of migration to

TABLE 26

RESIDENT MALES WORKING OUTSIDE VILYATPUR, 1848–1968
(full-time and part-time)

	Ag. labor (wage)	General labor	Industrial labor	Manufacture (sepidar)	Manufacture (general)	Trade	Services	Professions	Percent of total resident male workers
1848					20			1	11
1884				3	10		3		7
1898				2	15	2			12
1910				6	21	4			16
1922				4	28	4			14
1934	8			3	36	3			17
1946	19	1		7	44	5		2	28
1958	49	7	9	8	35	5		3	35
1968	56	12	36	4	44	9	1	9	43

SOURCE: Family biographies.
Sample: Resident adult males working outside the village.

the canal colonies. An increase in the number of weavers and potters, and the addition of some tailors and several peddlers, accounted for the change.

The developments in the period from 1910 to 1934 are important as transitions and indicators of things to come. A significant shift in the proportion of owner cultivators to the rest of the work force started in 1946, and the decline in the percentage engaged directly in agriculture dates from 1958 (Table 25). Their place has been taken by the growth in the categories of general and industrial labor, work unknown among Vilyatpur residents until the early 1950's. Industrial and general labor have drawn off some villagers previously engaged in agriculture, not only as a percentage of the work force, but in terms of specific individuals as well. Half of the factory and general laborers in 1968 are from property groups of Chamars who had worked as agricultural laborers; one-fourth come from landowning Sahota groups; and slightly less than a fifth represent two property groups of Nais who have farmed as tenants in Vilyatpur for more than one hundred years. Accompanying the shift in the occupational structure, there has been a rapid growth in the number and percentage of resident males working outside of Vilyatpur. Because there are no factories in the village all industrial and general laborers must commute to other places. Agricultural laborers work in Vilyatpur and in neighboring villages, and weavers who produce their wares in the village but commute to purchase inputs and market the final product, form a large part of this group (Table 26).

An indication of the extent of change in outlook and attitudes in the process of occupational differentiation, the disappearance of complex ties associated with economic activity, and the decline of the village as a meaningful economic unit even as a place to work, is the large number of men who have made several changes in occupation in the twentieth century. We will come to the question of migration later. Here, the number of men who *returned* to the village after working outside for a number of years is the important point. More than half of the Weavers, in 1914, joined the army as mechanics and metal workers and, after their service, returned to the village. Later, many of their sons worked for a number of years in textile mills and powerloom workshops in various cities of the Punjab, and then came back to Vilyatpur. The sons returned because the cost of living was much lower in the village, which means that the amount they earn in Vilyatpur is competitive with urban wages. One Barber has worked as a tenant farmer in the village, as a watchman in a factory nearby, as a milkman going from village to village buying milk to sell in the city, and now as a lathe operator in a factory which makes ball bearings. A Chamar, who first did year-round agricultural labor, went to Assam, where he worked in road and bridge construction for four years, before he returned to Vilyatpur. He now lives in the village with his family during the wheat harvest, but leaves them to live and work at a brick kiln for much of the rest of the year. Behind the changes in Vilyatpur occupational structure and the trend toward an increasing number of residents living in the village and working elsewhere (43% in 1968) lies a great deal of experimentation on the part of individuals. On this level, change in occupation is not simply a single event in the life of the individual, but a continuous process requiring considerable flexibility. Migration, to which we will now direct our attention, is an important part of the process. It provides experience, wealth, and know-how. Those villagers who do come back to Vilyatpur seldom return to their former occupations.

Incountry and Overseas Migration

Chapter III dealt with the magnitude and timing of migration from Vilyatpur in some detail to show its role in the history of village population. Movement to other parts of Jullundur district occurred gradually over the years mainly by single individuals and families. Emigration from Vilyatpur to other districts in the province, elsewhere in India, and to foreign countries was characterized by group movements concentrated in particular periods. The movements started in the 1890's with the opening of the canal colonies in western Punjab and the beginning of overseas migration to Australia. The next group movement was to another canal colony in the 1920's, followed by the return of the colonists and their descendants at the time of Partition and Independence in 1947, and the departure of the Muslims from the village. A second large-scale movement overseas started in the mid-1950's, running about ten years, with most migrants going to England. Migration was an important

TABLE 27

OCCUPATIONS OF EMIGRANTS, 1848–1968

(adult males only)

	Owner cultivator	Ag. labor (wage)	General labor	Industrial labor	Manufacture (sepidar)	Manufacture (general)	Trade	Transportation	Services	Professions	Total
1848	8									1	9
1884	17				2		7	1		10	37
1898	14	7	22		1	2	6			6	58
1910	14	8	29	1	1		2			6	61
1922	22	18	28	2	3	2	7		1	14	97
1934	50	22	18	1	3	9	10		6	5	124
1946	52	30	17	4	3	15	9	4	3	15	152
1958	70	4	19	22		21	10	7	3	22	178
1968	65	3	16	44		19	5	19	3	23	197

SOURCE: Family biographies.
Sample: Adult males born in the village, living and working elsewhere.

factor in the growth of the village, particularly after 1920 when epidemic disease declined and disappeared.

Before examining the motives for the movement from the village and the goals of migration of particular individuals and property groups, we should look at a development which parallels changes in village occupational structure over time and can best be considered by looking at the migrants as a group. In the late nineteenth century almost three out of four adult males who emigrated from Vilyatpur, were employed in agriculture in their new homes as owner cultivators (24%), laborers (12%), and as unskilled laborers (38%). The canal colonies attracted most of those in agriculture; in Australia the migrants worked on sugarcane plantations, roads, railroads, and general construction.[3] More than half of the remaining migrants were working in well-established occupations requiring little change other than a shift from the village to a new location.

[3] D.G., 1904, 52; Kondapi, 193.

Occupations in which this kind of adaptation had been taking place for a very long time were *sepidar* carpenters, priests, traders, and animal-keeping transporters. By 1934 change in this nineteenth century pattern was evident. Seventy percent of the men living and working outside the village still fell into the categories of agriculture and general labor. But for the first time the number of owner culti-vators exceeded those in agricultural and unskilled labor. The others either learned new skills or invested in business. The professions, trade, and general manufacture—accounting for 14 percent of the total—included military service, businessmen in urban firms, power-loom operators, and a construction contractor. It was the beginning of a trend that continues to the present. By 1958 40 percent of the migrants were owner cultivators, and an equal proportion were in industrial labor, manufacturing, trade, and the professions. Over the last ten years there has been an acceleration in the trend toward skilled and investment-based occupations among the migrants, along with a sudden expansion in the number of men working in industry and transportation. Together they account for almost one-third of the men living and working outside Vilyatpur—about half in each category in England, and half in India. In 1968 less than one migrant in ten was employed as an agricultural laborer or unskilled worker.

Table 28 shows that migration has not been equally important for members of different caste groups in Vilyatpur, and that the place of migration varies from one caste group to another. Of the four largest groups (Jat, Chamar, Julaha, and Brahmin) overseas migra-tion has been most important to the landowning Jats. The percent-age of Sahotas born in Vilyatpur but living abroad exceeds that of all others.[4] The importance of the opening of the canal colonies to the Chamars is indicated by the sudden increase of migration in 1898 (just after the settlement of the first colony) and the sharp drop in the percentage living and working outside the village in 1958, the first reference year after Partition and Independence when most Chamars returned to Vilyatpur. For a low status group, the Weavers have demonstrated remarkable mobility with a consistently significant percentage of men outside the village; they represent the largest proportion working elsewhere in India of all of the major groups. Migration began comparatively late among the numerically

[4] Children born of parents living abroad are not included.

TABLE 28

CASTE AND PLACE OF MIGRATION, 1848–1968

		Jat	Chamar	Julaha	Brahmin	Nai	Chiir	Tarkhan	Faqir	Chuura	All castes
		Percent of caste group born in Vilyatpur living									
1848	Abroad										
	Punjab	4									2
	India	1									...
1884	Abroad										
	Punjab	9	2	10	10						12
	India										
1898	Abroad	7	2	1	6						6
	Punjab	7	27	15	24			14			10
	India	1									...
1910	Abroad	12	1	3							8
	Punjab	7	22	3	11						9
	India	1									...
1922	Abroad	10		9			38				7
	Punjab	8	38	17	37					25	16
	India	*		6			17			25	1
1934	Abroad	7									
	Punjab	16	35	10	60		10	30	15	20	20
	India	1		14					8	20	2
1946	Abroad	5					33				3
	Punjab	16	35	20	64	6	9	17	7	17	19
	India	4	1	9	7		9	17	13		4
1958	Abroad	8	...					5			4
	Punjab	16	9	23	23	16	8	13	23	11	15
	India	4	3	2	18	3	23	21	12		4
1968	Abroad	24	1								8
	Punjab	24	11	41	29	17	33	25	32	17	14
	India	7	1	7	18	4	9	50	16		4

SOURCE: Family biographies.
Sample: All resident and nonresident males.

small groups, the Nai, Chiir, Faqir and Chuura, whose members were primarily concentrated in the services. With the exception of the Chiirs, who entered the army in the First World War and migrated to Malaya after demobilization, these groups have found overseas migration impossible. For them in general, movement from the Punjab to other parts of India is a recent phenomenon, growing in importance primarily since Independence.

But caste groups are not the relevant level of village society for studying migration. While focusing on the different castes reveals the general trend, it cannot explain the motives for the movement from the village and the use of new incomes, particularly after 1934, when virtually all caste groups contributed migrants. Changes in village occupational structure and the kind of employment emigrants secured elsewhere render impossible any simple evaluation of the factors that "pushed or pulled" migrants. In 1898, when the migrants were few in number, the canal colonies and Australia the only locus, and agriculture and general labor the only employment for migrants, the caste-group level is sufficiently revealing. Afterwards, the focus must be the individual *khandans* and property groups.

The Stimulus to Migrate
and the Use of New Incomes

The importance of the differential growth of individual property groups as a stimulus for migration can be demonstrated by returning to the baseline families to show patterns of population expansion in Chapter III. The baseline family is an artificial unit. The total number of men in all of property groups descendant from an ancestor in the village in 1848, and the aggregate size of their holdings were never considerations in an individual group's decision to send a member from Vilyatpur in search of work. But these factors were so pervasive, and the situation of most groups in each baseline family so similar, that a definite pattern is evident at this level. The close relationship between the baseline families' history of growth and their experience in migration is evident in Table 29. I have separated the Jats from the other castes, not to stress caste as the significant variable (which it is not), but to isolate the baseline families owning land over extended periods of time from those that are either landless, have little land, or have only recently ac-

TABLE 29

MIGRATION PATTERNS OF BASELINE FAMILIES, 1848–1968

	Terminal	Straight line	Diamond	Slight pyramid	Rapid pyramid	Total
			Jats			
No migration	22	3	0	1	1	27
Incountry only	3	1	4	5	0	13
Abroad	1	0	1	7	13	22
			Others			
No migration	27	1	0	4	0	32
Incountry only	0	0	0	7	6	13
Abroad	0	1	3	1	4	9
			Total			
No migration	49	4	0	5	1	59
Incountry only	3	1	4	12	6	26
Abroad	1	1	4	8	17	31
Total	53	6	8	25	24	116

SOURCE: Family profiles.
Sample: All baseline families, resident and nonresident.

quired it. Since land provided a base for emigration, a common
point for continued membership in the property group, and a focus
for investment, the families with land over a number of generations
were in a different situation than the landless.

Migration among the Jats was a function of the size of the baseline family over time. Of the fourteen families with the rapid,
pyramid-type growth, all but one have sent members elsewhere in
India or overseas. Half of them have been providing migrants since
the 1890's, and seven of the baseline families account for nearly 80
percent of the Sahota migrants until 1946. The Jat families that
grew more slowly also show a high rate of migration, but illustrate
more of a tendency to confine their movements to India rather
than overseas. Settlement in the canal colonies accounts for the
migration of four of the five families in the gradual pyramid-type
that participated only in incountry migration. The relationship between migration, and the place of migration, and baseline family
growth pattern holds throughout the table for the Jats. The families
with a straight line history—one adult male in each generation—

migrated with much less frequency and never went abroad. The pattern holds for the nonlanded groups, although not with the same degree of uniformity. I attribute the difference to the absence of land as a link between property group members and Vilyatpur.

The behavior of individual property groups within each baseline family mirrors the distinctions between baseline families with different patterns of expansion. The baseline family of Dasonda Singh, an example of the rapid pyramid-type of growth, illustrates this well. In 1848 Dasonda Singh and at least three adult sons controlled the largest holding in the village. Possessing more than fifty acres of land, they were able to cultivate forty acres themselves because of the number of men in the family. But between 1848 and 1884 the group suffered a marked decline in fortune about which I could discover little beyond the fact that some of their holding was held in trust for a property group outside the village in 1848 which reverted to the owners on their return. Not only had the holding of the baseline family fallen from more than fifty acres to about eighteen, but there were now three property groups in the place of one, and nine males instead of four to be supported and employed. Mann and Jawara, two of Dasonda's sons, were still alive, forming two of the groups; the third group was composed of the three offspring of the other son who died before 1884. Each group owned about six acres of land. Mann Singh had only one son and therefore did not pursue the possibility of migrating either to the canal colonies or Australia, as it developed over the next ten years. But Mann's brother, Jawara, who had three sons, decided to send Naurang, the second son, a boy of about eighteen, to Australia in 1896 with the group of the first overseas migrants from Vilyatpur. Isher, one of Dasonda's three grandsons who formed the baseline family's third property group, went along with his uncle, although he was hardly fourteen years old at the time.

In the case of the Dasonda baseline family, two of the three property groups took advantage of developing opportunities because they had sufficient manpower left in the village to operate family holding and assure the continuity of the group even if the migrants failed to return. The third group was in a different situation—much like a baseline family that did not grow over a number of generations. Mann Singh had about the same size holding as the other two groups, but could not afford to send his only son from the village. Besides, with only a family of four, the holding provided a sufficient base to work from, allowing Mann Singh to select a different alternative. In 1898 Mann Singh cultivated his own land plus two acres on rent. By 1922, when his son, Gurdit, had grown up, they cultivated twenty acres, six of their own and fourteen on a rent and sharecrop basis.

Isher's stay in Australia was fruitful. When he returned in 1908 he had sufficient funds to take about eight acres on mortgage. By 1922 he had purchased six acres, which doubled his property group's holding. Naurang never returned to the village, remaining in Australia until his death many years later. He sent enough money through the government post office in the first ten years after his departure to put the property group into the mortgage market. His brother added three acres to the holding by 1922 and constructed a good-sized brick house in the village. Naurang also acquired some property in Australia during his long residence there. For a few years after his death his nephew received occasional remittances from his uncle's agent. The later generations in Dasonda's baseline family repeated the same pattern. Only one of Naurang's two brothers had a son, so there was no stimulus to migrate. But he in turn had five sons, two of whom went to England in the late 1950's. Isher had a son before his death, but neither of his brothers had a male offspring that survived them. Gurdit Singh, however, had five sons, three of whom now live in Vilyatpur and two in England.

Naurang Singh's life story shows why fewer people migrated, despite the financial advantages, and why migrants were drawn only from baseline families and property groups with an abundance of adult males. Until the migrations to England after 1947, most emigrants who traveled abroad never returned to Vilyatpur or India. Some, like Isher, did come back, but many died overseas. News of their deaths reached the village via other migrants from Vilyatpur. Thus, while the benefits to be derived from overseas migration were generally acknowledged, they were never sufficient to jeopardize the continuity of the family in the village. The emphasis on the family and the community had an important bearing on the motives and character of migration to foreign countries, and illustrates an important facet of rural society in the Punjab.

Although only individuals migrated, not whole property groups, it is the latter rather than the individual that is the focus of Punjabi society. This contrasts with the emphasis on the individual in contemporary Western society. An individual's status and position in the community depends not on his achievements or property (unless they are extraordinary), but on those of the group to which he belongs and on property groups to whom he was related. Migration of a member required the efforts of the whole property group. The resources needed to muster the finances were considerable. The cost of passage from India to Australia was about Rs. 200, an equivalent to the value of about three-fourths of an acre of village land in the 1890's. From the point of view of the villagers, Naurang Singh was successful only because he added to the group's holding and wealth in Vilyatpur. A man who emigrated without contributing later was a failure in the eyes of the community, no matter what he achieved for himself. This truth was brought home to me in the course of interviews when I inquired about the marital status of some men who lived abroad for long periods of time and who did not return to the village. With one exception these men were considered single and without heirs whether or not they had entered into some kind of union in their adopted country and produced children.

This does not mean that everyone who left Vilyatpur kept in touch and sent money. A number went abroad and were never heard of again. Examples of deviations from prevailing values are not hard to find. There was *pagal* (crazy) Pakhur. In the 1930's he dissipated his holding by playing the future's market,[5] sold two acres to buy a hand-driven carbonated water machine, and fled from the village with a girl from another Sahota family (thereby committing incest). He broke almost every convention considered important in the village. The motive of the groups who send a member overseas (families with rapid growth rates), was to augment the position of the property group by acquiring land in Vilyatpur through resources from abroad. Migration was a group effort, even in terms of the sacrifices made by the individual who left. Leaving Vilyatpur meant separation from family, community, and, in most cases, the impossibility of producing legitimate heirs. Given the values held in Punjabi society the cost to the migrant was high. His only return was achievement for his family. Though these

[5] D.G., 1904, 52.

values did not inhibit migration, they gave it a distinctive pattern.

That overseas migration paid off in general is apparent in Table 30. I omitted from the calculations all groups in baseline families that died out. Their share in the village property (which diminished over time) and the land either owned as common waste or devoted to residences (which expanded) account for the unexpressed portion of the land. The families that engaged in overseas migration were most numerous and owned 51 percent of the land in Vilyatpur in 1848. The initial figure for those who migrated only within India is depressed because three families living outside the village in 1848, who returned later to claim their land, fell in this group. The 1884 figure of 16 percent is probably the more accurate reference for following their development. Little change is apparent in the proportion of land held by the three classifications of baseline families until the beginning of migration in the late 1890's. The impact of money from Australia is evident by 1910 when the share of the families with members overseas began to increase, a trend which has continued, except during a decline in 1922 for which I have no explanation. The families with the other two types of migratory histories have almost identical patterns. They expanded slightly in the early part of the twentieth century as they acquired some of the land belonging to the twenty-seven Sahota baseline families that had died out, and then declined. There are several other developments that support the thesis that land acquisition is the goal of travel abroad, and illustrate the success of migrant's families in reversing the downward trend in the group's position

TABLE 30

ACQUISITION OF LAND BY BASELINE FAMILIES WITH DIFFERENT HISTORIES OF MIGRATION, 1848–1968

	1848	1884	1898	1910	1922	1934	1946	1958	1968
	Percent of land owned by baseline families with								
No migration	12	11	12	14	13	11	10	11	10
Incountry only	11	16	17	15	16	15	11	11	10
Abroad	51	50	52	60	56	62	64	69	71

SOURCE: Family profiles.
Sample: Resident and nonresident Jat property groups.

and holding. After 1910 more than 60 percent of the mortgages, involving 80 percent of the area mortgaged, was held by baseline families with members abroad or recently returned. All of the land purchased by residents of Vilyatpur in neighboring villages belongs to groups within these families as well. The group consisting of the two brothers, Partap Singh and Hardit Singh, made the first purchase of land in a contiguous village in 1914, after Hardit returned from Canada. In the last ten years several others have bought a total of forty-four acres in two adjacent villages with money from England.

The benefits of migration among the nonlanded have been less tangible but perhaps as important as the acquisition of land among the Jats. In a few cases the results have been dramatic. One Chamar who migrated to England in the late 1950's remitted enough money to purchase ten acres of land in another State. His family has now left Vilyatpur to work its own property. A Weaver and a Chamar who went to Australia were among the first in the village to construct brick houses, quite a distinction for their time. But achievement within the community does not hold the same importance for the other castes as for the Sahotas. A substantial portion of the nonlanded caste groups now live and work outside the village; they rarely return to Vilyatpur. But this is not to say that the village holds no importance for them. At the time of Partition all refugees from the canal colonies came directly to Vilyatpur, even though in some cases they or their families had not been in the community for over fifty years.

For the most part, however, migration—incountry and abroad— has been important for widening horizons, gaining familiarity with technological changes, and inducing transformations in some aspects of the organization of work, even when the migrants return to the village for good. Darshan Singh, the Carpenter, who owns a flour mill and tractor, worked for several years in Delhi as an office clerk. Then he returned to enter business using new equipment. He feels it was the experience he gained, rather than the money he earned, that was important in his transformation from the role of *sepidar*-carpenter to mechanic-food processor. Prem Singh's shift into full time production of *khes* came after he had worked five years as carpenter in Baluchistan and traveled around the Punjab doing different kinds of work. The Chamars date the final disappearance of the *sepidar* system from 1947. The Partition brought the return of Chamars in large numbers from the canal colonies with their long experience in wage and piece work.

The Decline of the Community as a Referent

Since the First World War the occupational structure of Vilyatpur has been undergoing a process of transformation. Until the mid-thirties the changes were primarily in the organization of work—the type and amount of payment and the relationship between worker and customer—rather than in the task itself. These changes, therefore, have not been recorded in the Census, which employs static categories, or by anthropologists and economists, who see the same groups who had dominated particular occupations before continuing to perform them in their altered form. For the weavers, carpenters, and leatherworkers, the changes meant a decline in the network of noneconomic ties between themselves and the Sahotas. The process was slow, with a distinctive course of simplification and differentiation in the case of each occupation. As opportunities expanded the proportion of men living in the village but working elsewhere grew slowly. The results are a decline in the community as a discrete economic unit and as a place of work for the residents, both developments with many sociological ramifications. From the First World War to the mid-thirties change was slow, but significant when contrasted with the nineteenth century economic and social organization. These dramatic developments form the subject of most of Malcolm Lyall Darling's books on the Punjab.[6]

The developments since the 1940's modified agriculture's dominance of the village economy. In one sense there is little change. A majority of men in Vilyatpur still depend upon agriculture for their livelihood. But work in agriculture, and the distribution of surplus to laborers and servants, is no longer the core of the social and political organization of the community as it had been in 1848. Agricultural laborers work in neighboring villages, find off-season work all over the Punjab; opportunities in manufacturing and industry, furthermore, provide alternative forms of employment and

[6] Darling, *Punjab Peasant; Wisdom and Waste in the Punjab Village* (New York: Oxford University Press, 1934); *Rusticus Loquitur* or *The Old Light and the New in the Punjab Village* (New York: Oxford University Press, 1929).

wealth for many who continue to live in the community. Future development will most likely continue along this line, rather than that of the migration of workers in industry, manufacturing, and transportation, to the cities. The ambitious development of paved village roads now taking place in the Punjab, will facilitate the growth of this semiurbanized rural pattern.[7]

Migration, incountry and abroad, has been common in Vilyatpur since the end of the nineteenth century. After the founding of the village, Sahotas have never migrated as whole families or property groups. Migration has been one of the alternatives for adjusting the supply of family labor to its resources. One or two members of the group could find productive employment and a means of support without being dependent on the family's holding. The principal motive behind movement out of the village, however, has been the acquisition of wealth to purchase land and construct brick houses in Vilyatpur. This reverses the downward trend in the property groups' fortunes produced by expansion in size and division in inheritance. Property groups used developments in the provincial economy and the opening of opportunities for overseas migration as external means to advance their position in village society and economy, or at least to prevent their decline.

Whether push or pull is the primary stimulus to migration is too complicated to answer. To some extent the economic circumstances of particular property groups functioned as a push. In discussing the alternative means available for adjusting the supply of family labor to the group's holding, I found a relationship between migration and land ownership (Table 22). Property groups with more than ten acres of land migrated with less frequency than others because the land was sufficient to absorb the labor of all members, apparently no matter how many, particularly with the intensification of cultivation after 1920. The striking feature, however, is that there was little difference in the rate of migration between the landless, and the small, or middle-size land holders. Absolute economic welfare (the amount of land) cannot account for this lack

[7] Cohn, *Anthropology of a Civilization*, 164. Cohn speaks of a "semirural" urbanization pattern to highlight the rural characteristics of many Indian cities. Given the changes in Vilyatpur, it is also accurate to speak of a semiurban rural pattern to emphasize the citylike features of life today—diverse occupations, commuting for work, and orientation toward society outside the community.

of variation; neither can per-capita land for adult males. Men with
very small holdings did not migrate if they were the only adult male
in the group because it meant an end to the family in the village.
It is the goal of bettering the property group's position in the local
social system that accounts for the behavior of groups with different
size holdings. New opportunities pulled migrants from Sahota
property groups in Vilyatpur, but it was the differential growth of
individual groups and the existence of the village community as a
referent that determined which groups took advantage of the opportunities and the use of the wealth acquired.

From the 1890's through the 1930's wealth and incomes acquired
outside Vilyatpur were used to advance in the village social system.
Success was measured in terms of the local community and not a
wider framework. This phenomenon was not new. It had probably
occurred in the Sikh period when military and civil service were
often means for enhancing the family's position in the village. The
settlement officer, for instance, noted in 1881 that

brick houses are rare, except in some villages with a special history. When
found, they usually belong to traders or to persons who are themselves, or
whose forerunners have been in [government] service.[8]

After 1890 the number and types of opportunities to acquire wealth
outside the village expanded greatly. This enabled a larger portion
of the community to acquire desired goods and symbols of achievement.

But the increasing participation in a wider society and economy,
both by resident villagers and an expanding number of migrants
who retained their village ties, made it progressively more difficult
to isolate the internal social and prestige system from the more
generalized one of the district and region. Therefore, as more and
more property groups successfully used the external system to augment their position, the hold of the village declined and lost its
importance as a reference group for measuring success. In 1946,
for the first time since records are available, a Sahota landowner
sold his entire Vilyatpur holding to purchase a more substantial one
in western Uttar Pradesh. Unlike *pagal* Pakhur, a generally deviant
type by all reports, Rattan Singh's move was a calculated attempt to
better his economic position, not vis-à-vis other landowners in

[8] S. R., 1892, 59.

Vilyatpur, but in terms of a general standard (the amount he could raise for his own use and sale). Although many property groups still use wealth remitted from members in England to purchase land in Vilyatpur or a contiguous village at inflated prices, or more commonly now, to install electric pumping sets, one group took the money and purchased thirty acres in Rajasthan in 1965. Just as I left the village, nine acres of land with an electrically powered well were put up for sale. This sale represented the largest single block of land ever offered on the market. The sellers, two stepbrothers, plan to purchase land in Rajasthan with the money received and hope to multiply their holding ten times in the process. The character of overseas migration has also changed in recent years. Most villagers who have settled in England within the last decade have taken their families with them. Although they continue to remit money to the village, every effort is made to purchase houses and, if possible, to start businesses in their adopted country. Vilyatpur continues to exist as the home and home base for residents and migrants. But as a local prestige system, it is declining in importance.

Chapter VI

SOCIAL CHANGE 1848–1968: FAMILY AND KINSHIP

In India, until ten years ago, the proposition that the joint family was disappearing and the prediction that the trend would accelerate in the foreseeable future were widely accepted. Census commissioners, scholars, even the general public in India, treated the "decline" as an article of faith.[1] Because general social theory, as developed from the European experience, saw the decline as necessary consequence of industrialization and urbanization, empirical work on Indian society, until 1960, took the decline for granted and sought to show how it occurred instead of collecting data to test the validity of this view of the past, the present, and the future of the family.[2] Most scholars attributed the alleged transformation from joint to nuclear family structure to general changes in Indian society and economic organization. In an article devoted to formulating a general framework for the study of family structure in India, for instance, Bailey argues that change in the family can only be understood "by taking it in the total context of social relations," changing relationships between family members and institutions being responsible for all transformations in the family.[3] Changes in Indian social organization are seen to result from commercialization, industrialization, and westernization, or the imposition of an alien administrative and legal system. The argument in each account of the impact of these developments on family structure is essentially the same; the joint family (the norm) is assumed to be disappearing and the cause of change is external to the family itself.

More recently, attention has been directed toward the study of the actual course of change in family organization over time. Using statistical data covering an extended period, several scholars have arrived at a different conclusion, namely, that little change has

---

[1] George H. Conklin, "Social Change and the Joint Family: the Causes of Research Biases," *Economic and Political Weekly* IV (1969), 1445–1448.

[2] *Ibid.*, 1147.

[3] F. G. Bailey, "The Joint Family: A Framework for Discussion," *Economic Weekly* III (1960), 348.

taken place in the incidence of different types of the family. The lack of change is explained by the continuity of the joint family as the culturally valued form which remained unchallenged despite numerous changes in the "quality of life" in rural India. These studies, however, suffer from a number of difficulties relating to the data available, the definitions employed, and the techniques used to show change, thereby raising serious questions about their findings and conclusions.

Problems in the Study of Change in the Indian Family

In the most recent of a series of papers on the family in India, A. M. Shah has isolated the source of much confusion in the study of family structure and social change. Scholars studying nonwestern societies have frequently noted the distinction between the domestic group and the family in their accounts of the demographic and social structure of the communities they survey. Shah points out that social scientists who have worked in India do not observe the same distinction when examining the Sanskrit literature for data on the family as either a cultural ideal or the incidence of different family types in the past.[4] He finds the information on the family in the classical literature to be primarily of two kinds, "pertaining to the property aspect of the family . . . and pertaining to certain family rituals." [5] Regarding property, he says:

The legal definition of the joint family is based on that of the co-parcenary: it consists of all males included in the coparcenary plus their wives and unmarried daughters. The latter are not coparcenors but have only a right to maintenance.[6]

The group eligible to perform the *shradda* ritual is "virtually identical" to the coparcenary. Shah points out that in neither case is there any indication that persons constituting the joint family should reside in a single household. Because of the "coincidence of the legal and ritual definitions of the joint family, he concludes that the definition [in the sacred texts] came to be accepted as the general

[4] A. M. Shah, "Changes in the Indian Family: An Examination of Some Assumptions," *Economic and Political Weekly,* III (1969), 131.
[5] *Ibid.*
[6] *Ibid.*

definition of the Hindu joint family"; and the problem of residence was pushed into the background and forgotten. This "Indological definition" took hold and gained general usage because

most of the early studies were carried out by Indologists (including historians, Sanskritists, and Orientalists) on the basis of the sacred literature, and as both Indologists and lawyers were dominant in the academic field in India, the Indological idea carried a lot of weight and gained popularity.[7]

To illustrate the process Shah cites Henry Maine's use of the definition and the influence of his work.

Two points in Shah's essay are particularly important for the consideration of change in family structure in Vilyatpur and rural communities in general. Although the need to distinguish between the domestic group and the family seems commonplace once the point is made, a glance at the recent literature reveals the extent to which discussions of family structure have been contaminated by the confusion. An excellent indication is Kolenda's "comparison of twenty-six sociological and anthropological studies, all carried out since 1949, which contain quantitative data on the frequency of various types of families."[8] Because most studies take commensality as the defining criterion,[9] we have, in reality, comparative studies of household or domestic groups rather than of family composition. Desai and Ames avoid the difficulty by clearly differentiating between various "dimensions" of family life—commensality, residence, property ownership, the network of mutual expectations, and the cultural ideal—and then showing how they are related.[10] This distinction solves the definitional confusion and, more importantly, comes closer to approximating the nature of kinship and family relations in India. But neither Desai nor Ames has any data on the past and therefore cannot come to terms with the question of change.

[7] Ibid.

[8] P. M. Kolenda, "Region, Caste and Family Structure: A Comparative Study of the Indian 'Joint' Family," in Singer and Cohn, 339–396.

[9] Ibid., 344.

[10] I. P. Desai, Some Aspects of Family in Mahuva (New York: Asia Publishing House, 1964); and Michael M. Ames, "Structural Dimensions of Family Life in the Steel City of Jamshedpur, India." Paper presented at the Conference on Occupational Cultures in Changing South Asia, University of Chicago, 1970, (mimeo).

The need for adequate baseline data in the study of change is the second important point in Shah's essay. The Indological litera-ture is unsatisfactory as a starting point for the study of trends in the size and composition of residential groups because there is no information on the subject. The texts are insufficient for examining family organization since they yield data on one dimension only, the cultural ideal of the joint family. Moreover, they contain no data about the ideal's actual incidence at a particular moment in time. Commercialization, westernization, industrialization, and the imposition of an alien administrative and legal system are all his-torical processes which can be located in time and space. To arrive at a conclusion on the nature and extent of change wrought by these processes, historians need data on domestic and family group structure from the time before their inception.

So far there have been no systematic examinations of the history of family organization in India, although scholars have made some significant speculations. The primary problem has been the absence of baseline data other than the sacred texts, which results in the assumption that before the change, the cultural ideal of the co-parcenary group (consisting of all kinsmen genealogically qualified to be members) was universally achieved. That is, when joint owner-ship is taken as the defining criterion for the family as suggested by Shah, the traditional or earlier organizational form, in the ab-sence of any data, is generally assumed to have included all living kinsmen.[11] Bailey's study of the transformation of Warrior family structure in the Orissa Hills following the introduction of British administration exemplifies this type of analysis. Bailey argues that the ideal joint family (coparcenary group) disintegrated in the face of new occupational opportunities for family members as indi-viduals which came with the extension of the "economic frontier." [12]

[11] The use of the terms "joint" and "extended" to describe families comprised of more than one married couple is confusing. In general, the former is em-ployed when the defining variable is common residence, and the latter when some other criterion is used. Because the extended family is usually defined by kinship alone and therefore tends to merge with the minimal lineage (Raymond T. Smith, "Comparative Family Structure," *International Encyclopedia of the Social Sciences*, V, 304), I choose to use the term "joint" to refer to coparcenary groups with more than one adult male. This use has the advantage of distin-guishing a group of kinsmen who elect to hold property in common from the pool of kin of a certain degree of relatedness.

[12] Bailey, *Caste and the Economic Frontier*, 10.

The end product apparently was an increased number of smaller-sized property groups, some joint and some nuclear, but none as large or as complex as those before British annexation.

The position regarding history of residential groups is somewhat more satisfactory. There are at least two works (both called family studies) that employ a baseline for the study of change. Orenstein's examination of Census data on *households* over the period 1911–1951 shows that, if anything, a slight increase in the number of persons per household (commensal group) occurred.[13] His study is inconclusive, however, because household size is a poor indicator for composition and structure, particularly in view of the tremendous growth of the population during the period. For instance, many changes in composition may be concealed by an increase in the number of children. A second problem with Orenstein's paper is that Census data before 1911 cannot be used, either because it is unavailable, or because it is not comparable to the information available for the period 1911–1951; for our purpose 1911 is too late a date to consider many processes, especially the effects of British administration and improvements in transportation facilities. Kolenda's restudy of Lony in Maharashtra, which uses household data from Thomas Coates' survey in 1819 as a baseline, avoids these problems.[14] By reworking Coates' figures, she arrives at an estimate of household composition for the year after British annexation. These figures are then compared with distributions of household types in 1958 and 1967; she concludes "that there were not more joint families (sic) in 1819 than in 1967." [15]

Although Orenstein's and Kolenda's work are an advance over the assumptions previously held, there are a number of problems inherent in the technique of examining household and family composition in terms of the frequency of types at different dates. The natural cycle of growth and division which results from birth, marriage, procreation, and death, as discussed in connection with the *ghar, tabbar,* and *khandan,* is one complicating factor. Using data on forty-three domestic groups in a village in eastern Uttar

[13] Henry Orenstein, "The Recent History of the Extended Family in India," *Social Problems,* VIII (1961), 349.

[14] P. M. Kolenda, "Family Structure in Village Lonikand, India, 1819, 1958, 1967." Paper presented at the Interdisciplinary Conference on Processes of Change in Contemporary Asian Societies, University of Illinois, 1970.

[15] *Ibid.,* 419.

Pradesh, Gould shows that a decline of 10 percent, which occurred in the number of nuclear domestic groups over a five-year interval, reflects "the random vicissitudes of the development cycle," [16] and, therefore,

it should be obvious . . . that a mere counting of nuclear families in a community or region can in itself yield very little information about changes in family structure unless the developmental cycle has been worked out. For at two different points in time, the ratio of joint to nuclear families will almost never be the same, simply because the families comprising the population being studied will be so differentially affected by the development cycle.[17]

Before trends in the percentages from various points in time can be taken as either an indication of change *or lack of it,* the consequences of the "normal rearrangement of domestic organization through time" must be factored out.[18] Gould's discussion also demonstrates that it is not necessary to establish a different family or household type for every variation found in a particular population, since the inclusion of some individuals, like a widowed mother, is incidental to the development process and represents neither an important transition from one phase of the cycle to another, nor a basic structural change.[19]

There is still another problem that confounds the usual statistical approach to the study of change in household and family groups, raising additional questions about Kolenda's and Orenstein's conclusions. The examination of demographic trends in Vilyatpur in Chapter III revealed that before 1920 the village population failed to grow because of a low survival rate—a result of a combination of high mortality owing to epidemic disease and a low birth rate. The impact of the insecurity of life for village social structure can be seen in the large percentage of nuclear families lacking kinsmen with whom the family head might combine if he so desired. Or, to put it the other way around, in 1848 one-fourth of the property groups had only a single adult male (and were therefore nuclear) neither by choice nor as the result of the patterned rearrangements of the domestic cycle, but because its head had no father, uncle, brother, or adult son or nephew with whom he might form a more complex structure. And since the population increased substantially

[16] Gould, 419.   [17] *Ibid.*   [18] *Ibid.,* 420.   [19] *Ibid.*

after 1920 and life expectancy has continued to rise, the percentage of families nuclear "of necessity" has continually declined. The technique of studying domestic and family group structure through percentages of each type does not take this change into consideration. Although there is some variation in the categories used in the literature on India to label families and domestic groups, the work of twenty-six different scholars have enough in common to enable Kolenda to develop a typology of twelve compositional types applicable to virtually all data they presented.[20] In this typology each commensal group (and the same would be the case for families) is treated as an isolate. The existence of kinship ties between the units is never examined, and the possible importance of an increasingly large portion of nuclear groups being eligible for some other form is ignored.[21]

Domestic Groups in Vilyatpur

Table 31 shows the average size of domestic groups in Vilyatpur, rural Jullundur, and rural Punjab for those years in which Census data are available. Orenstein used the same information on the district and the province; it shows an increase in the size of households defined by a common hearth between 1911 and 1961. Because manuscript Census materials exist only for 1848 and 1961, it is impossible to disaggregate these figures to discover the relative importance of an expanding population with an increased number of children and an actual change in structure at various points in the interval. But the average size of households in Vilyatpur, calculated from unpublished Census records, does reveal an important aspect of domestic group structure through time related to the question of change. While the district and provincial averages show increases, those for Vilyatpur fluctuate quite sharply, indicating a decline in the intervals 1848–1911 and 1941–1951. There is nothing unique in the history of the village's growth that would account for the fluctuation (see Table 9). I suspect that variations of this sort are

[20] Kolenda, *Region, Caste and Family Structure,* 436–437.
[21] The necessity to take eligibility into consideration is discussed in Edwin D. Driver, *Differential Fertility in Central India* (Princeton University Press, 1963), 35–36, n. 6; and A. M. Shah, "Basic Terms and Concepts in the Study of Family in India," *Indian Economic and Social History Review* I (1963), 24.

TABLE 31

AVERAGE SIZE OF HOUSEHOLD, 1848–1961
(for years when Census data is available)

| | Vilyatpur | | Size of household (average) | | |
	Houses	Population	Vilyatpur	District (rural)	Punjab (rural)
1848	123	565	4.6	4.1	na
1911	195	705	3.6	4.2	4.4
1921	186	700	3.8	4.4	4.5
1931	153	687	4.5	5.1	4.8
1941	163	875	5.4	5.3	5.2
1951	248	1,092	4.4	5.5	5.6
1961	165	1,197	7.2	5.9	6.0

SOURCE: Punjab and Jullundur District: Punjab Census, Imperial Table I for the year indicated. For Vilyatpur, "District Census Register," 1911–1941, Sadr Kanungo's Office, District Courts Jullundur; District Census Handbooks, 1951 and 1961.

quite common at the local level, although they are averaged out by fluctuations in the data on other communities.

In a certain sense the problem is one of definition. Given the nature of the housing described in Chapter II, the task of deciding where one household ended and another began is not easy. Even in 1911 the defining criterion for the Census changed from a separate structure, or group of structures with a common courtyard, to a *chulla* (hearth), remaining constant through 1961. The frequency of rearrangements in Vilyatpur's domestic groups made the job of the census enumerator extremely arbitrary.[22] The variation in the number of commensal groups from one Census year to the next indicates the extent of the problem. Between 1921 and 1931 the population fell by thirteen, but the number of commensal groups decreased by thirty-three. An even more drastic variation occurred in the returns for 1941, 1951, and 1961.

But the figures for the number of commensal groups in Vilyatpur should not be dismissed as erroneous; the fluctuation is at least in part indicative of the nature of the domestic group. The structure of the household over time causes the difficulty both for the Census

[22] Punjab Census, 1961, IA (i), 105.

official and the historian studying social change in rural Punjab. Three types of groups were noted in the discussion of Sahota social structure in Chapter I: the *khandan,* the *tabbar,* and the *ghar.* The *khandan* is a large unit composed of kinsmen from four or five generations who trace their descent from a common ancestor, act together in ritual matters and at times of calamity, but who seldom own land in common and almost never live in the same household. The *khandan* is usually composed of a number of *tabbars,* a smaller group ranging from a couple with their unmarried children to a three generation cluster of lineally related kinsmen. These kinsmen usually coincide with the property owning group but may or may not live in a single household. Both the *khandan* and the *tabbar* are kinship rather than localized groups. Individuals dwelling in other commensal groups or outside of the village are still considered members, and even the *tabbar* may be represented by several *ghars* in Vilyatpur. The cycle of growth, division, and growth in all three units has already been considered in detail. The process is relatively slow in the case of the largest unit—the *khandan,* and somewhat faster in the *tabbar* where it approximates the period for the maturation and marriage of children. It is most frequent for the household in which rearrangements take place almost every year because a member leaves the village for work, a mother and daughter-in-law or several sisters-in-law fight and begin to cook separately in the courtyard, or two adult brothers decide to run distinct households while continuing to farm together.[23]

The point is not that the number of commensal groups (houses) indicated in Table 31 for any one year is statistically correct. But the fluctuation conveys the extent of variability in arrangements which is part of domestic life in Vilyatpur and which forces the enumerator to make a decision between existent *chullas* as opposed to those actually in use—the usual pattern in contrast to the one in vogue on the Census night. The *chulla* is a simple thing in most village houses, often little more than brick or *adobe* ridges for holding pots over a fire built between them. Most homes have several of them, and they come in and out of use depending on circumstances. Even recombinations are not uncommon as the result of death, illness, or migration.

[23] For an excellent description of these different groups, their relationships, and how they change over time, see Leigh Minturn and John T. Hitchcock, *The Rajputs of Khalapur, India* (New York: Wiley, 1966), 25–26.

By its very nature the domestic group is an inadequate focus for the study of social change in Vilyatpur. Transformations are too frequent to find out what, if anything, is happening to structure and composition. The household is not even useful for the study of family roles, relationships, and other aspects of socialization because most lines of authority and influence transcend it.[24] Until the property of the family is divided, household members are usually subject to the authority of the most senior male member and his wife. In other respects the arrangements in the village are too complex for a simple association of socialization with the domestic groups. There are at present two instances of brothers who live in houses more than one hundred yards apart but cook in common. In another example, all of the *ghars* in one *khandan* reside in houses surrounding a common courtyard, own land and farm together, and still cook separately. Given the complexity and variability in arrangements often contingent upon short term circumstances, the domestic group (defined in terms of residence or commensality) is of limited value as a focus for studying change in values and social structure in rural Punjab from 1848 to 1968.

Changing Family Composition in Vilyatpur

In contrast to the domestic group, the family defined by joint ownership of property has many distinct advantages. This unit is of primary importance in the lives and minds of village residents; the group operates the family farm and sends out members to find new jobs, either in the immediate neighborhood or at considerable distance, in an effort to adjust resources to available manpower. Abundant information on family composition over an extended period of time exists in the individual entries of the revenue records. The property group is stable enough to discover whether any change occurs in its composition, structure, and internal relationships. The family so defined is central to the processes of change generally considered to be at work in rural India since the mid-nineteenth century, thus facilitating the evaluation of the causes of change.

In Chapter II, I argued that the significance of the joint control of the village land by the *bhaiachara* before British annexation was political—designed to protect the local lineages' position on the land

²⁴ *Ibid.*, 26.

and in the community. With the detailed recording of each family's holding in 1848 and treatment as private property, the necessity for the corporate body disappeared which resulted in a shift in emphasis to the constituent lineages and *khandans*. Did this minute recording of rights and privileges in the British land revenue settlements also increase the importance of the individual vis-à-vis the family? To answer the question we should look at how property was recorded and divided over the next one hundred twenty years. Similarly, if the commercialization of agriculture and the increased role of the market in economic relationships since 1890 (and more dramatically since 1920) produced a shift in attitudes toward property, as the general social theory might lead one to expect, the change should be apparent in how the land is recorded in the *jamabandi*. The examination of the manner in which Vilyatpur residents chose to record their holdings provides an opportunity for testing a number of hypotheses on the causes of change: Bailey's theory that new occupational opportunities led to the break-up of joint property groups; Darling's argument that the spread of western values and ideas emphasized the individual at the expense of the family group;[25] and the possible effect of migration on family structure.[26] Looking at the history of property groups also reveals changes in relationships between members of the coparcenary.

Table 32 summarizes the history of family composition in Vilyatpur by showing the distribution of different types at nine intervals in the period 1848 to 1968. The primary distinction here is between the groups with only one adult male, and those with more than one—roughly approximating the nuclear family and the joint family as conventionally defined. My concern, however, is with the ownership of property and its transmission over time. There are several differences between the types I have used and those generally employed in the study of family and domestic group composition.[27] Perhaps the most radical departure is the absence of any concern with marital status. In this typology the focus is on the number of adult males

[25] This theme runs throughout Darling's work, finding its fullest and most explicit expression in *Rusticus Loquitur,* especially 106, 340–343.

[26] See T. N. Valunjkar, *Social Organization, Migration, and Change in a Village Community,* Deccan College Dissertation Series 28 (Poona: Deccan College, 1966), 38, 74.

[27] Kolenda's typology (*Region, Caste and Family Structure,* 436–437) is the most detailed available and seems to be coming into general use.

TABLE 32

FAMILY COMPOSITION, 1848–1968
(percent)

| | Single adult male | | | | More than one adult male | | | |
	No adult male	Without an heir	With heir/heirs	Total	Different generations	Same generation	Both same and different generations	Total
1848	2	10	40	50	10	24	14	48
1884	6	24	27	51	12	24	8	43
1898	4	20	25	45	14	23	14	51
1910	11	28	27	55	10	12	13	34
1922	7	33	24	57	11	12	13	36
1934	12	25	30	54	17	7	11	35
1946	11	32	20	52	12	12	13	37
1958	11	24	18	42	16	11	19	48
1968	5	26	31	55	15	7	18	40

SOURCE: Family biographies.
Sample: Resident property groups.

who can potentially own property individually (in the eyes of the law, 18 years of age), and on underaged males who will become co-owners or individual property owners in time. Gould's point that in view of the processual development in the domestic group a separate type need not be specified for every minor variation in composition applies even more forcefully here. A property group composed of a single adult male, for instance, is treated the same as a man and wife because over time they are equivalent from the point of view of choices regarding the sharing of property and opportunities for its transmission until the latter produce a male offspring. And, given the insecurity of life, particularly before 1920, the production of heirs cannot be assumed. Similarly, a family composed of a widower with two unmarried adult sons (and any number of daughters) is no different than when the wife-mother was alive because her absence is of no consequence to the family as a property group, and the marital status of her sons does not alter it, even though as adults they have chosen to continue to hold property in common with their father. In all these examples there is obviously a difference between the family as a coparcenary and what might be called the sociological family defined in terms of joint property ownership.[28] Certainly, the designation of a family made up of man and wife and several daughters as something less than a nuclear family ignores a set of roles and relationships which might be considered complete. My typology admittedly produces some distortions. But given the central position of relationships between agnatically related males in rural social structure and the importance of male offspring to perpetuate the family line, to perform death and commemorative rituals, and to inherit the family's property, the distortion is minor compared to that which results from forcing the Indian data into a social science mold derived from Western experience. A family composed of a man and his orphaned nephew is a perfectly acceptable and complete family to the people of the village, although it would not be considered a nuclear family in Kolenda's typology based on Western society. The categories used here miss certain aspects of the sociological life of the family but do less violence to indigenous ideas and values regarding the family as they work out over time.

Table 32 indicates that property groups composed of more than one adult male tended to decline slightly over the period 1848 to 1968. The change is small, however—less than 10 percent at the extremes—and there is considerable variation from one reference year to the next, rendering impossible a definite conclusion regarding anything but the general direction of change. One development that is quite clear is a marked decline in the proportion of families that are joint and composed of two or more men in the same generation —brothers and, in a few cases, cousins—who own property together. But Table 30 does not take changes in eligibility into consideration. After the turn of the century, as life expectancy and the population increased, more families of each type were eligible for a more complex form because they had more living relatives with whom they might combine if they so desired (Table 33). While nearly one-fourth of the families with only a single adult male in 1848 included all kinsmen in the village, only 9 percent were forced into this category by 1968.

[28] Shah, *Changes in the Indian Family*, 131.

TABLE 33

FAMILY COMPOSITION AND ELIGIBILITY, 1848–1968
(percent)

D—composition the result of a division from other kinsmen
I—includes all living kinsmen

| | | No adult male | Single adult male | | | More than 1 adult male | | | | Grand total |
			Without an heir	With heir/heirs	Total	Different generations	Same generation	Both same and different generations	Total	
1848	D		6	20	26	5	5	5	16	42
	I	2	4	20	24	5	18	9	32	58
1884	D	3	12	16	28	6	4	3	31	44
	I	3	12	11	23	6	20	5	30	56
1898	D	2	10	15	25	7	5	5	17	45
	I	2	10	10	20	7	18	9	34	55
1910	D	6	18	23	41	5	6	6	17	64
	I	5	10	4	14	3	6	7	16	35
1922	D	4	24	18	42	8	7	8	22	68
	I	3	9	6	15	3	5	7	15	33
1934	D	7	17	23	41	14	5	9	28	76
	I	5	8	6	14	3	3	1	7	25
1946	D	8	26	15	41	9	7	9	24	73
	I	4	7	4	11	3	5	4	12	27
1958	D	9	18	17	35	12	6	16	36	79
	I	3	7	2	8	4	5	3	12	22
1968	D	3	20	27	47	14	5	13	32	81
	I	2	6	3	9	2	2	5	8	19

SOURCE: Family biographies.
Sample: Resident property groups.

Before reaching any conclusion as to changes in attitudes expressed through joint or individual ownership of property, therefore, I must subtract from the total, those who had no choice—that is, who by force of circumstances had only one adult male. But the families in Table 33 do show one dramatic change. Among the families with two or more males in 1848, over two-thirds reached the ideal of embracing all genealogically eligible kinsmen in the village, while only one in five fulfilled this goal in 1968. From 1848 through 1898 more than half of the families in Vilyatpur included all living kinsmen residing in the village, but thereafter the position was reversed and the proportion of families which were the product of a division from other kinsmen began to grow, reaching 81 percent in 1968. A clear change in the norm occurred between 1848 and 1968. In the nineteenth century most property groups included all of their close relatives in the village. Other families were generally outsiders in two senses: property ownership and kinship. After 1910 this was no longer the case; most families had at least one other property group in the village to whom they were closely connected through ties of kinship.

Before looking at the pattern of change in family composition adjusted for eligibility, there is one factor that will prove important for determining the extent of change in family relationships that must be introduced. Tables 32 and 33 are based only on persons actually resident in Vilyatpur, omitting family members living outside the village, temporarily or permanently, as is common in most studies of rural family structure in India. But since I am defining the family in terms of joint ownership of property, there is no longer any justification for limiting the study of the family in Vilyatpur only to kinsmen living in the village. Punjabis do not exclude members of the coparcenary living outside, and including them here avoids distortions of reality that would result from considering cases like a group composed of husband's mother, wife, and several minor children as a fragment because the household head works and lives outside of the village while continuing to support the family. Table 34 incorporates family members living away and distinguishes between property groups that include all kinsmen and those that had experienced a division. When contrasted with Table 32 it shows a number of differences in degree, although nothing dramatic.

The importance of considering all kinsmen, however, is apparent

TABLE 34

FAMILY COMPOSITION AND ELIGIBILITY INCLUDING KINSMEN LIVING OUTSIDE THE VILLAGE, 1848–1968
(percent)

| | | No adult male | Single adult male | | | More than one adult male | | | | |
			Without an heir	With heir/heirs	Total	Different generation	Same generation	Both same and different generations	Total	Grand total
1848	D		6	20	26	5	5	6	16	42
	I	2	4	19	23	5	19	9	33	58
1884	D	3	12	15	27	5	4	3	12	42
	I	3	12	11	23	6	21	5	32	58
1898	D	2	10	15	25	7	5	5	17	44
	I	2	10	10	20	7	18	9	34	56
1910	D	3	16	18	34	6	6	4	16	53
	I	6	9	4	13	2	14	13	29	48
1922	D	2	21	15	36	13	4	7	24	62
	I	3	8	5	13	2	11	10	23	39
1934	D	5	14	20	34	16	6	7	29	67
	I	5	10	6	16	3	5	5	13	34
1946	D	4	23	15	38	8	7	13	28	70
	I	4	7	4	11	4	6	5	15	30
1958	D	4	14	17	31	11	5	18	34	69
	I	3	7	1	8	7	6	9	22	31
1968	D	2	15	24	39	13	3	17	33	74
	I	2	5	2	7	3	5	10	18	27

SOURCE: Family biographies.
Sample: Resident and nonresident males.

in Table 35 where the history of family composition adjusted for eligibility, is shown on the left for kinsmen in the village and on the right for all family members. In making the calculations I subtracted from the total number of families all those with one or no adult

TABLE 35

FAMILY COMPOSITION ADJUSTED FOR ELIGIBILITY, 1848–1968
(percent)

| | Kinsmen living in village only | | | | All kinsmen | | | |
| | One adult male or less | | | More than one | One adult male or less | | | More than one |
	No male	One	Total		No male	One	Total	
1848		35	35	65		35	35	65
1884	4	37	41	59	4	37	41	59
1898	2	31	33	66	3	31	34	66
1910	7	51	58	42	4	42	46	54
1922	5	51	56	45	2	43	45	56
1934	8	50	58	42	6	42	48	52
1946	9	48	57	43	4	45	49	51
1958	10	39	49	51	4	34	38	61
1968	3	52	55	45	2	43	45	55

SOURCE: Family biographies.
Sample: Resident and nonresident males.

males. The table, therefore, includes only those families that expressed a choice between individual ownership and joint ownership
of property, and the percentages have been calculated on the basis of
this group alone. Considering first only the kinsmen in the village,
we notice that a rather significant shift has taken place from the
nineteenth century, when joint families were statistically more common, to the period starting in 1910 when groups with one adult male
became the most frequent type. But when kinsmen who have migrated are included, the degree of change is reduced considerably.
Even as late as 1968 joint property groups remain the predominant
family type, accounting for more than half of all the cases in which
a choice was possible. A decline occurred, the 1910 reference year
being the turning point, but even as late as 1968 the degree of change
was not large enough to make groups with a single male the most
common form. The number of groups without an adult male is reduced by including members living outside, showing how commonly
a household head might work and reside elsewhere, while leaving his
family in Vilyatpur.

The results of Tables 32 through 35 can now be summarized to answer the first problem posed in this chapter, the nature and extent of change in family composition in the village 1848–1968:

1. Substantial changes in eligibility have occurred dating particularly from 1910. Since the proportion of families not eligible for more complex ties has declined, all studies of changes in preferences for particular forms must be adjusted for eligibility.

2. There has been a general decline in the proportion of families that embrace all of the appropriate kinsmen. This is true whether or not migrants are included. Before 1910 coparcener and close kinsman were likely to be synonymous; afterwards they seldom were.

3. If only the population resident in Vilyatpur is considered, the family with just a single adult male has replaced the joint group as the statistical norm. But this change is largely an artifact of the exclusion of migrants who are still important members and cosharers in resident property groups. With their inclusion the joint family remains the norm today, although in a reduced proportion compared to the nineteenth century.

4. Joint families composed of two or more brothers have declined as a percentage of families in excess of the general reduction of joint groups of all types.

5. The involvement of persons living outside of Vilyatpur in the affairs of resident property groups has increased, especially since 1910.

The conclusions show that qualifications are necessary in both the unsubstantiated statements about the decline of the joint family that characterize most writings on rural India, and the findings of empirical studies like those of Kolenda and Orenstein which argue that little modification has taken place. Changes have occurred, but they are too complex and subtle for the approaches and conclusions of earlier studies.

Family Structure: Causes and Nature of Change

Although the joint family has remained the statistical norm in Vilyatpur, experiencing only a slight decline in numbers from 1848 to 1968, important changes have taken place in the structure of the family and relationships between family members. As we have seen, since 1910, a growing number of families in Vilyatpur were joint only if members living outside the village but still coparceners, are included (Table 35). This arrangement calls for numerous alterations in relationships within the family as compared to its nineteenth century counterpart. Although all members of the coparcenary had never necessarily lived under the same roof, they all lived in the village working together under the direction of the head of the family, or each using part of the family property portioned out by him. As an increasing number of property groups consisted of members separated by considerable distances, the head's control of the daily economic activities of family members has declined. Men living elsewhere continued to consult the family in the village on important matters; major decisions about work, further migration, match making, and the like. They were part of the family in Vilyatpur, not only in this social sense and in that they retained a share in the title to its land, but because they remitted money for investment in mortgage and purchase of land and to increase the productivity of existing acreage. When a father received money and, perhaps, technical advice from his son who is a truck owner-driver in Delhi, a foundry worker in Bradford, England, a soldier in the army in Jabblepore, or a school teacher in another village in the Punjab, the relationship between the two changes from one of unambiguous deference and obedience on the part of the son to something more of give and take.

The change in relationships in families still joint after members have migrated is not the only new development. A slow but marked transformation in the development cycle, dating from the turn of the century, indicates that a more general alteration has taken place in relations between family members. In Table 36 I have tabulated the means by which each new family came into existence in the interval between reference years. The process that produced each new name or group of names appearing in one revenue record when compared with the record for the preceding reference year has been identified and counted. Families continuing to exist under the same head were excluded from the calculations. The results are striking. Almost all new families that appeared between 1848 and 1884 were the product of ordinary succession upon the demise of the former head (father, uncle, or brother). Another 3 percent of the new families came into being following a split between brothers, a division that is a normal development over time. While the pattern holds with slight variation over the next interval—separation from a father during his lifetime

TABLE 36

ORIGINS OF NEW FAMILIES, 1884–1968
(percent)

| | Succession | Recombination | Formed by division from | | | | No. of cases |
			Father	Brother	Other	Total	
1884	94		2	3		5	89
1898	70	2	5	24		29	56
1910	75		19	6		25	79
1922	66	5	12	17		29	41
1934	58		21	19	1	41	67
1946	56		26	18		44	84
1958	35		33	30	2	65	43
1968	49	1	37	11	1	49	91

SOURCE: Family biographies.
Sample: Resident and nonresident property groups.

remaining quite rare—a new variation emerges by 1910. Three-fourths of the new families still resulted from orderly succession, but nearly 20 percent came about through a split from a father who was still alive. The proportion of new families of this type is roughly constant from the interval 1898–1910 to 1934–1946, although divisions between brothers became increasingly frequent, yielding a falling percentage produced by succession. Then, in the two post Independence reference periods, divisions between sons and fathers during the latter's lifetime became increasingly frequent and common enough so that, together with splits between brothers, some sort of division challenges succession as the usual means by which new families come into being in Vilyatpur.

How could such a dramatic shift occur in the development cycle without an equivalent decline in the proportion of joint groups in the total? I think two considerations will answer the question. First, the discussion of demographic change showed that the growth of the village population occurred through a disproportionally large expansion of some baseline families rather than an equal increase of all families in Vilyatpur in 1848. Twentieth century property groups are therefore both larger, and eligible for more complex forms, than those of the nineteenth century. This means that a division between members of the coparcenary does not necessarily produce two groups with one adult male each. Two recent cases illustrate the point. Kabul Singh has five adult sons. In 1960 he gave some of his property-group land to the two eldest who work it together. Kabul Singh farms the rest with the youngest of the five while the other two live and work in England, remitting money and visiting the village from time to time. The result of the division is two joint property groups: one composed of a father and three sons, and a second of two brothers. In another example, Battan Singh farms his land with two of his adult sons, while the eldest, Rabinder, uses a few acres given him by his father and works in a foundry six miles away. Here the split yields two new groups, one joint and one with a single adult male.

But the question of reconciling dramatic change in the development cycle with only a slight alteration in family composition is an artificial problem, a product of the assumptions detailed in the first section of the chapter. The only reason why scholars should make a shift in composition *the* criterion of change in the study of the family in rural India are preconceptions based on general social theory. Bailey's hypothesis of new occupational opportunities and Darling's assertions about the spread of individualism can be dismissed even without evaluation as causes of change in the sense of an increased number of nuclear families simply because no such development occurred. Individualism, either as a product of occupational opportunities or new ideas, is not a factor in Vilyatpur. The whole discussion of the family farm suggests that outside occupations and individual efforts to exploit economic opportunities is an asset rather than a liability to the family. Migration in particular involved single individuals, although migrants were financed by the family because the principal goal of movement outside the community was to enhance the family's position.

Several factors explain the change in the development cycle, the increased tendency for new families to come into being by acquiring property through division rather than inheritance. The minute recording of the holdings of particular families and individuals had led to a new phenomenon of some importance, most clearly indicated in Table 35 which shows family composition adjusted for eligibility. In 1848 no one chose to be part of a property group without at least one adult male. But from 1884 there were always several groups of this type—even when kinsmen living outside of the village are in-

cluded in the calculation. The contrast between the first year and all
the rest is significant; the absence of any groups without an adult
male in 1848 reflects the situation before the elaborate recording
system of the British revenue system. Such groups were not viable in
the village before annexation; even in 1848, all orphans and widows
of property holding groups were listed as wards of some relative or
kinsman in the *patti* rather than as owners of separate holdings. The
new records system enabled widows and orphans to own property,
which they usually rent out since they cannot cultivate it themselves.
Groups of this type have accounted for a considerable portion of all
rented land since the turn of the century; a few widows have even
become important moneylenders in Vilyatpur.

It is impossible, however, to attribute the more general change in
family structure and the development cycle to the recording system
and the institution of privately owned holdings. Punjab's Land Code,
in contrast to that of most of the rest of India, was not based on the
British interpretation of the Mitaksara text, according to which any
adult male member of the coparcenary could obtain his share of the
family property on demand.[29] Punjab law did not recognize this
right; sons could obtain part of their patrimony only if presented by
the father during his lifetime or by inheritance at his death. If it
were not for this difference the increase in divisions during the
father's lifetime (see Table 36) could be seen largely as a product of
the legal and recording system, although it developed quite slowly
in time. Since the divisions tabulated occurred either with the consent of the head of the group or through the purchase or lease of land
by a son independently of his father, other causes must be sought.

The explanation lies in the complex of developments apparent
from the late 1890's which have grown in importance since the end
of the First World War: in village agriculture and occupational
structure, migration, and working arrangements for agricultural
laborers, weavers, and other artisans. The most dramatic shifts in
Tables 36 (origins of new families) and 35 (family composition ad-

[29] In a detailed review of law in the British period relating to the Hindu joint
family, Derrett outlines the factors contributing to this difference between the
Punjab and most of the rest of India. By the mid-nineteenth century British
administrators felt that the decision to apply Mitaksara law to family property
in land was mistaken and was leading to an undesired transformation in rural
India. J. D. M. Derrett, "The History of the Judicial Framework of the Joint
Hindu Family," *Contributions to Indian Sociology* VI (1962), 17–47.

justed for eligibility) take place in the interval between 1898 and
1910. This is the same period as the first large scale migrations to
Australia and the canal colonies, the disputes about the right of a
Chamar to leave his family in Vilyatpur and work elsewhere and the
freedom of village Weavers to set their own prices, and the first increment in the proportion of resident males working outside of
Vilyatpur (Table 26). The slight change in family composition and
the rather dramatic alteration in the development cycle are indications of adjustments in the family to these changing conditions.

Throughout the period under study family composition has shown
a fairly consistent relationship to occupations (Table 37). With the
year 1958 as the only exception, groups engaged in agriculture have
usually been composed of more than one adult male. Families of
laborers, in contrast, usually have only one male (exceptions: 1884
and 1898). The number of families with the head engaged in manufacturing and services is very small and, therefore, the results here
are probably not significant. There has, however, been a consistent
tendency toward joint families amongst those in manufacturing in
the village. The changes in agriculture, occupations, and working
conditions in Vilyatpur produced numerous adjustments in family
structure and relations between family members.

TABLE 37

OCCUPATION OF FAMILY HEAD AND FAMILY COMPOSITION
ADJUSTED FOR ELIGIBILITY, 1848–1968

	Percent with single male or less				
	Cultivator	*Labor*	*Manufacturing*	*Services*	*Total*
1848	29	66	21	29	35
1884	42	39	33	30	41
1898	33	15	42	60	34
1910	39	58	45	63	46
1922	37	65	46	30	45
1934	48	50	35	57	48
1946	52	50	30	58	49
1958	35	47	35	32	38
1968	39	60	35	39	45

SOURCE: Family biographies.
Sample: All resident and nonresident adult males.

The rate of change increased after 1934 with further developments in agriculture and new occupational opportunities. But since 1934 still another factor has come into play, producing an even higher percentage of new families resulting from divisions between fathers and sons. After 1931 Vilyatpur's population began a period of constant expansion. As more people lived longer, joint families grew in size, becoming too unwieldy to function successfully. Fathers and elder brothers lived longer, which made it increasingly difficult for younger men in the family to wait for a more responsible role in its affairs. Although the growth of the population contributed to the increased frequency of divisions within the lifetime of the father, there was no marked growth of the nuclear family with a single adult male even in this period. It is also important to note that there is no evidence that population growth outstripped the resources of the village, a factor which would force a change in the family's development cycle.

Given the nature of change in family structure, Conklin's finding that Indian informants' generally feel that the joint family is declining is not surprising. The data presented here show that, although the joint family remains the preferred type, it is different in form and content than in the nineteenth century. Before 1910 more than half of the families of all types (58%) included all of the appropriate kinsmen. By 1922 those *not* including all kinsmen had reached about the same level (62%), and by 1968 almost three-fourths of all families were in this category. This development, combined with changes in origin of new families and migration, makes the twentieth century family very different from its predecessor. The norm of the patriarchical and patrilocal joint family, usually embracing all kinsmen of a certain degree of relatedness, has declined. However, it has not been replaced by the nuclear family and a growing spirit of individualism. Instead a new type of joint structure has emerged as the norm in Vilyatpur, responsive to new types of opportunities and related to long-standing values concerning the family in rural Punjab.

CONCLUSION:
SOCIAL AND ECONOMIC CHANGE,
1848–1968

Vilyatpur in 1968

Vilyatpur in 1968, the end product of the changes discussed in the preceding chapters, is a different place from Vilyatpur in 1848, the baseline year. Many changes occurred in the layout of the residential site, the quality of the buildings, and the use of space. These developments are indicative of the modifications in social and economic organization, and the relationship of the community to the outside world.

Had the revenue party that surveyed Vilyatpur in 1848 been able to return, they would have been struck by a number of new features. In place of several ill-defined wagon tracks between the village and surrounding communities, a graded road, raised above the level of the fields, now connects Vilyatpur with a second improved dirt road running from Barapind (the parent village) and Phillaur (the tehsil headquarters and nearest market). These roads are well drained, and therefore not subject to flooding during the monsoon as had always been the case in the past. Vilyatpur's portion of road was already covered with bricks in 1968 and the block development officer had approved plans for paving it and the section of the road into Barapind. Since there is a one-lane paved road and a regular bus service from Barapind to the Grand Trunk road, Vilyatpur, like many Punjabi villages, is on the verge of being tied into the nation-wide network of all weather roads.

The residential site is much larger than at the time of British annexation. Fifty acres of agricultural land have been incorporated into the *abadi,* partly to provide for the larger population (from 565 to 1353), but primarily to accommodate changing tastes in residential structures. Not only has brick replaced adobe as the most common building material for residences, but wealthier landowners clearly prefer bungalow type structures with courtyards and considerable open space on the sides, modeled after newer houses in the cities of

Punjab. The village gate, now made of brick, still functions as a focal point, but it is well inside the residential site rather than on its periphery. There is little trace of the old village wall. Inside the original portion of the *abadi* most pathways have been paved with brick and provided with drains, facilitating passage in the rainy season. A few mud houses still exist in the Sahota section of the village, but most of them are either used for storing fodder and other agricultural produce, or have been sold to artisans and laborers by their owners who now live in the new houses on the edge of the residential site. Other Sahota families have replaced their old single storied adobe houses, with two and three storied brick and plaster structures. It is only in the section of the village where the untouchables have always lived that reminders of former days exist in the form of numerous small adobe houses. Yet even here more than half of the homes of Weavers, Leatherworkers, and Sweepers, are at least partly made of brick: the walls facing prevailing wind and rain pattern are made of brick and the rest of adobe. Slightly less than one-third of the homes are all brick.

Modifications in the use of the *abadi* have accompanied its growth. The spreading of houses outside the old site, and the sale of some residences to artisans and laborers, have blurred the lines between the four *pattis*. Some Chamar and Julaha families live in old Sahota *pattis* and the newer homes are located without much attention to former subdivisions. The three village wells, once common meeting places, are no longer used with much frequency because of the installation of hand pumps in all but a few village homes. The Chamar's well is the only exception. It is used for washing clothes and livestock by women in the quarter, since they do not have the alternative of using agricultural wells like the Jats and do not have courtyards in which to work.

In 1848 the movement of men and livestock from homes in the village to the fields had made sunrise and sunset times of great activity in the pathways of the *abadi*. The bustle has, if anything, increased, but it has changed in character. Most of the Jats now tether their livestock at the wells, eliminating the crush of animals through the narrow passageways. Agricultural implements and carts are stored at the wells in brick sheds built to accommodate the livestock and new electrically driven pumping sets. Seven families have even built houses at their wells. But if movement to and from the fields has declined, it has more than been replaced by the daily trips of children going to middle school in Barapind, the high school six miles away, and the college eleven miles away. About seventy boys and girls attend school outside Vilyatpur, going daily by foot to Barapind, and on cycles to more distant institutions. Thirty-six men commute to workshops and foundries, six as far as eleven miles away on a daily basis, another nineteen travel daily as traders, school teachers, and government clerks. Agricultural laborers, and weavers travel with less regularity, but about one hundred of them work outside Vilyatpur at some time in the year, contributing to the stream of commuters. The bicycle, the principle mode of transportation for students and working men alike, makes the movement possible. All but nine Vilyatpur households have at least one cycle, and many have several. Bicycles are also used by itinerate tradesmen who hawk vegetables, fruits, cloth, and trinkets from village to village. Villagers use the buses and Tempos from Barapind for special occasions: shopping trips, travel for weddings and festivals, and trips to the courts in Jullundur city.

The contrast between the village in 1968 and 1848 is evident in almost all of the tables which form the data base for this study. There has been a demographic revolution. Population growth in the village brought an increased pressure on local resources. The increase from 565 persons in 1848 to 1353 in 1968 meant a decline in per-capita land from .95 acres to .36, and a subdivision of the forty-one original holdings into one hundred and forty-six ownership units. While 66 percent of the holdings had been larger than ten acres in the baseline year, 78 percent of them are less than five acres at present. Almost all land (90%) had been owned in holdings larger than ten acres in size whereas now almost half (48%) is in units less than five. The figures on the use of land show the same general trend, although with a significant variation. The number of farms has increased (61 to 127) but the rate of increase is slower than in the number of holdings. Seventy-one percent of the farms are less than five acres in contrast to 48 percent of ten acres and more at the middle of the nineteenth century. Only about half as much of the total acreage is cultivated in the category of relatively large holdings of ten acres and more (43% vs 81%).

Improvements in village agriculture, however, have more than absorbed the additional pressure on the land. The growth of village production from new seed varieties and more double cropping alone has kept up with population growth. This calculation does not take into account increases in production from better irrigation facilities in the form of a 37 percent increase in the number of wells since 1848 (from 30 to 41) and improvements in lift technology. Thirteen are deep tube wells (100–200 feet) equipped with electric or diesel pumps and the rest are fitted with at least one Persian wheel, most have two. Nor did I give weight to the intensification of labor on all crops, the use of fertilizer on crops other than wheat and sugarcane (in which the fertilizer input is included). The fact that in 1968 there were seventy-three carts as against seven in 1848, sixty-two sugarcane presses as compared to three, and that the efficiency of these contemporary appliances is greater than their nineteenth century counterparts also indicates that agricultural production has increased more than the resident population. The price of land has increased dramatically from Rs. 200 per acre in 1885–1890 to Rs. 9300 at present, and the mortgage value from Rs. 90 per acre to about Rs. 4000. Sales and mortgages are more common than at the end of the nineteenth century (1960–1964: 28 mortgages and 59 sales; 1885–1889: 10 mortgages and 19 sales) supporting the view that they are part of a saving and credit mechanism necessary to village agriculture and life and not indices of disorganization and decline.

But agriculture no longer holds its position as the only source of livelihood for Vilyatpur residents. Occupations have become more diversified since 1848, reflecting developments both in the village and the surrounding area. The proportion of the population in agriculture as owner cultivators has fallen from 63 percent in 1848 to 44 percent at present. Agricultural labor is more common now (rising from 10% to 20%) but many of them work only at peak seasons and have a range of nonagricultural occupations for the rest of the year. Employment in workshops and small factories is a new development, accounting for almost a tenth of the work force. But taking advantage of new opportunities—factory jobs and off-season tasks for agricultural laborers alike, requires movement. Forty-three percent of the resident men now work outside Vilyatpur either full-time or part-time. In 1848 only weavers and carpenters, 11 percent of the work force, dealt with people from other communities, completely on a parttime basis. Migration presents still another alternative. Opportunities elsewhere in the district, the province, the nation and abroad, have attracted people from Vilyatpur in large numbers. Whereas there were only nine people with ties in the community living elsewhere in 1848, there are now at least 259.

Demographic changes and the development of agriculture and other sources of livelihood make social organization in the community very different today. The consequences of the demographic revolution are not limited to an increased pressure on land and a stimulus to migrate. The range and nature of kinship and family ties is different now because there are more kinsmen in general and they live longer. In 1848 one-fourth of the families in the village had only one adult male because there were no other relatives to make a more complex family possible, and through 1910 (when accurate data becomes available) 69 percent of the heads of new households were under thirty. In 1968 only 10 percent of the families had a single adult male "of necessity," and 73 percent of the heads of new households were *over* thirty when they inherited or took their position. The joint property group has remained the most common form of family organization (actually a slight decline from 65% to 55%). However now only 27 percent of the families include all genealogically eligible kinsmen whereas 58 percent did so in 1848 which means the distinction between kinsmen as insiders and nonkinsmen as outsiders has blurred for most property groups in the village.

Occupational differentiation, commuting, and migration have affected social relationships within both the family and the community. Members of the property group are no longer concentrated in Vilyatpur, sons who still live there often do not work with their father on the land, but have their own occupation and contribute their earning to the family pool, changing the terms on which they participate in family life. The fact that new families come into being as frequently by division of existing groups as by succession (49% in each) in 1968 while succession accounted for 94 percent in the middle of the nineteenth century indicates the influence of these developments. Job opportunities outside the village for residents has changed social relationships between individuals and groups within the community as well. The Chamar agricultural laborers in particular are no longer subject to the authority of the

Sahota landowners, while others are free to earn their livelihood without the kind of interference and control that was the case in the economic and political context of 1848. Differential migration and growth means that there are fewer castes in the village today (12 in contrast to 16 in 1848), and that the Chamars stand as an important numerical block vis-a-vis the Jats (1848: Jats 52%, Chamars 9%, 1968: Jats 42%, Chamars 30%). In the context of democratic village, state, and national government, numbers count.

With these developments, Vilyatpur has for many of its inhabitants, particularly the nonlanded, become little more than a place to live and work. Many have only a small interest in the community as such, and younger men clearly know less about the community today than the older men. The nonlanded are active in village politics only in areas that directly concern them, and here they have been very effective, allying themselves with one of the Jat lineages and electing one of its members as head of the new village *Panchayat*. In return they receive the assistance of the *Surpanch* in disputes between them and other Sahota groups.

In general the contrasts evident in comparing the village in 1848 with the community in 1968 are the results of gradual incremental change stemming from the interaction of several developments. The radically different political context, however, is the result of the independence of India and the government's explicit commitment to democratic self-government and social justice. There are a number of other areas where government programs since 1947 have had an impact on Vilyatpur, hastening and shaping social and economic change. In addition to providing the moral and legal framework for greater equality among different groups, development policies have provided the economic opportunities for individuals to take advantage of the changed circumstances. Villagers have responded to the Community Development Program's provision of improved varieties, fertilizer, and incentives for increased production, by increasing the area double cropped by over 20 percent and investing heavily in agricultural equipment. Since the decade 1940–1949 four new wells have been dug, and twelve have been redrilled and fitted with power-driven pumps. The number of carts in the village is up 160 percent, sugarcane presses by 67 percent and there are nine threshers and two tractors. Developments outside the village are indicated in the appearance of industrial labor as a new occupation, and sharply increased rates of employment of village residents, and both the volume of migrants and the nature of their occupations in the two reference periods since 1946 (Tables 25 to 27).

Stability and Change

However, Vilyatpur in 1968 is not the *end product* of the processes which are the subject of this study; the community and its families will continue to exist and to participate in social and economic change. Some processes will go on, new ones will appear. The description of the village in 1968 is, like the baseline village of 1848, an artificial framework for measuring, understanding, generalizing about, change.

The meaningful study of the social and economic history of rural India hinges on the distinction between what is changing and what is stable, and the demonstration of how aspects of rural life, which seem to continue immutably, are related to areas of obvious change. A detailed understanding of the past is a prerequisite for identifying new developments and measuring the extent of change. The background also provides a clue to the selectivity apparent in response to new opportunities, and the general direction of change. The development of an accurate picture of the past and its use in the study of change is primarily a historical and methodological problem rather than a theoretical one. Recent efforts to reexamine the theory of modernization, and the relationship of tradition and modernity are less relevant at this juncture than the search for historical data and the development of new methods for their use. Of recent works on India, the Rudolphs' in particular have stressed the dialectical relationship between traditional forms and ideas and modern ones.[1] But their work suffers from a lack of specificity as to the meaning of tradition,[2] and the new meaning for persistent ideas and institutions in changed contexts.[3] Much careful historical work must precede any attempt at theoretical formulation.

---

[1] Lloyd I. and Susanne Hoeber Rudolph, *The Modernity of Tradition* (University of Chicago Press, 1967), 8.

[2] Richard Fox, "Avatars of Indian Research," *Comparative Studies in Society and History* XII (1970), 60.

[3] Toru Matsui, "A Methodological Consideration in Modern Indian History," *Quarterly Review of Historical Studies*, VI (1966–1967), 75–79.

Several factors complicate the study of the past and the establishment of a baseline. Conditions in contemporary Indian villages render the scholar's own senses an obstacle rather than an aid to his efforts. Since most observers—scholars, travelers, and officials alike—consider Indian villages poor and primitive in comparison to their own backgrounds, the possibility that any improvement has occurred is inconceivable. The absence of sanitation, the use of animal and human power for most tasks, the simplicity of tools and techniques, and the monotony of the diet, clothing, and housing—especially for landless laborers—all suggest that there has been little improvement in the quality of life. And yet, though relatively poor and backward, present conditions do not preclude the possibility that the general state of things was worse in the past.[4] Although there has been no wholesale revolution in daily life, there have been a number of improvements making the village in the 1890's different from what it had been at the time of annexation. By the 1920's there was further development, and still more by the time of Independence. The rate of change has increased since 1947.

By their nature and means of occurrence, the detection of the developments requires the use of more subtle methods than those conventionally employed in the study of rural India. New features, particularly in the late nineteenth and early twentieth centuries, were of a type that do not register in the usual techniques of measurement. The common approach shows that there has been little change and that any new developments are very recent. Agriculture still dominates the economic life of the village, no new crops are grown, indebtedness, mortgages and land sales are still a problem, cultivators, artisans, and landless laborers still follow the same occupations as their forefathers, and there has been little change in family structure. To identify areas of new developments and to measure the degree of change it has been necessary to look for alterations in the terms and modes of compensation for laborers and artisans, increases in the use of agricultural inputs purchased outside the village, and the growth in the proportion of residents working outside Vilyatpur. The study of shifts in family structure requires the calculation of changes in eligibility with population growth, a close look at the development cycle in the family, and the

[4] Morris D. Morris, *Economic Change and Agriculture,* 192.

inclusion of migrants living outside the community but still contributing to the economic activity of the resident property group.

The practice of viewing rural India from outside, which makes it
appear to be a closed and static system, is another source of difficulty. The view of the village community, economically (except for
the payment of taxes) and politically self-sufficient, that dominates
the literature on rural India is, of course, the most extreme example
of the misconception. Even though the information on rural Jullundur before British annexation is incomplete, there is ample
indication that local society was neither static nor isolated. The
process by which Vilyatpur came into existence shows one type of
change, a recurrent development which at certain times yielded new
settlements as part of the lineage hived off. The turmoil during
the period of the *misls* and the career of Gulab Singh Sabota as a
local adventurer illustrate how general political events reached the
villages, producing change in the structure of power in rural Jullundur.

The external view of village society and economic activity as a
closed and static system also obscures the nature and extent of the
changing processes in rural Punjab after annexation. Of course
there is no evidence that Vilyatpur, or any other village, produced
a general stimulus to change in the regional economy or transformed
themselves completely in the face of the imposition of an alien
administrative and legal system, improved transportation, or increased urbanization. In this sense the study of Vilyatpur closely
parallels Epstein's examination of the canal's construction in Madras. She compares the results of a single external development—
canal irrigation—on two villages. One village received canal water
and shifted from dry to irrigated agriculture, while the other, although not irrigated, benefited indirectly from the general development of the region. Epstein's findings are significant for our understanding of the relationship between social change and economic
development. Although economic development (an increase in per-
capita income) occurred in both villages, social change was for the
most part confined to the dry village. This fact she explains by
looking for conflict between the new opportunities created by the
canal and existing economic, social, and political organization in the
different settings of the two villages. Exploitation of the canal's
potential in the irrigated village did not require any new forms of

organization. The old order continued and became more elaborate with the new prosperity. In contrast, residents of the dry village were forced to look outside, to the surrounding region, for new opportunities. As new modes of economic activity and organization developed for participation in a larger and more diverse economy, they came into conflict with traditional village organization, which resulted in social change.[5] Epstein's study contrasts stability in the wet village with social change in the dry village. She explains that all economic development was a response to a single external stimulus and the difference in the consequences in terms of the organization necessary to take advantage of the new opportunities.

Although the ultimate source of economic change is external to the village—the canal in Epstein's study, and a combination of several less dramatic developments which occurred over an extended period of time in Vilyatpur—it does not follow that rural society is passive, acted upon in some undifferentiated way. The study of Vilyatpur over a one-hundred-and-twenty-year period at the level of its constituent property groups reveals an internal system of ideas and institutions that together with an internal cyclical process of change influences the form that external developments will take in the community. The most important elements in the internal system are the property group and its farm and the local community which forms the reference group for measuring success. The differential growth of individual property groups results in changes in the amount of land owned and provides for social circulation within the village. The relative positions of particular groups change vis-à-vis one another without any alteration in the basic structure of the community.[6] Externally the system is stable but

[5] T. Scarlett Epstein, *Economic Development and Social Change in South India* (Manchester University Press, 1962), 314–326.

[6] Godfrey and Monica Wilson suggest this distinction:

"Within all societies there is social circulation: that is, the members of the various categories and groups change, and leaders and subordinates change. Social circulation—the change of occupants of existing positions—is to be distinguished from social change, that is, change of the positions to be occupied in society."

The Analysis of Social Change (Cambridge: University Press, 1954), 58–59. See also Ellen M. MacDonald "Elite Recruitment in 19th Century Maharashtra: A Case of Old Wine in New Bottles," paper presented at the annual meeting of the Rural Sociology Society, Washington, D.C., August 26, 1970.

internally there is a process of circulation of very real importance to members of the community.

It is the interaction of the internal system with external developments which explains the nature and extent of changes in Vilyatpur from 1848 to 1968. Changes in the behavior, preferences, and ideas of local residents, which range from the adoption of improved agricultural practices to new patterns of migration, occupation, and family structure, all are determined by the internal system even though the original stimulus in every case originates outside. New opportunities provide a means for groups that have experienced a decline in the size of their holdings, through growth and excessive partition in inheritance over time, to acquire additional land, add to its productivity and thereby raise their position in village society. The conclusion on social and economic change in Vilyatpur supports Leach's contention that

The ultimate 'causes' of social change are . . . nearly always to be found in changes in the external political and economic environment; but the form which any change takes is largely determined by the existing internal structure of a given system.[7]

Epstein's study, though an important contribution, is, in several respects, incomplete. Since she does not notice the internal system, the different reactions of individuals and families receive only *ad hoc* explanations. The motive for a particular choice at this level is generally stimulated by the local system. This is why, for instance, groups with large holdings are less innovative in agriculture and less likely to migrate. By taking only an outside view of and examining only the response to a single external development, Epstein limits the value of her study; she even precludes the possibility of examining further developments. She treats change—both the stimulus to change and its effect in the two villages—as a single, terminal event. It is, however, a process initiated by alterations in the external political and economic environment with continuous ramifications over time because of additional, though less dramatic, developments outside the village, and the continued functioning of the internal system with its own process of circulation. Small scale developments have been occurring in various parts of India for well over one hundred years and the examination of their importance

[7] Leach, 212.

for rural society and economy is as important as the dramatic changes stressed by Epstein and discussed in more general terms by Anstey for the period through 1940.[8] It is, moreover, through continuous interaction with these developments that the internal system of village values and institutions undergoes considerable modification.

Family, Caste, and Village

The individual family is the most important element in Vilyatpur society and economy throughout the period 1848 to 1968. Even before annexation, when the property group did not own land in the sense that became the case under British rule, the family was the unit of economic activity. Although there is little detailed information for the period before 1848, it is known that land was *not* equally divided among all Sahota groups in the village as is at least implied by most studies. In fact, the distribution of holdings was markedly skewed. The three largest holdings represent 15 percent of the farms and account for more than one-third of the village acreage. British annexation brought a private title to property, and a number of developments presented the property group with new alternatives for pursuing its interests. The family, then, with its property, pool of labor, and the complex of values regulating its behavior, is the best focus for identifying economic development and social change in rural Punjab, and understanding the considerations that give it direction and limit its extent.

For the Sahota families, the landowners and numerically the largest caste group in Vilyatpur, the ownership and management of the family farm has always been the central concern. Land is at once the principal source of social status, a form of employment for family members, a basis for credit in times of need, and a form of investment and savings in times of plenty. Its product provides sustenance for family members, a source of income for the payment of the government tax, the procurement of goods and services in exchange of grain in the village, and, increasingly, for the purchase of inputs and consumer goods from urban markets. Land is, therefore, something to be acquired, and most groups plan their economic

[8] Vera Anstey, "Economic Development," in *Modern India and the West*, ed. by L. S. S. O'Malley (Oxford University Press, 1941), 261.

activities in order to accumulate a surplus to purchase land. But
the market for land is highly localized. Since the referent for determining success in Vilyatpur for most of the period of this study
is the local community, the land must be located in Vilyatpur or in
one of the contiguous villages. It must be so situated that resident
members of the family can work it and so that it is visible to the
community. It is the range of holdings in Vilyatpur that sets the
scale for measuring achievement, and not any general consideration
including a larger region or the province. These are the factors,
highly localized and internal to the village, which motivate the
behavior regarding new opportunities for adjusting the family's
holding to the supply of family labor.

A number of developments provided means for Sahota property
groups to add to the size and the productivity of their holdings.
Peace, security, and the improvements in transportation facilities
stimulated trade and brought an increase in value of agricultural
produce in the second half of the nineteenth century, changes
which cultivators in the village certainly felt. The construction of
an extensive network of canals in the sparsely populated tracts of
western Punjab in the 1890's added a general stimulus and provided an opportunity for several Sahota groups to migrate. The
holdings they left in Vilyatpur went to relatives. A more important
development, particularly as an indication of things to come, was
the beginning of overseas migration to Australia. Returns followed
quickly. Money which came to the groups that had sent members
out, was used first to take land on mortgage and then to purchase
it. After the turn of the century, migration, overseas and within
India, increased. But these movements had a distinctive pattern and
purpose. Only property groups with an abundance of male members that had also recently experienced a decline in the size of
their holdings sent members out. The purpose of migration was,
in the short run, to adjust the supply of family labor to its holding. Over a longer period of time, however, the migrants acquired
wealth in order to purchase more land in the parent village. Property groups with few members or good sized holdings (relative to
others) usually did not participate in migration since nothing outside of the community was as attractive as continuity and good
standing within it. The volume of migration, however (particularly
since the 1890's), shows that there was no special restraint on migra-

tion in rural Punjab. Ties of family, kin, and community did not inhibit migration in Vilyatpur, although they did give it distinctive character and pattern.

From the First World War, and particularly since the 1920's, there were a number of improvements in village agriculture. Some of the addition to the total production of the village resulted from the initiative of village cultivators themselves. Investment in agricultural appliances—particularly carts and sugarcane presses—grew from the end of the nineteenth century. Since the 1920's there have been further increases in total production through more intensive cultivation, the extent of double cropping, and probably the intensity of labor. But a good deal of the growth came from the adoption of improved seed developed by the Department of Agriculture. By the 1930's improved varieties were used on most Vilyatpur farms, and a further investment in implements took place. The most important development was the replacement of the *charsa* by the Persian wheel. With these improvements, agricultural production rose throughout the period covered in this study to a degree sufficient to keep ahead of the growth of the village population. Blyn's study, which shows that this was the case for Punjab as a whole, supports my findings.

Developments in agriculture occurred within the context of the family farm and the iron chest system of accounting. Improvements that neither altered the capacity of the farm to provide foodstuffs for the family nor required the outlay of much cash (like improved seeds and the Persian wheel) were accepted rapidly and widely. Crops are produced for the market, but those that can be consumed at home and sold in the market are clearly favored. There is no evidence of any specialization. Because the labor employed is available family labor, practices like the manufacture of homemade, unrefined sugar (*gur*) continues, even though its return after computing the cost of labor in production is less than the profits from sending cane to the sugar mill. Even though the cost of the additional production is very high, land is still rented and purchased at rates far in excess of its productive value since it increases the per-capita production for members of the family. In view of the importance of land mortgage and sale as a saving and credit mechanism, and the nearly universal practice of renting land in and out to adjust family labor to its holding, much of the standard interpretation concerning the management practices common to the family farm in rural Punjab, must be called into question. They are not an indication of poverty, maladministration, or even the misapplication of a British system of land ownership to the Indian situation.

The developments in agriculture, however, have meant some modification in the operating principles of the family farm, changes of consequence to the nonlanded groups in the village and the wider regional economy of rural Punjab. In the mid-nineteenth century most inputs for farming were available in the village. Cultivators saved seed from the previous year's crop and most implements were fashioned in the village by local artisans paid through the *jajmani* system of customary grain payments at the time of the harvest. Exceptions were bullock carts and parts of the wooden sugarcane presses. Until the general growth of trade in agricultural produce following improvements in transportation, however, few cultivators owned the appliances. Cultivators even bred in Vilyatpur the livestock necessary for farming and the supply of dairy products, although it was occasionally necessary to purchase animals from wandering cattle dealers. But increased investment in carts and sugarcane presses in the last nineteenth century, the general use of improved seed varieties in the 1920's, the shift to iron Persian wheels and sugarcane presses in the following decade (all of which had to be purchased outside the village for cash), meant a growing participation in the regional market economy. Increased consumption of goods produced outside the village was not limited to agricultural inputs. Bricks and cement for the houses that grew steadily in numbers since the turn of the century, bicycles from the nineteen thirties, hand pumps since the nineteen forties, and a wide range of goods including radios and fans since 1950, are all purchased in cash in local markets and nearby cities. Sahota cultivators had previously taken part in the market economy, but the amount of produce available for sale was small and they purchased very little. Now with much larger surpluses through the use of inputs purchased in the market, villagers entered the market as buyers and consumers for the first time.

The transition from economic activity dominated by the iron chest system of accounting to a pronounced orientation toward the market has been gradual, and is not yet complete. But I would take the general use of chemical fertilizers in the late fifties and the heavy investment in machine powered irrigation wells in the early sixties as the turning point. The size of the investment in wells, and the necessity of repeated outlays of substantial sums for fertilizer and fuel, require the marketing of relatively large quantities of produce at good prices. The change in the role of prices in village agriculture is indicative of the transition. Previously, when some produce was sold to obtain a little cash to pay the government tax and purchase a few necessities, the rate of return per unit sold was not particularly important. Naturally, cultivators preferred a good return which meant that more could be invested in land or jewelry, and there is proof that adjustments within certain limits were made in cropping patterns to take advantage of good prices for certain commodities. Because the feeding of the family and the working capital of the farm did not depend on cash beyond that necessary for the tax, in most years it did not matter if a little less or a little more had to be sold to obtain some money. Now that most inputs must be purchased, their cost in the market, and the prices received for produce are crucial factors in village agriculture. Cultivators do retain a good measure of flexibility—indicative of the limited extent of the transition—in that they continue to grow most food required for family consumption and can therefore endure a year or two of poor prices. Given the need for cash in the working capital of the farm, however, crop prices have definitely become an incentive to further development.

There have been several changes in economic organization important for the consideration of social change. The transformation in the conditions of work for the Chamar agricultural laborers is the most dramatic. The growth of opportunities outside the village —the alternative of migration to the canal colonies being the most important example—led to the disintegration of the traditional *jajmani* relationships between Sahota cultivators and Chamar laborers with compensation for the latter in grain at customary rates. From the 1920's arrangements were made for only a year at a time, and payments gradually rose. By 1947 the last vestiges of the old system disappeared and labor was engaged on a daily basis at a cash or piece-work rate that fluctuated according to the demand. A similar transition from economic relationships embedded in a complex of ritual and social obligations and paid at customary rates to market-type relationships occurred among the artisans of the village.

Some left Vilyatpur, contributing to the growth of small towns that have appeared throughout the Punjab during the last sixty years as service and market centers for surrounding villages. The Goldsmith, the Oil Presser, some Carpenters, a tailor, and one group of Shoe Makers have made the shift to broaden their business opportunities. Most Carpenters have stayed in Vilyatpur but have taken new jobs like the grinding of flour, threshing of wheat, and constructing houses to supplement their role as repairmen and installers. These jobs are now done primarily for cash payment. The Weavers have, by and large, remained in the village, but since they sell most of their produce in urban markets, Vilyatpur is nothing more than a convenient place to live and work. The changes contributed to and were part of the general development of the nonagricultural part of the rural economy which created new opportunities for village residents from the 1940's.

Economic development and a growing involvement with the market and the wider, regional economy, apparent in the 1920's and well established since, brought several structural changes in rural society. There is no need to repeat the summary of changes in the family which occurred gradually throughout the period 1848 to 1968. Significant changes have taken place; the result is still consistent with long established values regarding family structure; the family and not the individual remains the essential focus in rural Punjabi society today.

Another important change has been the decline of the community as the predominant referent for measuring achievement by village families. Through greater involvement in a wider economy, and with the development of sources of wealth in rural Punjab other than agriculture, the local, internal village system of values and institutions has lost much of its hold as a motivating force. Now it is not enough to be the family with the most property in Vilyatpur or among several surrounding villages. A few groups have taken the drastic step of leaving the village entirely; they have sold their land or given it to close relatives for a minimal rent. Some have bought large tracts of land in Rajasthan and Uttar Pradesh with money from the sale of land or remittances from overseas. Although family members who emigrated continue to send back substantial sums, there is for the first time, a clear tendency for them to purchase property in their new homes. In a sense they have made the complete transition from peasant cultivators in a highly localized social and economic system to farmers, businessmen, and property owning factory laborers in the national economy.

The role of caste in the village has also changed, but many aspects remain completely unaltered. Sahotas see themselves as the cream of the community, avoid social interaction with other castes, and marry only Jats of other *gots* from nearby villages. But there have been substantial changes in the place of caste in social, and more particularly, political structure. Before British annexation politics was structured through the ties of caste of the Sahotas within the village and to others in the *ilaqa*. Members of the other caste groups in Vilyatpur participated only through their *jajmani* relationships to their Sahota patrons. With the establishment of British rule, which took the individual village as the unit of administration, connections between Vilyatpur and other Sahota villages were deemphasized. There was no need for solidarity throughout the *ilaqa* after the establishment of the *pax Britanica;* even within Vilyatpur the unity of the Sahotas was no longer necessary to protect their control of the land and dominance in the village. The period after 1848 saw considerable conflict between the three lineages in the village. The *Tehsildars'* inspection notes invariably mention factional conflict along these lines among the Sahotas. The Sahota monopolization of village politics began to decline with the related developments of the disintegration of *jajmani* ties and the growth in the proportion of the population working outside the village. With the weakening of ties between Sahota patrons and clients from the other castes, a numerically large counterweight to Sahota dominance potentially emerged, particularly after the disputes over the freedom of Chamars to work outside the village and of the Weavers to set their own prices. The realization of this potential change had to await Independence, the promulgation of the Indian Constitution with universal suffrage, and a responsible government for the Punjab. Individuals are now free to pursue opportunities and relationships as they see fit. As a friend (who happens to be a Chamar) succinctly put it, while strolling slowly toward me when I was leaving the village in a rush one day and had called him to hurry over and take the keys to our house: "Chamars don't run any more."

GLOSSARY *

abadi   a group of houses; the part of the village containing the houses of village residents

al   maximal lineage of all males who trace their descent from a common ancestor

amulguzar   a Mughal official charged with collecting taxes in the *subah*

amin   Mughal official subordinate to the *amulguzar* in each *pargana*

bahi   the register of pilgrims maintained by the *Pandas* at important places of pilgrimage

basti   a residential neighborhood

begar   forced labor taken from Chamars and other untouchables in the village

belna   sugarcane press

bhaiachara   the proprietary group in villages where all landowners are descended from a common ancestor and are treated as a corporate group by the government

chapatti   flat unleavened bread made of wheat or millet which is the staple village diet in the Punjab

charsa   a simple mechanism for raising water for irrigation consisting of a large leather bag drawn up by two pairs of bullocks

chullah   a hearth; often taken as defining a commensal group

diwan   Sikh official charged with the maintenance of records in the *sarkar*

doab   the tract of land between two rivers

faujdar   the Mughal official responsible for policing the *sarkar*

ghar   a house; a household

ghi   clarified butter used as a cooking medium in the village

got   subcaste, clan; the exogamous group within the *zat*

gur   unrefined sugar produced in the village

ilaqa   a region; an area containing several villages connected historically or by kinship ties

* I have followed the most common English rendering of Punjabi, Hindi, and Urdu words rather than attempting a systematic transliteration.

jagir a tract of land granted by a government to an individual in return for or in recognition of service to the government

jagirdar the individual holding the *jagir*

jamabandi the government tax record of land ownership and tax due compiled every four years

kamin a general term referring to all landless artisans and laborers who earn their livelihood by supplying landowners with goods and services

kardar Sikh revenue official in the *pargana*

khariff the summer cropping season

khandan the minimal lineage comprised of patrilineally related kinsmen who can trace their descent from an ancestor one or two generations earlier

khes a coarse cotton cloth woven by hand and used as a wrap and as a bed sheet

kotwal a Mughal police official

mahal the lowest division in Mughal revenue administration; in the British period another name for village

mahalwari a revenue policy in which tax was assessed on and collected from village landowners as a group

malikhana a fee paid by village cultivators to revenue collecting intermediaries like *jagirdars, taluqdars,* and *zamindars* in the Mughal period

maund a unit of weight, about eighty pounds

mauza a Mughal term for village

misl confederations of Sikh military leaders and followers which dominated Punjab in the late eighteenth century

muqaddam the term for the village headman in the Mughal period

munna the simple wood plow used until the late nineteenth century

nazim Sikh revenue official in the *sarkar*

pagal crazy

panchayat the group of elders from the landowning caste who acted as leaders, arbitrating disputes, and dealing with government officials

Panchayati Raj the system of elected village councils instituted after Independence in 1947

Panda Brahmin record keepers in important pilgrimage places

pargana the lowest level of administration in the Mughal and Sikh revenue systems *patti* a subdivision of the *abadi* inhabited by a single maximal lineage

patwari village record keeper

pind a village

prohit family priest

qanungo the revenue official between the *patwari* and the *tehsildar*

qasbah a large market village with a bazaar serving numerous villages in the area

rabi the winter cropping season

ryot village cultivator

ryotwari a revenue policy in which tax was assessed on and collected from individual landowners

sarkar a division of territory in the Mughal and Sikh states roughly equivalent to the district

seer a measure of weight equivalent to 2.2 pounds

sepidar an artisan, servant, or laborer who provides goods and services to a landowning patron in return for a share of the biannual harvest as part of an hereditary relationship

tabbar the family

taluqdar a revenue collecting intermediary in the Mughal period

tehsil a subdivision of the district in the British revenue system

tappa a region containing several villages settled by the same clan

zamindar in the Mughal and Sikh periods, an individual or group with hereditary rights to collect revenue from a number of villages; in the British period, a village landowner and cultivator

zat caste, clan; the endogamous group which is the functional unit of the caste system

INDEX

Because of the nature of the sources for this study I have not included a formal bibliography. References to the literature on various topics are italicized in the Index.

Absentee landowners, 81
Agriculture, 54, 60, 61, 102–104, 146, 159, 205; Punjab, 104–112; village, 112–129; technology, 110; statistics, 104, 106. *See also* Holdings, size of, Yields, Department of Agriculture, and Crops
Agri-Horticultural Society of Lahore, 105
Arenas, 5

Baseline, 4, 45, 46, 77, 167, 181, 208
Begar, 126, 161. *See also* Control of village residents and landless labor
Bhaiachara. See Proprietary body
Bicycles, 158, 204
Brahmin, 42, 96
British policy and the village, *31–34,* 77–82

Canal colonies, 12, 15, 85, 91, 92, 94, 113, 125, 128, 129, 163, 174. *See also* Migration
Capital, 122
Carpenter (*Tarkhan*), 159–160
Caste, 9, 50, 94–96, 219
Census, 53, 186–187. *See also Khanna shumari*
Cholera, 85
Clan settlements (*Ilaqa*), 39–40, 43, 78
Classical view of Indian villages, 2, 4, 25, 74–77, 78, 100–101, 156–157. *See also* Maine, Henry and Metcalfe, Charles
Commercialization, 177, 181
Conflict, 72, 73, 82, 127. *See also* Proprietary body
Community, 5, 174–176, 204, 210
Community Development Program, 78, 111, 207–208
Commuting, 161–163
Compensation, methods of, 57–58, 74, 123–128, 158–160, 216–217. *See also* Consumption, 148, 152, 159, 216. *See also* Houses
Context of the village, 2, 3, 4, 73–74, 83
Control of village inhabitants, 58, 73, 74, 126–127, 147, 154, 158–159, 207. *See also Begar* and Conflict
Coparcenary. *See* Proprietary body

Courts, 82
Credit, 136–138, 149, 216–217. *See also* Savings
Crops, 61–62, 102, 117–118, 119–121. *See also* Innovation
Customary Law, *81–82*

Demographic patterns of families, 98–100
Department of Agriculture, 104, 105, 106, 108, 109, 110, 112, 147, 151, 215
Development cycle in the family, 37–38, 51, 52, 139, 182–183, 197
Domestic groups, 50–52, 179, 180, 182, 184–187
Dominant caste, 53–55, *70–73. See also* Caste and Proprietary body
Double cropping, 59, 118–120, 126, 129, 144, 204

Epidemics, 85, 87, 88, 89

Family, 5; size and composition, 138–139, 142–144; structure, 177–201, 206
Family farm, 5, 129–130, 137, 138–153, 215
Family labor, 60, 62, 103, 123, 138–153, 162
Famine, 85
Farm accounting, 150–153, 215
Farms, 141. *See also* Holdings, size of
Fertilizer, 150–153
Fragmentation of holdings, 59, 60, 76, 130, 132, 145, 149. *See also* Holdings

Genealogy, 6, 7, 24, 38, 40, 42, 51, 97–100, 167–171

Holdings, size of, 62–64, 67, 68, 75, 104, 114, *115, 116,* 117, 141, 145–147, 153, 155, 167–168, 171, 204
Honorary Magistrate, 127
Household (*ghar*), 37–38
Houses, 48, 49–53, 140, 148, 155, 159, 170, 176, 202–203

Improved crops, 108–111, 113. *See also* Crops and Innovation
Indebtedness, *130, 135–137*

Industrialization, 177, 181
Inheritance, 68, 97, 131, 178, 179, 187, 188
Innovation, 109–110, 113, 148, 151, 207, 215, 217
Investment, 137, 140, 149, 150, 152, 171, 207, 217
Iron chest. *See* Farm accounting
Irrigation, 14, 59, 60–61, 107, 110, 121, 129, 147, 149, 205

Jajmani system, 55, 56, 57, 75, 123–124, 212, 216, 219. *See also* Compensation, method of
Jamabandi, 6
Jats, 34–35, 103; social structure, 36–38, 78
Joint family, 51, 76, 89. *See also* Family
Jullundur District, 14–16, 87

Khadi Bhavan, 158
Khandan, 37–38, 59, 61, 68
Khanna shumari (Household Census), 6, 7

Lal kitab, 6
Land: revenue, 14, 21, 31, 62, 68; tenure, 27, 31–33, 66, 80; sale and purchase, 69, 71, 129–134, 136, 137, 151, 171–173, 177, 213–215; ownership, 54, 74, 75, 103; management, 138–139; renting, 65, 69, 139, 140, 143–144, 152; price of land, 132–134, 147, 152, 205. *See also* Holdings, size of
Land reform, 31
Landless labor, 58, 64, *123–129*, 135, 139, 150. *See also* Compensation, method of
Leatherworkers (Chamars), 42, 94–96, 124, 160–161, 203
Linkages outside the village, *25*, *26*, 70, 73, 176
Livestock, 53, 54, 59, 202

Maine, Henry, 82, 180
Man/land ratio, 113, 115, 119. *See also* Holdings, size of
Market, 62, 107, 128, 148, 158, 216–218
Maximal lineage, 36, 40–41, 51, 67, 79, 80. *See also* Jat, social structure
Metcalfe, Charles, 25, 32, 43
Migration, 42, 75, 80, 89–94, 125, 128–129, 138–139, 145, 148, 155, 163–174, 193, 196, 198, 205–206, 218; and landownership, 155–156, 167–169; and caste, 165–167
Military service, 93
Misls, 21, 22, 24, 27, 34, 40, 210
Mitaksara Law, *199*
Modernity, *208*, 209
Monetization, 147
Money, 150

Mortality, 87–89, 98, 183, 189–191, 195
Mortgages, 135–137, 150, 170. *See also* Land: ownership, purchases and sales; and credit
Mughal administration, 17–20
Muqaddams, 18, 20, 44
Muslims, 52, 93–94

Occupations: structure, 156–157, 174–176, 206; new, 154–167; and family composition, 200
Overseas migration, 92–93, 155

Panchayat, 18, 20, 207
Panchayati Raj, 112, 207
Patron-client relationships, 57, 102. See also *Jajmani* system
Patti, 36, 51
Patwari, 18
Perspective on the village, 210–212
Pilgrimage records, 6, 35–36, 42
Plague, 85, 87
Polyculture, 130, 151. *See also* Crops
Population, 84, 147, 183. *See also* Mortality and Man/land ratio
Processing of agricultural produce, 50, 54, 59, 61, 159–160, 173
Profits, 150–152. *See also* Farm accounts
Property group, 55, 65, 66, 138, 142–144, 187–201, 213
Proprietary body, 66, 67, 69, 70–73, 80, 187. *See also* Dominant caste
Punjab, 9
Punjab Co-operative Societies Act, 83
Punjab Land Alienation Act, 83
Punjab Land Code, 199
Punjab Pre-Emption Act, 83, 132

Railroad, 15
Rajput lineages, 20, 22, 26, 29, 33
Reference years, 8
Rentiers, 140, 148. *See also* Absentee landowners
Revenue records, 81, 140
Roads, 15–16, 48, 202

Savings, 137
Segmentary political systems, *41*, 43, 70, *71*, *72*
Settlement process, 38–41, 43, 91
Shajra nasib, 6–7
Sharecropping, *152*
Shradda ceremony, 44–45, 179
Sikh administration, 21, 22, 23, 24
Smallpox, 85
Social change, 210–212

Social circulation, *211–212*
Sources, *5–7*, 16, *113*
Standard of living, 139, 140, 146, 147
Subsistence agriculture,
Surplus, 147

Tabbar (family), 37–38
Technology, 139, 148, 158, 173
Tenancy, 59, 65, 69, 139
Tradition, 4
Traditional shares, 68–69, 208–209
Transportation, 62, 113, 106–107, 147, 204
Trusteeship, 169

Values and attitudes, 100, 110, 146, 162, 170–172, 175–176, 190, 213
Village: definition, 5, 19, 26, 43, 44, 45; description, 48–50; position in administration, 19–21, 24, 78–83; histories, 24, *35–36*, 47, 48, 49; as a referent, 131

Weavers (Julahas), 42, 96, 157–159, 203
Wells. *See* Irrigation
Westernization 177, 181, 188

Yields, 129, 140, 215–216

Zamindars, 19–21, 23, 37, 39, 31, 33